WE SAW THE HOLY CITY

UNDER THE LAST SUPPER ROOM.

WE SAW
THE HOLY CITY

BY

LESLIE FARMER

If I forget thee, O Jerusalem,
Let my right hand forget her cunning.

PSALM CXXXVII. 5

THE EPWORTH PRESS
(EDGAR C. BARTON)
25-35 City Road, London, E.C.1

THIS BOOK IS PRODUCED IN
COMPLETE CONFORMITY WITH
THE AUTHORIZED ECONOMY
STANDARDS

Made and printed in Great Britain by
The Camelot Press Limited, London and Southampton

TO

MY WIFE

CONTENTS

LIST OF ILLUSTRATIONS

Maps

ACKNOWLEDGEMENTS

READERS of the books mentioned at the end of this volume will understand how much my thanks are due to the authors for the valuable material they have provided. I am especially grateful for the works of Professor Dalman and Canon Hanauer.

I appreciate also the help of Eric Gilboy, who drew the end-paper map, and of those who have contributed photographs for this book. Most of them were taken by members of H.M. Forces.

Most of all, and very sincerely, I thank Mr. C. N. Johns, M.A., of the Government of Palestine Department of Antiquities, for the great pains he has taken in reading my manuscript, and for much valuable advice.

I shall never forget the great kindness of my many friends in Jerusalem. May this book be for them and for the men who were exiled there with me a happy reminder of the days when 'we took sweet counsel together, and walked unto the house of God in company'.

LESLIE FARMER

CHAPTER I

CENTRE OF THE EARTH

God is my King of old,
Working salvation in the midst of the earth.
PSALM lxxiv. 12.

I HAD travelled a long way and was weary. The war had snatched me from the Old Kent Road, as it had taken a million others from their homes, and sent me half-way round the world. My beloved London had been sufficient world for me; I was content with it and was never happy away from it for long. And now I had circled Africa, and penetrated it as far as the Nuba Mountains in its pagan heart. I had stood on the borders of Abyssinia, and dwelt in a desert camp on the field of Omdurman for nearly a year. Twice had I made that week-long, thousand-mile journey on the Nile between Khartoum and Cairo. I had seen Upper and Lower Egypt, Suez and Alexandria. I had passed through Palestine and worked in Syria. Now, after a stay in the Sinai Desert, I was bound for Jerusalem, my future all unknown, to report to my superiors for further orders. No doubt I should be told to proceed into 'the blue', but I hoped that my stay in the Holy City would be long enough to enable me at least to see the Holy Sepulchre and the Mount of Olives.

The train climbed slowly on a single-line track up a winding valley between hills, bare and rocky for the most part, with occasional scanty crops between them, and here and there a shady pepper-tree at a wayside station where a few Arabs rested, wearing flowing white *kafiyehs* over head and shoulders, crowned with a black cord. I realized that this was the Valley of Rephaim up which we were creeping, where David routed the Philistines. I tried to picture him with his men making a circuit of the mulberry trees, waiting for the sound of marching in the treetops before he sallied forth to smite the enemy. There are cedars still in Lebanon, and olives at Gethsemane, but it was too much to expect to see mulberries still flourishing in this valley—or, rather, balsam trees, as the Revised Version margin renders 2 Samuel v. 23. The countryside must have been more fertile in those days. I was not to know until the rains fell some months later how green and pleasant is the Promised Land, where dry and yellow hills suddenly become bright with anemone, narcissus and the pale cyclamen, even if there are not so many trees as in Bible days.

The train jerked to a final stop at the platform, lined with eucalyptus trees, which is Jerusalem station. There was a tumult of porters clamouring for my baggage. I was in the Holy City.

A chaplain I happened to know slightly had come to meet me, and he whispered a secret:

'You're staying here.'

'Here?' I said incredulously. It was beyond my imaginings. I had not for a moment thought of the possibility that after all my wanderings I should settle for a while in Jerusalem, where I could 'walk about Zion' and become familiar with the holy places.

'Sh-sh,' he said. 'You're not supposed to know until you are told at the office, but I happen to know you will be posted here. There is no Methodist chaplain in the area and there's plenty to do, I assure you. I am your C. of E. "opposite number".'

And so it proved to be. My weariness began to drop away from me as we sped in a car along the smooth, wide curve of St. Julian's Way, and I saw across the valley to my right the grey, crenellated walls of the Old City, and the spires and turrets that rise upon Mount Zion above the dirty, smelly streets I was soon to know so well. My prosaic arrival at the railway station, only to glimpse next minute the timeless wonder of the Holy City, was a foretaste of many incongruities I was later to experience. Jerusalem is a city of contrasts. East and West are mingled, though not inextricably, for each community is careful to maintain its own identity: its speech, its dress, its customs. More than sixty languages are spoken by its people, with three official ones: English, Arabic and Hebrew, as in the days of Jesus they were Latin, Greek and Aramaic. Street names are written in three kinds of characters, as was His title on the Cross.

The ancient and the modern combine with the holy and profane to bewilder the newcomer and to fascinate him. I have sat on the hill of Calvary within the great gloomy shelter of the Church of the Holy Sepulchre, trying in the silence to think about the Cross, only to have that silence shattered by the shrill burr-burr of a telephone in the Orthodox priests' vestry below me. I was on Calvary, but could not concentrate my thoughts because a telephone was ringing! It seemed so fantastic. A Franciscan monk pottering about the Garden of Gethsemane provides an idyllic picture of contentment in this world of strife until he lights a cigarette and tells one in a broad Middle-West accent that he is longing to get back to the States. The women of Siloam still carry water from the pool, gracefully balancing on their heads—a petrol-tin! The Mosque el Aksa is a chapter directly out of *Arabian Nights*, with its prayer-rugs and arabesques and Moslems cross-legged before the Koran, until one beholds beside the praying place of Mohammed himself a solemn grandfather clock made in London. Solomon's Quarry is an air-raid shelter, and in a corner of the battlements of David's Tower I found an air-raid siren.

The Old City streets are unchanged from the Middle Ages. Arabs and Jews and Armenians, Sudanese and Indians, monks of many orders and priests of many faiths, mingling with donkeys and camels and children and black-veiled women and men bowed beneath immense burdens, all concentrated in the narrow, cobbled bazaars, must have presented a similar appearance for centuries past. Yet a stone's throw away are buses and Barclays Bank, modernistic blocks of flats and the Y.M.C.A. Along Mamillah Road comes an Arab with a long, dirty *galabieh* flowing behind him as he rides a motor-cycle. Outside the Ecce Homo Convent a brown and bearded water-carrier with a filled goatskin across his back stands aside to allow a giant, sleek Daimler to pass. Baggy-trousered Syrians suck their hookahs as they listen to the radio in a corner coffee-shop.

I shall have more to say about the famous Jerusalem Y.M.C.A. in a later chapter. For a few days I lived there until I settled in an officers' mess, and when the servant took me to my room and I lay for the first time for months upon a real bed, I was overwhelmed at the thought of the Providence which had led me there, not only to see the Holy City, but to live and work in it and to preach the gospel where Jesus and the Apostles preached it, to learn to love 'Jerusalem, my happy home', as later it became. I had only to raise my eyes to see through the window the ancient domes and spires behind the city wall, with the magnificent background of the Mount of Olives beyond. These surrounding hills, and the mountains of Moab on the far horizon on the other side of Jordan, were seen by Jesus. His feet had trod these paths. He had looked upon this city and loved it as a mother, and yet His tears were those of a young man. After all, Jesus was exactly my age when He wept over Jerusalem because it did not know the things that belong unto peace. All those centuries since His time had not taught us peace. The whole world was at war, and like the contesting empires of old, the aggressors sought to gain possession of Palestine, still at the strategic centre of world conflict. Is it a mystery that this city, geographically set at the centre of ancient and modern civilization, which has known throughout its history the clash of arms and the din of battle, should be named the Habitation of Peace? On one of the hilltops by Mount Scopus to the north of Jerusalem lie the beautifully kept grounds of the British War Cemetery, where ordered rows of headstones mark the graves of men who fell in the

1917–18 campaign. A white stone cross rises from its centre and all around are pointed, dark green cypress trees. About a mile beyond it, strangely enough, is another hilltop, clumped with trees, where not long ago was found an old Roman cemetery. It is thought that the men who were buried there were soldiers of Titus' army who fell in the battles against the Jews in A.D. 70, when the Romans besieged Jerusalem. The juxtaposition of these two war cemeteries, on similar locations outside the Holy City, with nearly two thousand years between them, is a silent, eloquent witness of the way mankind has gone through history. Battles have ever raged round the City of Peace, in the centre of the world. 'Pray for the peace of Jerusalem', said the prophet, surely to us all. Perhaps when there is peace here there is peace everywhere, for here is the heart of the world.

In the Church of the Holy Sepulchre there is a piece of stone with a metal cross set in the top. That cross marks what was believed long ago to be the centre of the earth. It was not mere superstition that made the ancients declare that Jerusalem was their centre. They were quite right. It was. Take an old map of the world as they knew it, mark the length and breadth of it, and you will find that the centre is right in Jerusalem. Put the point of a pair of dividers at this spot and describe a circle with twelve degrees of latitude for radius, and you will include the capitals of every great empire of history up to the time of Alexander. This can be said of no other city in the world. And there is a sense in which we can still say to-day that this City of Salem is at the centre of world affairs, as well as the focus-point of faith and peace.

In the far-off days before the Hebrews invaded the country this fortress in the midst of the Promised Land was called Uru-Salim. The credulous still call the chapel beneath Mount Calvary the tomb of Melchizedek, although the 'Salem' of which he was king and priest was, according to Jerome, in the Jordan valley. Letters have been discovered, written about 1400 B.C. by the ruler of Uru-Salim to Pharaoh of Egypt to request help against the Jebusites, help which Egypt was not able to send. It was in the Province of Beit Lahm, so in those days Bethlehem was probably more important than Jerusalem. It was left for David to capture the city some four hundred years later from the descendants of those same Jebusites, and to install himself and his army within its citadel, which he called Zion, or 'Height'. It is possible, however, that Jerusalem is referred to in even older records than these. Some writing was found at Luxor in 1925 which dates from about 2500 B.C. The author was cursing the enemies of Egypt, and he mentioned a Canaanite city named Wrwshlm, which may be a reference to Jerusalem. 'Shalom', the greeting which is heard every day in the streets of the Holy City, is a very ancient word. Possibly long ago Salem was a Semitic god of Peace, and so Uru-Salim meant originally 'the City of the God of Peace'. It belied its name then as now. Jesus saw its beauty from the Mount of Olives and wept; yet still within it, where meet the three great monotheistic religions of the world, lies the possibility of peace and goodwill for all mankind.

I soon found that there was plenty of work amongst the troops for a Methodist chaplain in Jerusalem. It is no part of the purpose of this book to tell of a chaplain's life and duties, his opportunities and difficulties and failures. All that is another story. It is one particular aspect of my life in Jerusalem that I want to describe, for I found that besides the normal routine of hospital and barrack visitation, of social work in hostels and clubs, of the busy round of Sunday and weekday services, there was an opportunity in Jerusalem for a special sort of ministry which no other place could provide. Far better than preaching sermons to the men from a pulpit or from behind a Union Jack at a parade service was to take them to the actual places where Biblical events had happened, and to tell them the story there. I decided that I would be a guide, and, please God, more than a guide, to the holy places. Surely men could be led more readily into the life of faith as they were shown the very place where Jesus was born, and where He died; as they looked upon Gabbatha and the Via Dolorosa, and the Tomb of the Resurrection! There were not only troops dwelling near Jerusalem, but a vast crowd of them flocked there when they had leave, often to be at the mercy of ignorant and extortionate 'guides', who told them fantastic tales in bad English, grinding the axe of the particular community to which they happened to belong. Men were sickened and disappointed where they might have had a glorious opportunity of understanding better the reality of their Lord's life and death, and the verities of the Christian faith. So I resolved to be a guide, not only to the men whom later I got to know so well after months of fellowship with them, but to visitors to the Holy City who had but a few precious days in which to see as much as possible of the holy places.

It was not a simple nor a speedy task to qualify in the way that I wished as a guide to Jerusalem and its environs. The place is full of sacred sites and historical monuments, many in queer out-of-the-way corners, all with an accumulation of legends which had to be understood and sorted out. Of course, I met some missionaries who had lived in Jerusalem for years and knew the stories of the holy places, and I listened to them. I went over and over the ground with parties from the Y.M.C.A. Information Bureau under the leadership of the most reliable of the local guides. I went along every street in the Old City until I knew my way about. I visited the Archaeological Museum, and secured a reader's ticket for its wonderful library, where I read guide books, travel books and history books, seeking for authority in the researches of scholars for the authenticity of the holy places, checking up on the stories I had heard, getting evidence for what I should tell the men. I used the invaluable Y.M.C.A. library, with its great section on religious subjects. And I read my Bible.

I accepted no story about a place without good authority. I wanted to be able to provide for the men in my care a truthful and reliable account of the history of the different objects of our pilgrimage in a way that they could understand. I give at the end of this book a list of some of the authorities I consulted and which I commend for a further study of the geography and history of the Holy City. Upon investigation, I may say, I found that some of the most popular writers on the Holy Land are very unreliable in many of the facts. Indeed, I preferred the accounts written by the ancient pilgrims to those of modern journalists who pay a hasty visit to Palestine for no other purpose than to write a readable book on the subject. The pious visitors of long ago were most credulous, and believed the most amazing things, but at any rate they were sincere, and recorded what they really believed was true. I came to the conclusion that some popular writers to-day are either very careless in their statements, being too hurried to seek proper authority for what they write, or they deliberately mislead their readers with inaccuracies in order to provide a description which they think will be more popular or more startling than the truth. And so I found myself correcting mistakes and delusions about the Holy City which the men had gained from too-eloquent guides or from too-popular books.

All this took time because it was in addition to my other duties, which were legion. Once a month from the Jerusalem station, I conducted a broadcast service for troops in the Middle East; I took my turn at a combined Sunday-night service of song for members of the Forces at Christ Church; I preached sometimes at St. Andrew's, the beautiful Scottish Memorial Church; I led a canteen service in the Y.M.C.A. which some of my men organized every Sunday; I had regular parade services in the barracks in the mornings. And this was only on Sundays. During the week there were the hospitals and interviews and office work and correspondence.

How much correspondence I had! I always seemed to be sitting at my typewriter. I kept in touch with hundreds of men I had met on my travels, for I knew so well the value of such links with them. I had formed a Fellowship in Khartoum, and did the same immediately I arrived in Jerusalem. We met on Wednesday evenings in an upper room in St. Andrew's Hostel in the centre of the newer city, and we had wonderful times together. There not only many of the Methodist troops met together, with the members of other Churches for whom I was responsible, but practically every week there would be present several men who were in Jerusalem on leave. I wrote to all of them every month, duplicating a news-letter which circulated all over the Middle East, and beyond it, as the men travelled about upon their duties in the far-from-static life of the Army in wartime. I was always receiving replies which needed answers, as well as a gradually increasing correspondence with their folk at home.

Like most other chaplains, when I was in action on the East Africa front and when I was a hospital chaplain at Khartoum I would write to the wife or parents of a man who was seriously ill or for any reason could not write home for himself. And I invariably wrote a letter to the next of kin of a man who died. But later, when I was in Jerusalem, it occurred to me that it would be a worth-while ministry to write to the homes of men who were fit and well. Why should a chaplain write to a man's wife or mother when it was only bad news that he had to give? A letter from a third person, somebody as responsible as a chaplain, to say that Johnny was looking fit and enjoying life in the Middle East, would surely not be unwelcome to the people at home? I asked those who attended my Fellowship, therefore, to include their home addresses when they recorded their names and units on their visit to the meeting, and I found that the response was almost overwhelming. For hours I sat typing on those flimsy pieces of paper which represented the first step in that amazing production, the airgraph. Each one was a letter which carried reassuring news about the well-being of a husband or a son, told of our fellowship together, and asked that we should be remembered on Wednesday evenings when we stood in silence at ten o'clock to think and pray for the folk at home. I did some each day at the beginning, and it was work that was amply rewarded, for I received piles of airmail postcards, airgraphs, and letters in reply, many of which resulted in increased personal contacts with the men and enabled me to know them better and help them more than would otherwise have been possible. Extracts from those letters, telling of personal troubles and revealing so often how acute was the pain of separation, and as often much courage and patience, would make fascinating reading. But they are not for the public eyes. The same can be said of the mounting pile of correspondence I received from men in the Middle East with whom I maintained exchange of letters. The effect of all this was the development of a bond of fellowship which linked up people of common interest over a wide area.

This fellowship had its focus point in the Wednesday Fellowship. Within a week or two at Jerusalem I had made friends with some kindred spirits amongst the men and about twenty men attended the first meeting, on November 14th, 1941. We decided to follow broadly the lines of the youth movement, the Wesley Guild, with which we were familiar in the church at home. On the first Wednesday in the month we would have a devotional service, followed by Holy Communion. At every meeting we would have a different member of the Fellowship to preside, announcing hymns and giving the prayer. At ten o'clock we would stand quietly for a moment for the Fellowship of Silence which linked us in thought with our people at home and with absent members. On Sunday afternoons we would organize rambles to the local places of interest. One man was appointed librarian, to dispense the books I had received from home for a chaplain's library. Another enthusiastic brother was appointed secretary.

The W.F., as we called it, grew beyond all our expectations. We met at 8.45 in the evening, when most men had finished work for the day, and soon our small room was overcrowded. We moved to the larger games-room, removing table-tennis equipment and filling the place with chairs, soon crowding that room. Attendance rarely fell below fifty men and sometimes it was nearly twice that number. The monthly news-letter reached every one who had attended the meeting, perhaps only once when he was on leave. The answers I received from men who were 'out in the blue' told me how much that regular touch with us was appreciated, how much it meant to them to be reminded of happy days of leave, and to know that they were still part of the Fellowship. Within a few months my mailing list for the news-letter had risen to several hundreds, and each one was usually read, I was told, by several other men. The attendance was always good on devotional evenings, and our 'devotional walks', as we called some of our Sunday pilgrimages, when we held a little service in the Garden of Gethsemane, were the most popular. Our meeting place at St. Andrew's was an 'upper room', we were quick to realize, and it was a wonderful experience for us to receive the Sacrament in such a setting, some of the men for the first time.

The spirit of the W.F. was a happy thing. On one occasion I invited a rabbi to come and speak to us about 'What Palestine means to a Jew', and he was very surprised to hear the Chairman making jokes and the men laughing in a meeting where a few minutes before they had been singing a hymn and joining in prayer. It was a completely new experience for him to join with such cheerful Christians, and he was greatly impressed by the idea of religion which was so linked with the vitality of normal men's lives.

We had speakers of many kinds on many subjects, for Jerusalem is the sort of place where it is not difficult to find a resident with an interesting story to tell, either of the land in which we were dwelling or of more distant places where he had travelled. We had talks about India and Greece and Yugoslavia, about Everest and Central Africa and Persia; we had literary evenings and debates on post-war reconstruction and evenings provided by the members themselves when they spoke about their own hobbies: the making of films; railway-engines; amateur photography. We had an eloquent Arab to tell us of the Palestine question from the viewpoint of his own nationals, and an equally eloquent Jew to present the case for Zionism. One lad who had qualified as a solicitor talked to us about crime. Lady Petrie came and spoke to us informally about archaeology. We had play readings, enjoying Noel Coward and A. E. Housman on the same evening. We learned about life in places as remote as China and the Argentine. And, best of all, we learned to know one another in a way that even the familiarity of Army life, with its own conventions and reticences, did not permit. We not only laughed together and learned things together, but we prayed together, and took the bread and wine from the Communion Table, and walked in company to the holy places, treading where Jesus trod.

Early in 1943, my friends of the Church of Scotland opened a larger hostel for troops in the Holy City, and invited me to take a part of it for my headquarters. So in March of that year Wesley House was opened in Jerusalem, and it became a social and religious centre for troops on leave. One room was dedicated as a place of worship—the first Methodist chapel in the Holy City—and I was able to hold my services there. Wesley House became the meeting-place for our tours and pilgrimages.

The Sunday afternoon outings—open-air Sunday school, as we termed it—were popular from the very first. I always had a large party to lead, sometimes over thirty of us, and we became a familiar sight to the custodians of the holy sites. We visited them all, and we found so many places to see that it was many weeks before we started on the round again, revisiting them, as we were invariably ready to do, especially as there were always newcomers who had not been to them before. It was mainly for this that I read so hard in the libraries and accumulated as much information as I could to tell the men as we went round about Jerusalem.

I soon found, as I had anticipated, that Sunday afternoons were not the only times when my services as guide were required. Jerusalem was naturally one of the most popular leave centres in the Middle East, and the Y.M.C.A. had created an Information Bureau that arranged sightseeing tours for the troops. This performed an invaluable service for the men, and it employed, of course, the most dependable of the local guides. The demand would sometimes be so heavy, however, that the chaplains received requests to take parties of men on leave to such centres as the Holy Sepulchre, the Mount of Olives, the Temple area, and Bethlehem. So I found that a good deal of my time during the week was spent in guiding groups to these holy places and telling them their history and significance. Sometimes it would be a party of troops or R.A.F. men straight from the Western Desert, jaded and tired, and ready for the refreshment to mind and heart, as well as to body, that the high altitude and fresh air of Jerusalem provided. Sometimes it would be a group of black Basutos, or of Dutch sailors, or a party of sisters and medical officers from a military hospital. Nearly every chaplain in the Middle East came to Jerusalem for an arranged course of lectures and tours, and I was often called upon to guide them.

I found myself telling the same story over and over again, so I had to guard against 'vain repetition' which lacked sincerity. That was difficult, and was attained only with an effort. I can understand how a professional guide drops into a glib, parrot-like spate of words which so offends a newcomer to a place, especially a holy place. The other thing I had to guard against was an undue familiarity with the sacred sites, which had impressed me so much when first I saw them. But that was a private problem with which I had to deal personally. I think I may say truthfully that I succeeded in avoiding the threatened results of seeing too much of them. Indeed, I learned to regard them so that they meant more to me as time went on, and I was able to have a maturer and more balanced judgement about them than any hasty visit could provide.

We explored places on our Sunday afternoon outings, of course, that were beyond the range of the visitors on leave who wished to see only the chief centres of interest. This book is an attempt to describe what we saw and what we learned as we made our weekly excursions in and around the Holy City. Sometimes I will describe the members of my party as wearing battledress, sometimes there will be a reference to the heat, when we will be clad in khaki drill. This is because the rambles I describe were sometimes in winter, sometimes in summer, for I was privileged for two years to minister in this way in Jerusalem. It was scarcely ever too hot for us to sally forth for our weekly outing, even at the hottest part of the day, for the air there is nearly always fresh and pleasant, with a breeze to be found somewhere. That is always the first thing the traveller notices when he arrives in Jerusalem from the stifling summer heat of Egypt. And in the winter we often wore great-coats and gaitered boots as we splashed through the snow.

I shall not soon forget a trip to Hebron to peer into the Cave of Machpelah, where the sepulchres of the Patriarchs have been hidden for centuries. My car was snowbound, amid freezing wastes, until natives on camels that slipped silently through the snow came and dug us out. And the memory will remain with me of an all-day donkey ride amid torrid heat across the hills and valleys to see Anathoth of Jeremiah, and Gibeah of Saul, and the two crags at Michmash over which Jonathan and his armour-bearer climbed to attack the Philistines; and then I was plodding along on my donkey through such heat, striking back from the white rocks, that it seemed to me greater than anything I had known in tropical Sudan. And that reminds me of a story.

In *The Romance of the Last Crusade*, Major Vivian Gilbert tells a story of the capture of Michmash by his brigade in the campaign against the Turks in 1917. The enemy occupied the village, and the British troops the hills across the valley. That night, the Brigade Major was reading his Bible, and happened to turn to the account of Saul's first victory against the Philistines, in 1 Samuel xiii and xiv, where he read of Jonathan's tactics against Michmash when the Israelites were encamped at the very place where the British now were. When he read how Jonathan and his armour-bearer went through a narrow pass between two crags named Bozez and Seneh, and climbed the hill to a 'half an acre of land, which a yoke of oxen might plough', and surprised the Philistines that way, he awakened the Brigadier and suggested that they follow the same plan. Scouts were immediately sent out, who discovered the two crags which were obviously Bozez and Seneh, and what is more, located a flat piece of ground higher up, suitable for ploughing, which must have been the very 'half an acre of land'. So previously made plans were scrapped, Saul's strategy was adopted and, like the Philistines, the Turks were routed. One can still go to Michmash and see the very place where Jonathan climbed the hill, dragging his armour-bearer with him, and in the pass the two rocky headlands stand sentinel as they have done for thousands of years.

The W.F. suffered by reason of the changing character of Army life in wartime. At no time could a man be sure that he would not be posted away by the following week. We lost a large number of stalwarts in this way, keeping in touch with them, however, by means of the news-letter. But we always seemed to maintain our numbers with others who added themselves to us. At first we had no Methodist Church in Jerusalem which could be a centre of our activity. But the Scottish Church welcomed us, as I have described, and until we had premises of our own we enjoyed there the privileges of Methodist fellowship. When we became responsible for an informal service in the Y.M.C.A. canteen, some local preachers and I formed a 'plan', conducting the service in turn, and thus extending the practical work of the W.F. The secretary kept a diary of all our activities, which was read every Wednesday at the Fellowship. One of the lads was an artist, and he designed a crest for us: hands clasped in friendship before a cross.

Through the hardships and separations of war, not one of us carried his cross alone. Ours was the fellowship of suffering, with each other and with the Christ whose Way of Sorrows led through these very streets: our living Comrade, strong and tender. These pages hold the record of but a few of the happy days, strenuous days, memorable days that we knew when we saw the Holy City.

CHAPTER II

BETHLEHEM

Beginne from first where He encradled was
In simple cratch, wrapt in a Wad of Hay
Betweene the toylfull oxe and humble ass,
And in what Rags, and in how base Aray,
The glory of our heavenly Riches lay,
When Him the silly sheperds came to see
Whom greatest Princes sought on lowest knee.

EDMUND SPENSER, 'The Babe',
sixteenth century.

A BUS runs to Bethlehem every twenty minutes from the Jaffa Gate. The distance is five miles and the fare is 20 mils. A mil is worth a farthing. So it was possible for the troops in Jerusalem to get there quickly and cheaply. It was a popular outing, when the men had a few hours to spare, to take a return trip to Bethlehem. I went there more times than I can remember by bus, by car, and, best of all, by foot on a sunny morning with a friend with whom to yarn, and a pipe to smoke, and now and again a pause to appreciate the magnificent scenery or to locate this or that place of special interest either by the roadside or in the distant view.

Many times was I called up on the telephone from the Y.M.C.A. Information Bureau to inquire whether I was free to take a party of soldiers on leave to Bethlehem, and I have acted as a guide to such parties sometimes four days in succession. Thus I became very familiar with the road and with the little town itself, balanced on the top of a hilly ridge, with the Church of the Holy Nativity in its midst. On such occasions cars were hired for the party and, strange as it may seem, the Mount of Olives was usually included in our itinerary, although it is in almost the opposite direction. This was because Bethlehem and the Mount of Olives are the only places visitors are anxious to see sufficiently far from Jerusalem to need a car to get there in the short time, the one or two precious days' leave that troops usually had in the Holy City. They are near enough, however, to be visited in one journey, although the whole of Jerusalem lies between them; and the rest of the time of leave could be devoted to seeing as much as possible of the Old City.

Some of the routes I describe in this book follow those suggested for troops on leave. When a man arrived at a troops' hostel,

as scores did daily, to ask how best he could see the sights round
Jerusalem, he was invited to join parties that were being formed
of men on leave like himself, to economize by sharing a car
with them. A guide would lead them to the holy sites they
desired to see, and if there was a large party, a chaplain would
guide them instead. Thus a man would be able to visit the Temple
Area, the Wailing Wall, and the Old City markets on his first
morning; the Church of the Holy Sepulchre, the Via Dolorosa and
the Ecce Homo Convent in the afternoon; Bethlehem and the
Mount of Olives on the next morning; and then the Garden of
Gethsemane, the Kedron Valley, and the Pool of Bethesda. If he
had another full day to spare, he could get a seat in a car for a
twelve-hour trip through Samaria to Galilee and see Nazareth and
Capernaum, returning sometimes by way of Haifa and Jaffa. Other
itineraries, such as a car journey from Jerusalem to Jericho with a
chance to bathe in the Dead Sea and to see the River Jordan, or to
wander to other sites and churches around the Old City were
suggested when more time was available for him. A valuable all-
day work was done in this way by the ladies who volunteered their
services at the Y.M.C.A. Information Bureau and at various hostels
for troops in Jerusalem.

I never begrudged the time I spent in leading parties of men
around the holy places. I invariably found it to be a ministry in
itself—'open-air work' of the best and happiest kind. Troops who
had the good fortune to be stationed in Jerusalem, of course, took
advantage of these facilities when their time off duty permitted, but
as I got to know them during the weeks and months that passed, I
took them on our Sunday afternoon rambles over much of the
ground again, this time more carefully. We went farther afield, too,
and we took a good deal of interest in learning the local stories of
certain places and in reading more of their history together.

When a party passed quickly in a car over the Bethlehem road it
was not possible to do more than indicate to the men one or two
famous landmarks. But at greater leisure a few of us were able to
walk along the road and pause at will to look about us. I want
to describe a 'hike' I took in this fashion with one or two others
on a pleasant afternoon not long before Christmas. I shall tell in
a moment of our visits to Bethlehem on Christmas Eve and
Christmas Day.

We set off at a long, steady stride past the few scattered streets of
modern houses south of the city, and we were soon in the open
country. The road was a good and a fairly busy one, and we
were passed by cars, War Department vehicles, and an occasional

low, rickety omnibus full for the most part of Bethlehem Arabs, the women wearing tall medieval head-dresses. They were probably returning from shopping in the narrow, crowded markets of Jerusalem. Along this road in their day had marched Israelites and Philistines; Egyptians, Assyrians, Babylonians; Greeks and Romans and Persians; Moslem invaders and Crusader liberators; Saracen and Turk and, later, British soldiery. Abraham the nomad had driven his sheep this way to Hebron; Samuel the prophet had visited the house of Jesse to find the David who later roamed these hills and plains; Rehoboam had trod this road to build a fortress at Bethlehem; Mary and Joseph had made their way to the City of David for the enrolment in the days of Caesar Augustus. We followed the steps of Byzantine Emperors and Crusader kings and of prelates and pilgrims of succeeding generations. In our rough khaki battledress, tramping along with pipe in mouth, we represented our own age and were but part of the mighty pageant of history.

Around us lay the rolling hills of Judea, the fields yellow and rocky beyond low stone walls, and dotted with an occasional twisted olive tree. The sky above us was a cloudless blue and the air fresh and clean. We felt full of vigour, and as we swung along we talked of days gone by, of Bible times and more recent history, until we stopped to look at an old stone well-head by the roadside on our left. This is an ancient piece of white stone with a great circular hole cut through it, perhaps by Arabs some five hundred years ago, and at one time it apparently stood at the mouth of a well. It might be one of the stones of a Roman conduit. It is known as the Magi's Well, and the legend is that having lost sight of their guiding star the Wise Men paused to drink and saw it again reflecting brightly in the water. It is perhaps inevitable that there should also be a local story that Mary rested here on her weary journey and refreshed herself at this well.

Nearby is a field with the stony soil lightly ploughed after the manner of the Palestine peasants, and I recalled a tale I had heard of a certain Russian nobleman of last century who visited the Holy Land and was impatient to learn all the events associated with the places he saw. He was constantly pestering his guide to tell him what had happened here and what had happened there—a somewhat natural keenness not to miss anything not uncommon among pilgrims then and now, which often results in the use of a guide's fertile imagination in order that he might satisfy a client's curiosity. When the Russian passed this field he demanded:

'And what happened here?'

'Here,' said the exasperated guide, 'is the place where God obtained the soil from which He made Adam.'

So, somewhat to the surprise of the man who was tilling the field, he was paid a large sum for a sackful of its soil and it was duly exported to Moscow. Whenever that credulous Russian nobleman or his friends suffered from headache they found that a spoonful of the soil stirred into a cup of tea proved to be a wonderful remedy. The earth from which God made Adam possessed, of course, great curative properties.

It is said that the Orthodox Patriarch received subsequent orders for the despatch of consignments of this soil to Russia, and made quite a considerable profit thereby, but this allegation may very well be a great injustice to that good man. In this manner local legends arise. We at any rate resisted the temptation to remove any more of the field and decided to continue to rely upon aspirin for our headaches.

At the top of that rise stands the roadside Greek monastery of Mar Elyâs. This is a seminary for priests of the Greek Orthodox Church and we saw entering it some almost beardless youths in the black garb of Greek theological students. A rocky seat with an old stone shelter by the side of the road is said to be the place where the prophet Elijah rested when he 'went for his life' from Jezebel, fleeing from Jezreel to Beersheba in the south. As the monastery was built by a bishop named Elyâs or Elias, however, it is probable that his name gave rise to the legend that Elijah sat here. It is a good place to rest, though, not only because of the steepness of the hill, but because of the wonder of the view. Holman Hunt's widow placed a lovely carved stone bench on the spot where the artist was accustomed to sit. It is on the brow of the hill to the right of the road, and we thankfully rested on it.

Some people say that from this hilltop is the finest view in the world. I have stood upon many an eminence and marvelled at the vista before me: the Bay of Naples from Vesuvius, the panorama from Anacapri, Cape Town from Table Mountain; but never have I seen so much history linked with beauty as we saw from Holman Hunt's seat. From here and from here alone is it possible to see both the Mount of Olives to the north and Bethlehem to the south, with the mountains of Moab across the Dead Sea to the east. Behind us lay the distant domes and towers of Jerusalem, with the Russian Tower on Olivet lifting like the point of a slender dunce's cap. On the flat top of Mount Moriah the Temple of Solomon once had gleamed in gold and marble, and from this hilltop the Hebrew traveller would have paused to see the column of smoke rising to heaven from the Altar of Sacrifice. On this summit, surely, Mary and Joseph rested and gazed at the tiny city of their fathers on the hilltop to the south before they began the last stage of their journey to the inn, only to find that swifter travellers had already crowded it. The distant Frank Mountain to the south-east was dim on the skyline. It is flat-topped like a volcano, and although it is now named after Crusaders it was once the site of a palace of King Herod, and was called Herodium. Falling away from us on every hand and then rising again were the timeless hills that David knew. A flock of sheep and goats clustered in the little valley at our feet. There was at that moment little traffic on the road, and we were looking at a scene of Bible days. Except for a few buildings, the view can be very little different from that which lay before the partriarchs of old and the countless travellers through the ages who had rested on this hilltop.

I remembered another story I had read of a field by this roadside, a story much older than the one about the Russian nobleman. It probably dates from the Middle Ages. Along on the right near Rachel's Tomb, a piece of land dotted with stones is pointed out as a garden in which peas were growing when Mary and Joseph passed that way. Joseph asked the farmer for some of the peas, as they both were hungry, but his request was refused. So he cursed the ground, and the peas turned into little stones. They lie there to this day. It is not explained why every other field in Palestine is also covered with little stones. Perhaps some over-curious abbot on pilgrimage in the days of long ago had also been a victim of a guide's imagination, this time of some impatient Knight Hospitaller with a flair for fiction.

The Moorish dome which covers what is known as Rachel's Tomb is about two hundred years old. The shrine is the only one in Palestine which is in the custody of the Jews. It stands to the right near a fork in the road, the right-hand prong leading to Hebron, some twenty miles distant, and the left to Bethlehem. This tomb has been a landmark certainly since the fourth century A.D., for more than one pilgrim writes about it, and Jerome a few years later describes a tumulus at the place where the road to Bethlehem turned from the Hebron road. He, however, called it 'the tomb of Archelaus, King of Judea', and R. W. Hamilton, of the Palestine Department of Antiquities, suggests that it is possible that the word 'Archelaus' has a resemblance to 'Rachel' and could very well have been mistaken for it in early times. The author of Genesis xxxv. 19–20 knew of a 'Pillar of Rachel's grave' which stood in his day 'on the way to Ephrath (the same is Bethlehem)'. In the

Book of Ruth 'Ephrathites' are obviously men of Bethlehem, and Micah refers to 'Bethlehem Ephrata'. But in I Samuel x. 2 Rachel's sepulchre is described as being 'on the borders of Benjamin at Zelzah', which would place it somewhere north of Jerusalem. There is an early tradition that Rachel's tomb was near there, at Er-Ram, the old-time Ramah, as far north of Jerusalem as Bethlehem is south, and Jeremiah in xxxi. 15 suggests that this was believed in his day to be where Rachel lay. On the other hand, this very passage about Rachel weeping for her children is quoted in Matthew ii. 18 as a reference to Herod's slaughter of the innocents at Bethlehem. So there is a little confusion about it. But there is no doubt that for many centuries, perhaps thousands of years, the great stone under this rough dome has been a landmark in the countryside and has been venerated as the resting-place of Rachel. Moslems revere this spot as well as Jews, and in the vestibule there is a place of prayer for them, facing towards Mecca.

The Jewish visitors congregate around the cenotaph itself, uttering their separate prayers in a wailing chant and sobbing and kissing the stone. We went in to see them, past two bearded Hebrews who sat studying the scriptures. But we did not remain very long in that confined space with so many people pushing about the tomb, weeping and rocking their bodies to and fro as they prayed. All the lamps hanging about were given by expectant mothers at the tomb of the mother of the Patriarchs. An up-to-date touch was given to the whole scene by an immense 'V', presumably intended to indicate 'Victory', which somebody had scrawled outside on the wall of the shrine.

We clambered over a low stone wall into a field between the forked roads to look at one or two blocks of stone, rather more than a yard square and a foot thick, that lay about there. They had large circular holes cut through them.

'I know what this is,' said one of my companions.

'What is it?' I said.

'This is Pontius Pilate's aqueduct, and it was discovered by H. V. Morton!'

'It's an aqueduct all right,' I said, 'but it doesn't belong to the time of Pilate. And, of course, its existence has been known for a long time. Actually, these blocks, and a few others scattered along its course, are all that remains of a pipeline made by order of the Emperor Septimus Severus in the second century A.D. Pilate's aqueduct is below the earthenware pipe, part of which you can see along this road on the other side. It followed a serpentine route round the hillside to enable the water to flow along it, while the idea of the newer one was to syphon the water as it went up and down the hills on a shorter course. It is thought that it was never finished. It led from Solomon's Pools, south of Bethlehem.'

'What is your authority for that?' asked one studious youth.

'The Government of Palestine's *Guide to Bethlehem*, by R. W. Hamilton,' I replied. 'You can get it at the Archaeological Museum for 50 mils.'

I added that about forty years ago Canon Hanauer traced in these stones the names of centurions who had been in charge of the work, which was in the hands of the famous Tenth Legion.

'They had some R.Es. attached to them, I suppose?' said somebody.

I replied that engineering was one of their specialities.

A house had recently been built in the corner of the field, and one lad noticed that, after the fashion of builders in Palestine for centuries, older stones had been incorporated into its walls. In this instance two of the stone blocks from Septimus Severus' aqueduct had been built into the side near the ground-level, with their wide perforations making fine circular windows for a cellar.

The members of my party all wanted to see Pilate's aqueduct, so we crossed the road a little way along the road to Bethlehem, and on the left we found it opening on to a deep quarry. Its course is represented by an earthenware pipe about a foot in diameter set in a wall of rubble and concrete. It has long been disused although it was restored and repaired many times in the past, and it lies in its original bed winding round the hills, now burrowing beneath the ground, now emerging, as it does at this spot for about a hundred yards. The present pipe belongs to the last repair.

We sat on it for a while to rest ourselves, and as we surveyed the grandeur of the countryside rolling before us to the east we realized that its contours must have remained unchanged through the centuries, for where we were sitting, unlike the changed altitude of Jerusalem streets, had been ground-level in the days of Pontius Pilate. He took the Temple taxes to pay for this water supply, we remembered, which proved to be a most unpopular action and led him into endless trouble. The story is graphically told in Frank Morison's *And Pilate Said*.

The surrounding fields we noticed were not carefully fenced, but were still divided by little piles of stones, the ancient 'neighbours landmarks' of the Old Testament. Away to the right on a pleasant hillside we could see the Christian village of Beit Jala, which was Giloh, the home of Ahitophel, David's boyhood friend.

We followed the road as it curved round the side of a hill, and

saw it sloping up ahead of us beside white stone houses and past a
great Franciscan monastery on the hilltop to the right. A path led
away to an old well which tradition declares is the very well at the
gate of Bethlehem from which David longed to drink when he was
in the cave of Adullam surrounded by his enemies. Three mighty
men went to this well and drew water for him, although Bethlehem
was garrisoned by Philistines. 2 Samuel xxiii relates how David
refused to drink it, but poured it out unto the Lord, declaring that
the water was the blood of the men who went in jeopardy of their
lives. It may have been clear and desirable water once, but now the
water in the well is unfit to drink. A well at the gate of Bethlehem
in those days is more likely to have been at the east of its main road,
possibly one of the cisterns at the Nativity Church. On the top of
the hill we could see a small belfry over the church which contains
the famous Bells of Bethlehem that ring round the world on
Christmas Day. Away to our left the view was glorious. Terraces
of olive trees went down into the valley far below us, and the Fields
of the Shepherds stretched away into the distance, not green with
grass, as we had always imagined, but stony and yellow-earthed,
with scanty pasture.

Most of the inhabitants of Bethlehem are Christian Arabs, and
Roman Catholic missionary work from Italy and America is very
pronounced here. More than one shopkeeper to whom we spoke had
visited the United States. The principal industry in the village,
taught by monks of the sixteenth century, is the manufacture of
ornaments in mother-of-pearl, and the shops are full of them. The
women have a fame for embroidery, and once when I was walking
through the village of Beit Sahur, down in the valley, I watched a
cottager working a most intricate pattern with gold thread upon
blue velvet. It was the sort of jacket that Arab women wear, heavy
with its embroidered design, a memory from Byzantine days.
They pay a great price for such a garment, but it lasts a lifetime and
is very beautiful.

Men sat about *café* tables in the main village street listening to
weird Oriental music from a wireless loudspeaker, and watched us
as we walked towards the courtyard of the church. Above them,
from the balcony of an upper-story flat, hung a board with the
strangest of all notices to be seen in Manger Square, Bethlehem. In
Arabic and English it said, 'Bethlehem Ethical Club'. The Arabs
of royal David's city are pretty highbrow. Do they ponder together over the modern implications of 'peace on earth and goodwill to men'? Many youths pestered us to act as guides, for *baksheesh*,
of course, and although we waved them aside, one or two insisted

upon walking a little way in front of us, pretending to be leading us. They would turn their heads constantly to see which way we went, and when we turned in a different direction they hurriedly went ahead of us again.

We crossed the famous courtyard beside old walls high to the right of us, and found the tiny entry into the church. Traces of older doorways can be seen in the surrounding stonework. Once, long ago, men could ride right into the church on horseback, and often did so. Later it was made smaller and men had to dismount, but they could stride in erect. Now every one must bow low his head as he enters the place where his Lord was born. This 'eye of a needle' was made for purposes of defence in turbulent days and to prevent animals from wandering into the sanctuary.

Suddenly, out of the sunshine, we were in a great gloomy church, with four files of big columns and many immense lamps draped with cloth hanging from the old roof. We were standing in the oldest Christian church in the world. In A.D. 330 the Emperor Constantine built a church here, which was probably damaged by a Samaritan rising in 529 and was then rebuilt on a much larger scale by Justinian. The present edifice, patched and renewed in subsequent generations, is substantially the one built by Justinian, and it is barely possible that the walls, or part of them, date from Constantine. The Persians in 614 invaded Palestine and destroyed Christian churches all over the country. But they spared this church. When they arrived at Bethlehem, intent upon pillage and destruction, they saw at its entrance, in glorious mosaics, pictures of themselves! The Magi clad in Persian dress were bowing before the infant Christ. So they entered the church and worshipped also. The Moslems at their conquest in 637 respected the church as the birthplace of their prophet Jesus and indeed worshipped in it along-side the Christians for many years. It was Moslem respect for it that probably preserved it through the waves of destruction that overwhelmed other Christian shrines in Palestine, notably the Holy Sepulchre, to which Moslems give no significance, since they do not accept the story of the Cross and Resurrection of Jesus. The advent of the Crusaders nearly caused the destruction of the Nativity church, or the Church of St. Mary as it was then called, by the Saracens, but it was rescued by the Normans, and there has ever since been a strong Latin tradition at Bethlehem.

St. Jerome, one of the founders of monasticism, dwelt here at the end of the fourth century A.D. and made his famous translation of the Bible into Latin, the present Vulgate, in a cave adjoining that of the Nativity, and his tomb is there now. He said that from the

days of Hadrian, in A.D. 135, until those of Constantine, a grove of
Adonis was venerated on the site, and 'where the infant Messiah
once cried, the paramour of Venus was bewailed'. It seems likely
that after the quelling of Barcochba's rising, when Jews were
banished, the pagan agricultural rites were observed. But were they
the survival of very primitive rites from ancient days? Beit Lahm,
the Arab name for Bethlehem, means the 'house of bread', and those
pagan festivities had to do with the spirit of the grain. It is the scene
of that idyll among the corn, the old story of Ruth and Boaz. We
need not infer from this, however, that Sir James Frazer is right in
the theory he puts forward in *The Golden Bough* that the birth of
the One who called Himself the 'Bread of Life' should have been
located here because of its old associations. As R. W. Hamilton
points out, the Christmas festivities have nothing whatever in
common with the Adonis cult, and the theory cannot be made to
fit the facts of history or the nature of the Gospel story.

It is not often realized that nowhere in the New Testament does
it say that Jesus was crucified on a hill, yet the fact that Calvary was
a hill has been an accepted tradition from the beginning. In the
same way, the stable in which He was born has been believed from
very early times to be a cave, although the Gospel writers do not
mention it. As early as A.D. 150, a cave is mentioned in Christian
writings, and this tradition is to be found in Justin Martyr's *Dialogue with Trypho*, some years later. Origen, who was in Palestine
in A.D. 215, says, 'they still show the cave in Bethlehem where He
was born', and the famous Eusebius, who lived in Caesarea at the
end of the third century, writes, 'the inhabitants of the place . . .
point out the cave in which the Virgin brought forth and laid her
child'. It is most unlikely that the cave over which Constantine
built this church is any other than the one known to earlier writers.

The troops, of course, were a little sceptical when they saw another
grotto. As one of them said, everybody seemed to live in grottoes
in those days. Were they cave-dwellers? Wherever there was a
hole in the rock near a traditional Bible event, it seems to have been
located on that very spot. The home of the Holy Family in Nazareth
is a series of grottoes; elsewhere in Bethlehem is the 'Milk Grotto',
where Mary suckled the Babe in the place where they dwelt before
the flight into Egypt; the Virgin was born in the grotto of St. Anne
in Jerusalem; she died in a grotto under the present Dormition
church; John the Baptist was born in a grotto at Ain Karim; and
there are many others. Since the pungent remarks of Mark Twain
on this subject, tourists have, I suppose, been sceptical wherever a
grotto was displayed as a holy site, and I have no doubt that most

BETHLEHEM UNDER SNOW, CHRISTMAS, 1941.

THE CHURCH OF THE NATIVITY

[Photo by J Meilutish

of such caves were chosen for that purpose because they were more indestructible than houses. They obviously had existed in the days in which the events took place, and it was not easy to prove that those events had *not* happened there. Furthermore, I can understand something of the feelings of investigators of early days, for when I was staying in Nazareth I would go exploring the surrounding hills and loved to imagine that the youthful Jesus climbed on these very rocks within sight of His village just below. Once I found a large cave in the hillside overlooking Nazareth. Without doubt this had been there in the days of Jesus. I entered it and looked about me at the age-old rocky wall and roof. Had Jesus known and entered this cave as a boy? It was quite possible. I could appreciate the emotions of some wanderer of long ago, who was blessed with a little imagination, finding a cave, not on a hillside, but in the village itself and thinking that maybe Jesus had walked there. If he communicated his thoughts to another less sensitive, more practical one, it is quite likely that the news would spread that Joseph's workshop had been found! A tradition would thus arise and a church be built by pious folk more credulous than critical.

But the cave tradition of Bethlehem is in a category different from this. It is a belief from very earliest times, and it was certainly nothing unusual to stable animals underground, in some natural, handy, ready-made shelter. I have seen several such places in and around Jerusalem with old tethering holes cut in the rock. I am not at all incredulous that the present grotto of the Nativity is the very place where Jesus was born. The Bethlehem site is probably the best-authenticated shrine in Palestine.

The nave of the church in which we stood is common to the Orthodox, Latins, and Armenians, and although it was resplendent with gilt mosaic in the Middle Ages, few scraps remain upon the walls now dulled and tarnished. Some visitors had secured the key of the large trapdoors, in the floor of the nave, and were peering down at the extensive remains of the mosaic floor of the original church of Constantine that were found in 1934. We looked down, too. About a yard below the present ground level we saw the many beautiful intricate designs in tiny stones that had been set there in careful artistry by the hands of men who lived only some 300 years after Christ. Around us, some of the reddish limestone columns had dim pictures of saints painted on them, including one of a king of England, St. Canute. One of the men in my party unkindly asked me to translate the Greek inscription he found on a massive octagonal font. I hastily turned to my guide book. It read:

C

'For remembrance, rest, and remission of sins to those whose names the Lord knoweth.'

This font had long been disused. It had been removed from the baptistery for some reason and was almost hidden in that forest of smooth and lovely columns. It was part of the church that Justinian built.

The Birthplace is under the sanctuary, which is shielded by an enormous Greek *ikonostasis* at the east end of the church, and we descended one of the two narrow stairways that led down to it from opposite sides, the steps worn by innumerable pilgrims. We stood in silence before a shrine with a silver star set in marble with an inscription round it. It read:

HIC DE VIRGINE MARIA JESUS CHRISTUS NATUS EST.

The Franciscans found the original eighteenth-century star with this inscription prised away, and nobody knows what happened to it. The Greeks had always objected to the Latin words. The Sultan of the Ottoman Empire gave the present one in 1852 in an attempt to prevent strife between the rival factions, but in vain. Incredible as it may seem, its loss was part of the great controversy about the care of the holy places in Palestine which led to the Crimean War. Vol. I of Kinglake's *Invasion of the Crimea* describes how the quarrel developed into an international war. On the other hand, some say that this squabble at Bethlehem, with Holy Russia threatening to take strong and independent measures to protect the sacred sites, and Turkey calling upon Britain and France to aid her resistance, was only an excuse for the war. In reality it was due to the fact that Napoleon III could not forgive Nicholas I that he did not address him in his letters as 'Sire et bon Frère', but simply as, 'Sire et bon ami', which he took as an insult!

But controversies and wars, even the present one, were far from our minds. We were looking at the place where Jesus Christ was born.

Above us the low roof of irregular rock was blackened with age and the smoke of countless candles. Around the walls of a space some 20 feet by 10 were dimly-painted fireproof curtains to protect the marble facings. Lamps were everywhere, hanging in scores from the roof, great golden vessels which the Easterns love. Down three more steps we went to look at a tiny chapel in a sort of niche in the rock where two altars opposite each other commemorate the situation of the manger and of the place where the wise men knelt to adore the infant Christ. Jerome wrote that the original clay manger had been replaced by a silver one, but now only a marble slab remains to mark its site. It was hard for us to picture the cave as a dirty stable with horses and donkeys tied to the walls and fodder in a manger of dried mud, waiting to cradle the King of Glory. It was possible to imagine this lower part as a manger and the upper main room as a tolerable dwelling place.

There is never any difficulty about accommodating people in an Eastern inn in normal circumstances. Space can always be found for an extra visitor. The Arabs have a saying, 'The house of a friend has a hundred rooms', meaning, of course, that no visitor is ever turned away. However crowded was the inn at Bethlehem, an ordinary visitor would have been given a corner somewhere. But an imminent child-birth was another matter. The Jews had cere- monial regulations about that, and there would be no suitable place for a birth in a crowded inn. The stable downstairs was the best thing the innkeeper and maybe his bustling, attendant wife could arrange for them. Babies in Palestine are still bundled in tight 'swaddling clothes', for the common idea is that such a practice enables the limbs to grow straight.

After a while we climbed the opposite stairs and, passing before the rather crudely decorated Armenian Altar to the Kings, we entered the modern Franciscan Church of St. Catherine, which was built in 1881 on the site of a medieval chapel. The old crumbling cloisters are still adjacent to it. We were looking for the way into the grotto where Jerome lived and wrote at the end of the fourth century. It is part of a series of caves joined to the Birthplace, but it is in the hands of the Latins, and so we must enter it from the Latin church. The Greeks have the custody of the Nativity cave, but the Latins and Armenians may use it, subject, of course, to strict rules. Many have been the unholy scrimmages between rival religious enthusiasts on the ground where the Prince of Peace was born.

We went down to see the underground chapel where Jerome translated the Bible and we saw his tomb and those of Paula and Eustochium, two holy women who were his disciples. Eusebius of Cremona is buried there, too. We found his tomb in a narrow passage. There was also an altar erected on the supposed place where the angel warned Joseph in a dream to escape into Egypt, and another in memory of the Holy Innocents slaughtered by Herod. Although the series of tunnels were lighted by electricity and a few lamps hung about, it was depressing, and we found that narrow space very stuffy. We soon moved away back up the stairs, and round the old cloisters into the open air.

It was wonderful to think of the old saint working away at his laborious task in that ancient cavern so many centuries ago. I tried to recall some of the things I had read about the life of Jerome, but the men were not greatly interested. They hustled me along to look at the Crusader stables—domed arches by the Greek chapel— and to find the Milk Grotto. We found this with difficulty in a side street, and marvelled at the *naïveté* of those who believe that the black cave turned miraculously white when Mary fed the child there, and who have decorated it with so many geegaws in honour of the Virgin. In *The Innocents Abroad*, Mark Twain says that a Methodist looks for a Methodist holy land when he goes to Palestine, and finds it, with everything to substantiate his own particular ideas. I did nothing of the kind. I looked for the simplicities of the Gospel story, the hills and vales where Jesus trod, and I found them. But I found a good deal of nonsense, too, perpetuated to their shame by the representatives of the great traditional Churches of Christendom. And the Milk Grotto is one of them.

At the end of that road, on the brow of the hill, we found a convent, and we were invited by a sister to mount to the roof to see the Shepherds' Fields. She was dressed in snowy white from head to foot, and we stood quietly beside her on that flat rooftop as she described the view to us in a gentle voice. It was truly a memorable sight in that afternoon sunlight. The Arab village of Beit Sahur (literally: 'the House of the Watching by Night') lay beneath us in the valley, and the fields, parcelled out to the peasants according to the old-time feudal system, were in orderly array beyond it. We could see men ploughing with a one-handled plough as in Bible times, sometimes following a horse or a donkey or even a camel. They only scrape the surface with a small coulter, usually of wood. The ground is covered with stones, so they must keep the 'hand to the plough' and not 'look back', in order to navigate the furrow round the stones, lest a jagged flint splits the implement. Sheep are still kept in that rough country, and once I went tramping over the very plains where David sang as he minded the flocks. An old Arab showed me a cave (another cave!) in which the shepherds sheltered on the first Christmas Eve. It is possible that Jesus was born in winter time, for the sheep could have been out in the open if it was a warm night. There is no serious objection to the traditional date. Perhaps the shepherds who heard angels singing were Bedouins who lived always in tents in the open air? Perhaps they were employed to tend sheep for the Temple sacrifices? The ruins of a Byzantine monastery lie in the traditional Shepherds' Fields. They are now overgrown with grass and a few olive trees, but a crypt remains, which is used for occasional Orthodox services, and in it I have traced the vestiges of some ancient mosaic on its floor. In A.D. 670 a pilgrim named Arculf found to the east of Bethlehem a church with the graves of three shepherds, who, he wrote, 'saw the Glory of God'. In the Middle Ages this shrine was known as the Church of St. Joseph, and it is probably the ruin that I saw. One tangled old olive was shown to me as the very tree under which the shepherds sat when they listened to the 'Glory to God in the highest'. The surrounding country is called the Fields of Boaz, and the natives of Bethlehem point to a beautiful rustic setting for that timeless story of love amid the corn. A little while after Christmas I conducted a service for troops in a big cave at Tell Boaz nearby. The Y.M.C.A., who have bought the ground, found Herodian potsherds in it. Maybe, who knows, the shepherds sheltered there?

Beit Sahur is an interesting and typically Arab village, of mixed Moslem and Christian population. The Arab headmaster of its school took my party of troops once on a tour round it, and led us into a house where wedding celebrations were taking place. A crowd of women, cumbered by their long red-and-black dresses, were dancing in a weird sort of stamping measure, to the accompaniment of shrill cries and clapping of hands. Little children ran among them, ignored by the adults, who had drunk too much *arak*, the potent native spirit. The grandfather of the bridegroom, whose house it was, was going to allocate one of his rooms to the happy pair. It was apparently unthinkable to them that a newly-married couple should set up a home for themselves. It was one big family establishment presided over by the 'old man'. I asked him his age. He laughed, and his answer was translated to us.

'Forty when my wife is listening,' he said, 'but seventy when she is not about.'

Apparently Arab women have ideas about the passage of the years similar to those of their Western sisters.

The village school was interesting. There were about 300 children in it, many of them Moslems, and the enterprising Head had initiated co-education with great success. The school, in wartime controlled by a missionary committee, was founded by the Shepherds' Fields Society, an organization that was established in Saxony with the object of teaching the shepherd boys of Bethlehem to read and write! At least one lawyer and six doctors received their first lessons there.

There are strange sidelines to war. It is an ironic commentary on the times that the only opportunity in a lifetime to visit Bethlehem on Christmas Day was given to me because I joined the Army. A dictator arose, minorities were persecuted, peaceful lands were invaded, tanks crunched their way across Europe, cities went up in flames, war spread round the globe, and I found myself in Bethlehem!

Nobody I met had known such rain as fell on the Holy Land at Christmastide, 1941. It rained without a pause for five days and nights: heavy, cold, and drenching. Troops on leave for Christmas in Jerusalem had perforce to remain in the Y.M.C.A. and Church of Scotland hostels or wherever they had found shelter, and make the best they could of amusements there, with an occasional sally into the downpour to visit another centre of interest. But they were not loath to go to Bethlehem. On Christmas Eve I had planned a carol-singing expedition. In the clear moonlit streets of the City of David we were going to sing 'O Little Town of Bethlehem', and in the Fields of Boaz, 'While Shepherds watched'. We had prepared 'Adeste Fideles' and 'Stille Nacht', 'Hark the Herald Angels' and many another. I had hired buses and borrowed a lorry, but I feared that I should be left to make the five-mile journey to Bethlehem alone or with a faithful few. But not a bit of it. The men came in their crowds through the drenching rain and piled into the waiting vehicles, and off we went. But, apart from our singing *en route* after the manner of soldiers as they travel—and, of course, we sang the songs of Christmas—there was no possibility of carols at Bethlehem. With macs and rubber ground-sheets over our heads, we ran from the buses across the courtyard into the Church of the Nativity. I must confess that we were all a little impatient as we waited in the rain for our turn to creep through the 'eye of a needle'.

Once inside the great church, away from wind and rain, every-thing was suddenly solemn and peaceful. It was like Jesus saying 'Peace be still', during the storm on Galilee. He was saying it again at Bethlehem to a stormy world, so it seemed to us. We stood in a group looking at the great pillars and the beautiful proportions of the Byzantine nave. We tried to picture the slow procession of priests in bright vestments and monks in quiet garb as it wound its way between these very pillars in those dimly distant days, when those gloomy walls were bright with the splendour of gilt mosaic. We tried to imagine St. Jerome as he toiled at his Bible, setting it into the vulgar tongue, in a cave almost under our feet; and pre-tended we could see Baldwin I, King of Jerusalem, crowned in this very church on Christmas Day, 1101; and we thought of the crafts-men paid by Edward IV of England to repair the roof of the nave with lead and oak in 1482. The roof we were looking at was placed

there exactly a hundred years before, in 1842. The Turks had
appropriated the Bethlehem lead to make bullets.

Groups of visitors moved about the church and the adjacent
buildings: the Greek convent and the Latin Church of St. Catherine.
Had the weather been only slightly less severe there would, of
course, have been very many more pilgrims there. The Eastern
Orthodox Christmas would not be celebrated until January 7, so
their sanctuary over the actual birthplace was unlit and silent. But
a few of their priests sat with tapers for us to use as we joined the
throng forming a thin file into the Grotto of the Nativity.

We stood in silence before the large silvery star set in marble.
Here, at the very Birthplace, was the focus point of Christendom
that day. Candles around us guttered and shone. Down in the
little chapel in the rock was a figure of a baby lying on hay in the
place where the manger is said to have been. The other altar
commemorating the place where the Magi knelt in adoration as
they brought their gifts was brightly illuminated. Anything less
like a wayside stable would be difficult to imagine. I am afraid
some of the troops were disappointed when they saw it. I explained
in a whisper that we must not expect the Eastern Orthodox Church,
or the Roman Catholics or Armenians, to have our tastes in decoration or our ideas of simplicity. These somewhat garish crudities
represented the Eastern notion of reverence. However childish the
baubles seemed to us, we must try to look beyond this veneer of
ecclesiasticism to the simplicities behind it. So we tried to picture
the cave as the dirty stable it was on the first Christmas Day.

We watched some faithful ones kneeling to kiss the stones. It is
strange to us who view a holy site with Western eyes and see a place
of historic interest, to realize that there are so many who believe
that there is some precious emanation from holy ground. A prayer
said there will be more efficacious than elsewhere. An altar must
be erected and lamps hung up and festoons of Oriental splendour
must add to the sacredness of the spot. We could dearly have
wished that it had been preserved as nearly as possible as it originally
was. But if the early Christians had that Eastern idea of the value of
holy ground, as is possible, then we must consider that therein lies
an additional guarantee that the actual places are the ones preserved.
It was an unforgettable moment for us.

When we had paid our Christmas homage at the Shrine of the
Nativity, we passed through the old Latin cloisters, where Franciscan
monks stood about, smoking and chatting. They were Americans
for the most part, as we discovered from their speech. In the
Church of St. Catherine was an immense throng of people crowding

the place to the doors. It was representative of many nations and we saw a strange variety of garb and complexion. There was a great proportion of men in khaki, of course, and Australians and New Zealanders stood with their comrades from England and nearly every Allied country, as well as swarthy Christian Arabs and others from Eastern lands. The Magi who made their way to Bethlehem 2,000 years ago were the forerunners of many men from the East who are beginning to follow the Star. One of my party asked what it was all about. I told them that they were waiting for the midnight Mass.

'Is that all?' he said.

'All!' I echoed. 'Pontifical High Mass by the Latin Patriarch! What more do you want?'

'A good Methodist service,' he replied.

We left that strange crowd standing there. They would be waiting, hushed and still, for several hours yet. Next day I met a Christian Arab lad I know whom I had seen there. He told me that he did not get back to Jerusalem until five in the morning and had spent nearly nine hours in that church.

We had hoped to hear the carol-singing being broadcast from the Greek Chapel of St. George across a courtyard near the Bells of Bethlehem, but the torrential rain made that impossible. The Choir of St. George's Anglican Cathedral in Jerusalem is permitted to sing there every Christmas Eve. We stood aside as the High Commissioner for Palestine, Sir Harold MacMichael, and Mr. William Bullitt, the United States Ambassador-at-large, His Excellency's guest, passed through the nave from the tiny chapel. A poor Arab woman wearing the high medieval wimple of the married woman of Bethlehem, which dates from the time of the Crusades, made her way through the crowd. The famous and the lowly, like the Wise Men and Shepherds, were kneeling at the place of the Nativity that night.

Once back in Jerusalem, we had coffee and cakes at a hostel and then we went through the rain to a simple Christmas Eve service at midnight in the beautiful Scots Memorial Church of St. Andrew. The church was full of troops and we hailed the ever-blessed morn with the timeless songs of Christmas.

Next morning, at ten o'clock on Christmas Day, I was at Bethlehem again, taking part in a church parade. It was still pouring with rain and we all sheltered as best we could under arches built by other soldiers of other times, when men went to the Holy Land to give battle for the holy places.

The service was broadcast by the B.B.C., and our folk at home, as they sat round the fireside thinking of us, as we thought of them, heard our voices singing carols at Bethlehem on Christmas Day.

The radio announcer told me how he arranges the Christmas broadcasts for various communities.

'Some say that Christmas comes but once a year,' he said, 'but for me it comes three times. The Western Christmas is to-day, the Orthodox Christmas thirteen days later, on January 7th, and the Armenians observe it at their Epiphany on January 18th!'

'Cheer up,' I answered. 'The Abyssinians keep Christmas every month, except in March.'

'Thank heaven they don't broadcast it, then,' he said.

Three days later the heavy rain turned to snow, and I saw a real old English Christmas scene at Bethlehem with a thick white blanket over fields and houses round the Church of the Nativity.

Before I left the church after the carol service, I went down again to the Birthplace. People were still filing slowly into the Grotto, and I saw that a priest was celebrating Mass at the altar of the Wise Men. He was clad in snowy white and gold. As he knelt and rose and bowed and knelt again, my thoughts went to that Christmas morning scene in T. S. Eliot's *Murder in the Cathedral*. I remembered the sermon of the saintly Thomas, as he explained the Church's act of commemoration of the death of Jesus on the morning of His birth. Jesus came to die. He knew our birth that He might die our death. The Incarnation is an entity, complete from cradle to cross. The Church has not forgotten the purpose of His coming. On Christmas Day at Bethlehem, where stood the humble manger, the bread is broken and the wine poured forth.

CHAPTER III

OLD CITY

How can we read this endless story of humanity with any thought of blame? How can we watch this restless quivering human life, this ceaseless effort of a finite creature to attain to those things which are agreeable to its created nature, alike in all countries, under all climates and skies and whatever change of garb or semblance the long course of years may bring, with any other thought than that of tolerance and pity— tolerance of every sort of city existence, pity for every kind of toil and evil, year after year repeated, in every one of earth's cities, full of human life and handicraft, and thought and love and pleasure, as in the streets of that old Jerusalem over which the Saviour wept?

J. H. SHORTHOUSE, *John Inglesant*, 1880.

A GREAT wall built by Suleiman the Magnificent 400 years ago encloses the Jerusalem which is known as the 'Old City'. Up to the middle of last century this wall marked the limits of the Holy City, except for a few convents and churches commemorating sacred places outside. But now Jerusalem sprawls across several surrounding hills, and the Old City is usually regarded as an immense museum of antiquities. Of the 130,000 residents in Jerusalem, at least 100,000 live outside the Old City and, indeed, most of them never enter it.

I suppose the troops who came to Jerusalem on leave, or those who were stationed there, only went within the walls when they were engaged in sightseeing. Their work lay outside, and their billets, and their entertainments. But on Sunday afternoons when I took a party of men in search of relics of the past, we often directed our steps towards one of the Old City gates and spent a few hours in the shade of gloomy churches, or in narrow streets spread with an awning of sacks to give protection from the summer heat.

Many of the bazaars are vaulted with stone arches, through interstices of which would pour the sunshine, sending bars of brightness down on crowds in the shady streets and sprinkling the people as they walked through dappled light and shade. There is scarcely a level street in all Jerusalem, for valleys run their course through the city, and so the passages between the houses are twisty and narrow and very steep. Scarcely anywhere is it possible for wheeled traffic to penetrate its labyrinth, and the donkeys and camels and bright-robed pedestrians preserve an aspect the city must have worn for centuries.

There is a great grey stone pile beside the famous Jaffa Gate, which

is known as the Citadel. Once Herod's Palace stood there, and when
Titus destroyed Jerusalem in A.D. 70 he used its stronghold to
garrison his legions when the rest of the city lay desolate. For that
reason the great substructure of one of Herod's towers, Phasael, as
Josephus tells us it was named, still stands, its huge margined blocks
of masonry, each weighing from five to ten tons, rising high above
ground and surmounted by the stones of a Mameluke fortress dating
from about the fourteenth century. There are sixteen courses
altogether of the ancient masonry, its dimensions approximating to
the forty cubits, or 65 feet, which Josephus gives as the size each way
of the base of the tower Phasael. The blocks are of fine limestone
and they are still beautifully jointed together without mortar.
Soldiers were apparently stationed here from New Testament
times until the British occupation in 1917, for within the wide area
of its courtyard, now surrounded by medieval bastions forming
part of the city wall, have been found the remains of Roman,
Crusader, and Turkish barracks.

The Citadel is a museum now. In one part it houses a collection
of Palestinian farm implements, household furniture, and native
clothes; and in another, at the side of Phasael, is a model displaying
the archaeological discoveries of the whole building. Only in the
last year or two, until the beginning of the war, have archaeological
diggings been possible here, when the ground was finally cleared of
the Turkish barracks.

One Sunday afternoon we explored it, mounting steps to its
entrance inside the Old City. We stood on the platform outside
an old gate with a drawbridge over a deep empty moat where
Allenby stood in 1917 and read the proclamation to the Christians,
Moslems, and Jews of the Holy City, declaring that—

> 'every sacred building, monument, holy spot, shrine, traditional
> site, endowment, pious bequest, or customary place of prayer, of
> whatsoever form of the three religions, would be maintained
> and protected according to the existing customs and beliefs of
> those to whose faiths they were sacred'.

The Crusaders believed the Citadel to be the Tower of David,
and the popular name remains to this day. From the top of Phasael
we were able to get a magnificent view of the city spread out below
us in a beautiful and bewildering maze of domes and minarets,
church towers, little huddled houses, and the roofs of synagogues.
The Armenian quarter, with a cluster of buildings round its Cathedral of St. James, lay to our right, and beyond it the elliptical tops
of two big synagogues in the Jewish quarter. To our left were the

dark domes, one large and one small, that cover the Holy Sepulchre and Calvary, in the midst of the Christian quarter. Far ahead rose the majestic Dome of the Rock, where once Solomon's Temple stood on Mount Moriah. Round that Noble Sanctuary, as the Faithful call it, were spread the teeming streets of the Moslem quarter. Below us, apparently at our feet, was Christ Church compound where we could see the roof of its none too pleasing Victorian Gothic church, and on the other side of two graceful pepper trees and a giant oleander massed with rosy blossoms stood the fine old Arab house where the first Anglican bishop in Jerusalem, Dr. Alexander, a converted Jew, began his services 100 years ago. Behind us, of course, were the modern massive structures which constitute the new Jerusalem outside the gates, notably the square million-pound luxury hotel, the King David, and towering beyond and above, the highest tower in Jerusalem, we could see the Y.M.C.A. building.

We were interested chiefly in the archaeological diggings that were open in the Citadel courtyard, but we looked, of course, round the Folk Museum and studied the fascinating array of head-dresses displayed there. For the initiated it is often possible to discern a Palestinian's religion, occupation, and native village by what he wears on his head. In Sudan every native wears a white turban, and in Egypt a red tarbush. But in Palestine, although the white *kafiyeh*, flowing over head and shoulders, is the commonest head-gear, an Arab wears very often a distinctive colour, shape and material to denote his faith, origin, and social status. We saw hundreds of styles of hats, all carefully labelled to explain their meaning. But it was impossible for us to remember them all.

Farming implements were interesting. We saw a winnowing fan, for instance, and it surprised us, for even after reading the lucid Seeley's *Ecce Homo*, the Biblical phrase, 'his fan is in his hand', meant a sort of Japanese paper affair to me and, I suspect, to the others. Actually a winnowing fan is a pole as long as a broom-handle with five or six flat wooden prongs at the end. Wheat and chaff are thrown into the air by means of this big rake, and the wind blows the chaff away. An ox-goad stood in a corner: a long pole with a vicious-looking spike at one end. We could appreciate both the valour of Shamgar, who killed six hundred Philistines with one of these things, and the difficulty Saul of Tarsus had in kicking against the destiny that was urging him on like a goad. One-handled ploughs and wooden yokes were familiar to us from our observation of the *fellahin* at work in the fields around Jerusalem. From Bible days until now he has toiled at his little patch of ground without change of method or style of implement. If you wish to find a genuine conservative, go to Palestine.

As we stood before the trench that the excavators for the Department of Antiquities had opened up, we could discern the layers of stone which constituted the wall here in the days of Jesus. Its presence had been suspected for many years, for Josephus gave minute details of its appearance and course in his *Wars of the Jews,* but only now has it been possible to explore the ground and reveal the very blocks of a wall that was old in Herod's day. There are indications that he breached an already existing wall—it was there in the period of the Maccabees—in order to erect this and two other towers whose foundations have now been disclosed. In one part there is some rough stone which may be part of Nehemiah's wall. The most interesting thing about these excavations lies in the fact that this old wall turns a corner at this point, instead of following the line of the present wall of the city. It goes eastwards in a line cutting the Old City in half, which gives another proof of the long-accepted idea that Jerusalem was on quite a different plan in the old days and that the Church of the Holy Sepulchre now stands on ground once outside the city wall.

I told the men with me how some Roman stonework had been found in the Citadel, and a drainpipe with the initials of the famous Tenth Legion, which was garrisoned here in the first century, and stayed 150 years. Crusader stables and stones with Crusader crosses have also been found. When Herod's Palace was here it spread over a much greater area. Pieces of masonry and mosaic from the floor of Herod's dining-hall have been discovered in Christ Church compound. The whole fortress was then a mighty edifice of stone which Josephus said appeared to be carved in one piece from the rock. Jesus was brought here when Pilate sent Him to Herod, and the remains of a prison found a little way within the city from this point, under the present Infant Welfare Centre, may be where Peter was imprisoned, and released by the angel, if not where Jesus was confined. It is generally accepted that Pilate's Judgement Hall was in the Antonia Palace by the Temple and that the pavement there, under the Ecce Homo Convent, is the Gabbatha of the Gospels. But certainly Pilate often used Herod's citadel, and one scholar, Professor Dalman, believes that it is very likely that Jesus was condemned here, and here He was loaded with His cross, to pass out of the gate to Golgotha nearby.

We turned to the right when we left the Citadel, to find the Armenian cathedral under a long cool arch towards the Zion Gate. We met Father Cyril at its vaulted entrance and he conducted us into the lofty, brightly coloured church. There is a long plank hanging on chains at its entrance, and a curved piece of iron hangs beside it. These, he explained, were gongs which once were beaten at times of services, for the earlier Moslem rulers forbade the use of bells, but had no objection to gongs, for they had a tradition that God commanded Noah to use a gong when summoning workmen to build the ark. The Moslem announces his time for prayer by shouting from a minaret, to be distinguished from the Jew who blows a trumpet and the Christian who rings a bell or, in this case, hammers upon an unwieldy gong.

I was very fond of visiting the Armenians. They are a kindly people, unembittered and on the contrary made gentle by their constant sufferings and periods of persecution. Their services are dramatic and colourful, and I went to more than one of their wonderful Easter ceremonies. The priests are mostly quiet and cultured men, and in Jerusalem, which is their centre of learning, Anglican teachers assist in their training. There is a magnificent modern library within the bounds of the convent, and once I spent an afternoon with a party of troops who were invited by Father Cyril to see some thirteenth-century illuminated manuscripts, bright with golden pages, which he preserves there. Their finest manuscripts are in Soviet Armenia, cared for by the Russian Government, which encourages the study of them by young students. It is said that the treasures in the Armenian Convent in Jerusalem are richer than those of the Orthodox Keepers of the Treasure in the Holy Sepulchre.

The ancient kingdom of Armenia used to lie in that large area between the Black Sea and the Caspian which is now covered by parts of Turkey, Persia, and Soviet Russia. It was a buffer state between warring empires and hostile faiths, and its history has been one of misery and persecution for centuries. All that remains to-day of its ancient glory is a Soviet state in Transcaucasia, south of Georgia, about one-eighth of the original size of Armenia, containing about two and a half million people, with a similar number of Armenians scattered throughout the world. Mount Ararat is traditionally located in this region, and their ancient Feast of the Deluge has become identified with the Feast of the Transfiguration, where a mountain also is involved. On that day the Armenians lightheartedly throw water over one another. Zoroastrianism was originally the religion of their country, and the god of fire has left his influence upon many of their hymns and ceremonies, in which there is frequent reference to light and fire. They call the saint who in the third century Christianized Armenia Gregory the Illuminator. They believe that two of the Apostles, Thaddeus and Bartholomew, first carried the gospel to Armenia, and their graves are shown near Mount Ararat to-day. Both Tertullian and Augustine rendered 'Armenia' in Acts ii. 9 instead of 'Judea'. Certainly there were very many martyrs there in early days, and from earliest times there have been Armenians worshipping in the Holy Land. In the fifth century Jerome describes how the Armenians lay down their bows and arrows in the Bethlehem grotto. In the seventh century there were no less than seventy-two Armenian monasteries round about Jerusalem.

There are about 10,000 Armenians living to-day in Palestine, perhaps 2,000 or 3,000 of them in this quarter of the Old City. There are several bishops and many priests, all ruled by a patriarch. Some of the priests—and every bishop—take vows of celibacy, while those who choose to be married are not ordained until they have a child as well as a wife. The monastic priests, the Vartabeds, wear tall, pointed black hats hanging with a black veil, which with their fine beards gives them a most dignified appearance. They are called heretics by the Orthodox and Latin Churches because they refuse to declare that Christ possessed two natures, although they themselves say that they merely retain the primitive theology. Their cathedral, which was founded in the Middle Ages, is dedicated to St. James, and has associations with both James the son of Zebedee, the first among the Twelve to be martyred, whose head is said to be buried there, and with James the brother of the Lord, the first Bishop of Jerusalem. The Armenians believe that his church was where this cathedral now stands, and they point to an old episcopal throne preserved beside the one their bishop uses to-day, and they say it was the one on which St. James sat. A little lamp hangs over its faded red brocade and the Armenian Patriarch sits on this throne for half an hour once a year. Father Cyril showed us in a side chapel the Altar of St. James, a little structure of white marble, where the head is believed to be buried, and we looked at the multitude of old pictures on the cathedral walls, many of them crudely painted and nearly all of saints in the act of being martyred or of bearded patriarchs looking exactly like one another. Several hundred lamps hung from the lofty roof, and the altar, set in the centre of the screen, stood upon a raised dais. The men with me were particularly interested in some wall tiles painted apparently by Chinese. Our guide told us, however, that they were painted by Armenians who had studied art in China several hundred years ago and so drew even their contemporaries and certainly Bible characters in the Oriental style, with a Mongolian cast of countenance. It was amusing to see

a portrayal of the beheading of John the Baptist, for instance, with
the Lord High Executioner holding a Chinese scimitar while
Salome danced in Chinese wooden clogs, and all the characters were
slant-eyed.

Before we left the convent we went through its twisting lanes to
see the House of Annas: a small, highly-decorated church; an olive
tree supposed to be the one to which Jesus was tied at His trial; and
an ancient piece of masonry, obviously Herodian, set in the corner
of a wall, with irregularities in it resembling a human face. This
stone was believed to be one that cried out 'Hosanna!' when the
multitude ceased their shouting on the first Palm Sunday, referring,
of course, to the saying of Jesus that the very stones would cry out
if the people did not. We were all very interested in this curious old
fable and one of the men quietly remarked:

'Obviously, this is a piece of the Wailing Wall!'

Our next objective, before looking for some tea at one of the
Army canteens, was the ancient Syrian Church of St. Mark. It is in
a back street behind Christ Church compound and is said to stand
upon the site of the house of John Mark. The difficulty about it
is that Herod's Palace and later Roman barracks probably spread
over this area, but their range is not quite certain, and maybe a
private house could have been there. The present building is part of
a Crusader church and remains were recently found beneath it of an
older church and—especially interesting—we saw an inscription in
what might be seventh-century Aramaic, which was disclosed in
renovations in 1940. It was hidden beneath plaster dating from the
sixteenth century, and it reads:

'This [is] the house of Mariam Mother of John who was sur-
named Mark, and was consecrated a church by the Holy Apostles
under the name of Mary the Mother of God, after the Ascension
of our Lord Jesus Christ into the Heavens. And [it] was rebuilt
again after the destruction of Jerusalem by the hands of Titus
the king [sic] in the seventy-third year of the Christian era.'

Such an ancient inscription provides an interesting confirmation
of the traditional connection of the Syrians with this church and of
its age-long association with the name of St. Mark. Apparently the
Crusaders incorporated this inscription in the wall of the church they
built on the site of the preceding church. But there is a theory that
the tablet dates from as late as the sixteenth century.

Was this place where the Christians met in apostolic times? Was
it where the Pentecostal fire descended? Was it where Peter went
when he was freed from prison? The jail was not far away, at any

HEROD'S CITADEL.

The only New Testament building still standing in Jerusalem. The great stones in the centre of the tower remain much as they were when Jesus saw them.

VIA DOLOROSA.

[See page 64

rate, and a narrow street leads from St. Mark's Church directly to where it might have been. It is possible to imagine the events of the twelfth chapter of Acts happening here.

We met the Syrian bishop, an old man with a patched robe who spoke only Arabic and the ancient language of his people: Aramaic, or Old Syriac, as it is called. In true apostolic style, the local minister of this little church has the title of 'bishop'. He showed us the place where the bones of a Crusader had been found a little while earlier; the font covered with beaten silver from the coins presented by women when they brought their babies for baptism; and a faded picture of the Virgin and Child which is said to have been painted by St. Luke. Illogically, the Syrians believe that the Virgin was baptized in this font. Babies are immersed three times in it when they are baptized, and are confirmed at the same time, as we saw when later we attended the ceremony.

The tradition that Luke painted portraits is a very old one. I remember seeing a picture of the Blessed Virgin in the church of St. Maria Maggiore in Rome, dating probably from the ninth century, which was ascribed to the 'beloved physician', and there is a similar one in Venice, dating from about A.D. 1200. A sixth-century writer, Theodore Lector, recorded that the Empress Eudoxia discovered such a portrait in Jerusalem in A.D. 460. I had no means of ascertaining the date of the picture we were looking at in St. Mark's. It belongs certainly to a school of art later than Byzantine. As is customary with many Eastern holy pictures, haloes of silver had been fitted on to the canvas round the heads of the Mother and Child.

All around are holy pictures in true Eastern style. Few of the people can read, and so the sacred history is depicted for them. The sanctuary is on very much the same design as that of the Armenians, with the altar in the centre of the screen, and like them, these people are fond of lamps and candles and discs like tambourines on the end of poles which are rattled to resemble angels' wings. The Syrians call themselves Assyrians, and claim to be descended from that ancient imperial power. But they are mistaken. The Assyrians are Nestorians, and their representation is very scanty in Jerusalem. The Syrian Church represents the earliest form of Palestinian Christianity existing to-day, and they have primitive liturgies and ceremonies. Like the Armenians and Copts, they are called 'monophysite heretics' by the orthodox Churches. The people are very poor and few in number, and this is their only church in Jerusalem. I have been in their church at Bethlehem, where they are making valiant efforts to complete a new one. Roulades and half-tones in

D

their chanting resemble the ritual prayers in a synagogue, as does their custom of separating men from women in the congregation.

The whole party, as we invariably did after our Sunday rambles, had tea together. We went to the canteen under the great Y.M.C.A. building. Later some more men joined us and we spent the evening profitably with our informal Sunday evening service.

The following week we went for another excursion into the Old City, pausing, as we often did, to look at the Jaffa Gate standing square and strong in Sulieman's old wall. The Arabs call it the Gate of the Friend, as it opens on to the road for Hebron, where dwelt Abraham, the Friend of God. I have seen an old picture of the Jaffa Gate surmounted by an ugly clock tower which had dials showing the time according to both the Western and the Arab reckoning. We were grateful that now the clock had been removed, and the battlements of the gate were much as they had been when it was built. Only pedestrians can pass through it, and Allenby did so in 1917. The contrast is often mentioned between his entry on foot and the ex-Kaiser's proud passage as he rode through the gap in the wall the Turks made for his reception when he came to dedicate the German Church of the Redeemer in 1898. Now that gap beside it enables traffic to enter a little way into the fringes of the Old City.

How can I describe the scene in David Street, down which we had to pass to reach the Christian quarter? It is very narrow and very steep, with wide cobbled steps, and is lined with Arab shops. These are stalls opening directly on to the street, and the wares are spilt in a cascade around the swarthy, robed proprietors, whose customers impeded our progress. The street was always crowded in daytime with perhaps the most colourful and fascinating throng in the world. It was a typical Eastern scene, with Arabs in long, dirty *galabiehs*; women with their faces hidden behind black veils or white muslin decked with roses; other Arab women from the countryside with brown tattooed faces unveiled, and clad in long black skirts and waistcoats intricately embroidered with red and gold; bearded Koran students wearing a white band around a red tarbush; girls barefoot and erect with immense bundles upon their heads; boys with baskets strapped to their backs in which for a piastre they will carry one's shopping; an old man bowed beneath so many wooden boxes, all tied together with rope to make a pile reaching from the ground to far above his head, that it seemed incredible that one man could lift such a load; orthodox Jews with wide, greasy hats sometimes trimmed with fur that had seen better days, and either with a bright praying shawl over the shoulder or wearing a long dark coat, as they went to or from the Wailing Wall; donkeys, and even camels, giants in that narrow space, pushing pedestrians aside with their protruding loads; and everywhere movement and colour and cries in strange tongues, and the ever-present smell of the East: an odour of animals, and of unwashed human beings, and of meat and spices from the open shops. Orthodox priests in flowing black, with tall hats and beards of grey, pushed past a Franciscan monk in a quiet brown habit or an Armenian with a pointed hood over his head.

We added our drab khaki to the motley, and perforce in single file we wound our way through the throng, and rejected with terse cries of 'Imshi!' the attempts of small boys to install themselves as our guides to the 'Hawly Sepaka' for baksheesh. With a sigh of relief, we turned to the left into the comparative quiet of Christian Street, and through a narrow doorway we found the remarkable old church of St. John the Forerunner.

As we passed under the entry into its courtyard, we were a little startled to behold above the door a rough, highly coloured picture of the head of John the Baptist on a plate, complete with appropriate details. One of the men who had been in Cyprus told us of a picture he had seen there in the Church of St. Lazarus. A man who was assisting in the removal of the stone before the tomb of Lazarus was shown holding his nose! French Crusader carvings from above the door of the Holy Sepulchre—now in the Rockefeller Museum— similarly depict the Raising of Lazarus.

The modern church is of little interest, so we went round to a little door at the side which leads down to the crypt. Several times had I been there before and asked to be admitted, but the few Christian Arabs living in the compound always had been at a loss to find the key, and anyway, could not understand why I should want to descend to a dirty crypt when their fine highly-decorated Ortho- dox church was open to me. I had discovered, however, that the apparently fast-closed door needed but a push to open it, so thus we went down the steps into its coolness. A dim light came through partially blocked-up windows, revealing a spacious underground church with graceful arches and a big stone altar within the apse. Some dirty wooden benches were facing it and in a corner stood some ancient giant waterpots. The whole place was covered with thick dust.

We were in all that remains of the beautiful Church of St. John the Merciful, an Egyptian patriarch who helped Modestus to rebuild the Christian churches destroyed in Palestine by the Persians in

A.D. 614. The church was restored in Crusader times, when it was part of a great hospital, but in the subsequent havoc wrought by the Saracens it became submerged in debris and was forgotten until it was discovered in 1847, by which time the ground level had risen so that it is now the crypt beneath a newer church. Hidden in the accumulated rubbish was found a fine piece of crystal, shaped like a mitre, with a sliver of the True Cross within it and little holes round it containing relics, either bones or pieces of the instruments by which they were martyred, of each of the twelve Apostles. One can imagine a priest of Crusader times, realizing that escape was impossible from the hordes of Saracen invaders, burying his precious relic from the eyes of the infidel, for it to lie unsuspected for all those centuries. It is now in the Orthodox treasury in the Holy Sepulchre.

The patron saint of this church has become confused with the Forerunner, and once a year, on June 24th, the Feast of St. John the Baptist, the Orthodox Patriarch permits members and friends of the Order of St. John of Jerusalem to celebrate Holy Communion in this wonderful old place of worship where the Order was founded. It is possibly the only time it is used for a service. I attended it when I was in Jerusalem, and the memory of that early morning service on St. John Baptist's Day, 1942, will always be a kindly one for me. Bars of sunlight came through the old east window on to the altar, then covered with cloth of gold, and with four lighted candles flanking a Greek crucifix with the letters I.N.B.I. above the Saviour's head. A few candles stood in sconces to light a little company of thirty people who knelt to pray where Christians had prayed 1,500 years before. The High Commissioner of Palestine and the head of St. John's Ophthalmic Hospital in Jerusalem, clad in a flowing mantle with a great crest, went forward with nursing sisters and leaders of Christian social work to receive the sacrament from the Anglican Bishop in Jerusalem at the altar where Crusaders had knelt long ago. We were invited to call to mind that the four bars of the St. John's cross represent the virtues of prudence, temperance, justice, and fortitude, the eight points of it represent the Beatitudes, and its whiteness the purity of the Christian life. As we came slowly up the steps from the service, I saw in a corner a heap of human bones with a grim skull above them. Had that man once received the holy sacrament at this very altar 1,000 years ago?

I led my party out of this remarkable old crypt of St. John Prodromos, and we went back to David Street to pursue the narrow, crowded way to its junction with the Street of the Chain which then continues on to the Temple area. Here, at a cross-road in

Crusader times, stood the Syrian Exchange, for currency difficulties were even greater in those days than to-day. Some stalls laden with vegetables were under the arches of what had been the Crusader Hospital of St. John, and in a little eddy from the main crowded thoroughfare we found an Arab coffee house.

It was interesting enough to see the men sitting around smoking their hubble-bubbles, drinking thick sweet coffee from tiny *finjans*, and playing backgammon. But what made it more interesting was the realization that they were sitting between the pillars of a Crusader church. Had a church been here then? Not according to the maps and records, for the money exchange was on this very spot. The orientation was wrong, too, for what might have been an apse was facing north, although, of course, it was not unknown for an artificial 'ecclesiastical east' to be created when there were architectural difficulties. The Franciscans have a legend, a very recent one, that the house of Zebedee, the father of James and John, stood here, where they sold the fish they had caught in the Sea of Galilee, and that is why the Crusaders built a church at this place. But that idea is quite groundless. There is no evidence that a church stood here. Almost certainly the pillars, with their capitals now covered with plaster, were taken from elsewhere to build this Arab coffee-house centuries ago.

To our right stretched the street leading to the Jewish quarter, which in the days of Jesus was known as the 'Upper Market', and to our left was the erstwhile Street of the Tanners and the Street of the Coppersmiths, unpleasant places which the Moslems had put close to the Holy Sepulchre. One of the thoroughfares there was called by the Crusaders 'The Street of Bad Cookery'. Along the Street of the Shoemakers can be seen in the wall an occasional inscription, SCA ANNA, a reminder that these shops once belonged to the medieval Convent of St. Anne.

We went forward down the Street of the Chain, pausing a little way along on our left to see an ancient Arab inn. Through a shop displaying straw mats, we passed under a stone archway and stood between stable doors under a gallery that ran along either side of us. Beyond the balustrade of this gallery above our heads we could see the doors of tiny bedrooms. A great gloomy vault roofed the place, and it was all built of fine old stone in the dignified lines of the thirteenth century. The Arabs call it the Khan of Sultan Zahir, and it has been an inn ever since the Saracens drove the Crusaders from Jerusalem. The Sultan who built it was called 'Baibars', the Leopard. It was he who conquered the strongest Crusader castles. His lions are to be seen on St. Stephen's Gate to this day. I am told that this *khan* is so popular to-day that its rooms are booked well in advance by Arab travellers.

We stood for a moment amid the excitement of shouting natives seeking accommodation, of cocks crowing, hens cackling, sheep and donkeys and horses everywhere, while some men sat idly by, smoking hookahs or roasting coffee beans or pumpkin pips over primitive fires. We could imagine the inn at Bethlehem with everybody too busy to bother about Mary and Joseph, who found rest in a stable below, possibly as dirty as these side stables were.

The Street of the Chain is in reality the top of a long bridge with its arches now filled up with rubble and covered with the ascending rooms and cellars of houses on either side of it. But once it was a viaduct over the deep Valley of the Cheesemongers, which lay between the Temple and the Upper City of Jerusalem, and it was one of two bridges by which the Jews entered their Sanctuary from the west. Until 700 years ago a street ran right under it from one side of Jerusalem to the other, along the bottom of the valley. But the level of the ground has so risen during the succeeding centuries that it is difficult to realize a deep valley was ever there, and now steps lead down on either side to the streets which are at right angles to the Street of the Chain.

About seventy years ago an English excavator, Captain Wilson, R.E., discovered one of the arches of this bridge beneath the street at the entrance to the Temple, and in 1931 the Palestine Government Sanitary Department found another arch a little distance westwards, the significance of which was recognized by the Department of Antiquities. We determined to see this for ourselves, so we inquired at a little cobbler's shop, and the Arab very obligingly lit a petrol lamp and conducted us into his cellar. There were twenty-five of us in the party that afternoon, and it was rather a crush in the dismal passage below the street level. There seemed to be a positive labyrinth of rooms and cellars under these ancient houses, and we surprised one old man who was lying in bed. He looked up startled while the twenty-five of us, clanking down in Army boots, apologized for disturbing his siesta. Then two furious dogs, fortunately chained up, began to bark at us. But we circumnavigated them successfully and at last came to the opening of the arch, which was almost completely filled with rubbish. We quailed at the sight of all the filth and bones that had accumulated there, and the stench was very unpleasant, but we clambered through the opening after the man with the light and found ourselves standing under the oldest bridge in the world.

The great stone blocks, neatly fitting together and clamped with lead by later Arab builders, had been there when Jesus walked across the bridge into the Temple. Five hundred years earlier than that, Nebuchadnezzar had destroyed the bridge, but Nehemiah had rebuilt it, perhaps with the original masonry. Scarcely a score of people had been under it for centuries now, and it was impossible to explore beyond it, as the 1927 earthquake had filled the end of the archway with earth. Now this chilly subterranean hall lay beneath the busy street unsuspected by the crowds passing above our heads. A trapdoor revealed a brick-built shaft leading down to flowing water we could see far below when our guide held his lamp over it. This underground channel is the Roman sewer—still being used—which passes through the centre of the city.

We were glad to get back to the sunshine. The cobbler gravely accepted my piastres, but I suspect that he considered the British Army to be completely mad to want to see his filthy cellars.

Down some steps to the right we went along an intricate way to see the Wailing Wall—the holiest place in the world accessible to a Jew. It is a very high wall skirting the Temple Area, about a hundred yards in length, with its lower courses consisting of great Herodian stones. It is known that the wall continues down into the filled-up valley below us to a depth of sixty feet. For over 1,000 years the Moslems have permitted the Jews to come only as near as this, the outer wall of Herod's Temple, to the site of the Holy of Holies, and here they have prayed for the restoration of the Temple and bewailed its loss. The hard stone, which has weathered the elements for centuries, is worn away in many places by the kissing and beating of heads on it for so long.

Sunday afternoon was not the best time to see the Wailing Wall, but we looked at it while we were in that direction. On Saturday morning, the Jewish Shabbat, it is crowded with orthodox Hebrews, men to the right and women to the left, wailing and lamenting in an abandonment of grief and with tears running down their cheeks. Old Polish Jews with fur caps and fringed shawls are particularly noticeable there. Many of them do very little else but pray at the Wailing Wall, and at all times of the day some are to be found there. In cracks between the stones we saw pieces of crumpled paper. They contained prayers that some Jews believed would be better received by Jehovah if inserted in the wall of the Temple. On the Feast of the Passover I was unable to get within several streets of the Wailing Wall, so dense was the crowd of worshippers. In 1942, on the 9th of Ab, the Fast in memory of the destruction of the Temple, more than 30,000 Jews wailed at the Wall within twenty-four hours.

Since A.D. 70 the Jews have prayed for the restoration of the

Temple. They have special liturgies to be said at the Wailing Wall, where a rabbi cries the prayers and the people chant the responses, twisting their bodies from side to side and setting up a concerted din of sorrow. I remembered the prayer that was offered at the Seder meal I attended on Passover Eve:

'O mighty God, glorious God, truthful God, perfect God, rebuild Thy house soon, rebuild it in our time. As a praise to Thee, as a glory to Thee, rebuild Thy Sanctuary in our time ... rebuild soon Thy Temple ... rebuild speedily Thy Sanctuary ...'

The Wailing Wall was a pathetic sight for us, and we did not linger.

A little farther along the Temple wall we saw an irregular projection of curved stone. It is all that is to be seen of the other bridge, parallel with the one we had just explored, that crossed the valley at this point. It is known as Robinson's Arch, after the archaeologist who identified it over 100 years ago.

It must have been a magnificent viaduct in the days of the glory of the Temple. Foundations of supporting bases have been found across the valley. It was destroyed behind them by Jews who retreated into the Temple at the advance of Pompey's army, and later it was surely used by Jesus after it was rebuilt by Herod.

Many historical places in the Holy City are named now after the archaeologists who identified them. We have Robinson's Arch, Warren's Shaft, Wilson's Arch, and Barclay's Gate. And some, I suppose, would add Gordon's Calvary.

We made our way round and up to the Jewish quarter past the Dung Gate, and up the steep steps out of the partially filled-up valley that still divides it from the Temple Area, as it did when it was the 'Upper City' in Josephus' day. There is no viaduct across it now and, instead of entering the Temple gate above, the Jews descend to the wall in the valley to pray. The Romans had a stadium at this end of the valley when they occupied the city after its destruction by Titus.

We went along the inside of the city wall where lepers' houses used to be. All the wall and buildings along here have a peculiar yellow appearance due to a shower of mud which, according to Canon Hanauer, fell in 1857. We were looking for the Synagogue of the Karaites, an heretical sect of Jews who can never worship in it because they are unable to gather the necessary quorum of ten men. They have a history that dates from the eighth century and they are to be found mostly in the Crimea. There are only two families of them in the Middle East and the key of their underground synagogue is with the one which lives in Cairo, so we found it impossible to enter. It is a gloomy, semi-underground building.

We were, however, able to enter the Great Synagogue of the Chassidim, with its elaborately decorated dais in the centre, and the interesting series of synagogues, almost underground, that we found in the corner of a narrow, obscure byway. The darkest and remotest of these is called the Synagogue of Elijah because that prophet once arrived there to make up the necessary quorum when there was a danger that the service would have to be abandoned. They are dilapidated little chapels with ancient, rickety furniture, and a musty smell. An old Jew was raising water from a well in the centre of one of the synagogues, but we declined a drink, in spite of the fact that we had been inoculated against paratyphoid. Water from those dark, unnameable depths did not attract us. Before the British occupation conditions in the Old City were much worse than they are now, from the reports of travellers in those days. When the Turks relinquished Jerusalem in 1917 they left the water supply worse than when they occupied it in the sixteenth century.

This Stambuliye section of the Old City, though picturesque, is comparable only with the Moslem quarter for poverty and misery. Perhaps the worst slums in the world are here in the Holy City. Tiny rooms, often without windows, shelter as many as a dozen people. Sick, senile, and lunatic men and women are herded together in indescribable poverty and dirt, with children everywhere, the boys with pallid faces and ringlets before their ears and their knees covered from the sun in orthodox fashion. The most elementary laws of hygiene are ignored: flies are everywhere, on food in shops, and in a cloud over sleeping beggars lying in a narrow fetid alley. The Jewish quarter of Jerusalem, we decided, was not perhaps the healthiest of places in which to spend a hot Sunday afternoon!

We found the Toc H hostel for tea, and the following Sunday concluded for the time being our explorations of the Old City.

There were two pools in Jerusalem we wanted to see. One was Hezekiah's Pool and the other the Pool of Bethesda. The Pool of Siloam, of course, is outside the present city wall away to the south, and we explored that when we were visiting Akeldama and Gehenna, which is another story.

It is not easy to see Hezekiah's Pool. It is hidden behind tall houses on all four sides of its quite extensive area. It is possible to traverse the lanes of Jerusalem all round it without being aware of its existence. I had made the acquaintance, however, of a shop-keeper in David Street whose back room had a window opening on to the Pool, and he was always pleased to allow men in uniform to pass amongst his bales of grocery and piled boxes of tea and sugar, to peer out of his window at the extraordinary view below. On the Sunday afternoon I refer to, his shop was open—he is a Moslem—and he willingly allowed us to file through to see the 'Birket Hammam el Batrak' as he calls it, 'The Pool of the Patriarch's Bath'; so named, it is thought, because at the northern end of it, opposite to our present vantage-point, the bishops of the Crusader kingdom had a palace, and one of the prelates is said to have built a great bath here. For long this stretch of water, nearly a hundred yards long, was believed to be the pool within the City of David that Hezekiah made when he formed a conduit to keep the water supply within the walls when invasion was threatened. But it is known now that the City of David did not cover this ground in those days, and that the facts mentioned in 2 Kings xx. 20 refer to the Pool of Siloam and the tunnel which runs to it from the Virgin's Fountain, away to the south of Jerusalem. This stretch of water is, however, the Amygdalon Pool mentioned by Josephus in his account of the Romans' siege of the city in A.D. 70. The name means the Great Tower, and obviously refers to the nearby Citadel. So the pool has no more to do with Hezekiah than the King David Hotel has to do with King David.

The scene was very pleasant. A soft breeze ruffled the surface of the water, which mirrored in its ripples the three- and four-storied houses which lined its edge, some with windows in overhanging rooms projecting above the water. Behind them rose the broad dome of the Holy Sepulchre, a minaret, and the white tower of the German Church of the Redeemer. Its picturesque aspect reminded me of the mildewed palaces that line the waterways of Venice. That dome might with a little imagination be the roof of San Marco, and the German church the Campanile. . . . But there were no pigeons on the piazza, and no gondolas on the water. A family of ducks quacked by beneath our window to look for food in a stretch of mud in one corner, and the smell that arose to us was not alto-gether pleasant. We used what Arabic we knew to say 'Thank you' to our host, and regained the crowded shopping-street.

To reach the Pool of Bethesda, we had to pass right across the Old City, rounding the Holy Sepulchre to St. Francis Street behind it and traversing the zigzag length of the Via Dolorosa. Along Christian Street the purveyors of candles and holy objects had closed their shops, but the undertaker at the corner had his shop open, with elaborate coffins displayed and a notice to the effect that he also did tattooing, of all strange combinations of occupation! Along the Via Dolorosa were trays of freshly-made cakes and loaves resting on the cobbled ground in front of bakeries, all with a great cloud of flies over them. We descended the street under the semi-arches made famous by a myriad of photographers, turned two corners at different Stations of the Cross, and mounted the hill that runs under the ancient Ecce Homo Arch, to descend again towards St. Stephen's Gate, the only entrance to the city in the east wall. Just within this gate to the left lies St. Anne's Church.

We were making for St. Anne's Church because the Pool of Bethesda excavations lie within its compound. Once the depression, now filled in, that lies between this spot and the Temple, was believed to be Bethesda. It was called Birket Israel, and many speculations were made about its significance. But since the White Fathers have dug up the ruins of a Byzantine church here and revealed the original five porches, nobody doubts that here is the twin pool beside which Jesus healed the paralytic. We entered the doorway and stood within the very pleasant compound with great shady pepper trees in the centre.

I pointed to the statue of Cardinal Lavigerie.

'He,' I said, 'was the founder of the Order of the White Fathers, who own this place. In those large buildings they train priests for the Greek Uniate Church—a branch of the Catholic Church which was originally Orthodox, and is still permitted to use the Greek Liturgy in its worship. Lavigerie, the Apostle of Africa, as he was called, had the idea of forming a band of missionaries who would dwell amongst the Moslems in North Africa and attempt to influence them, not by preaching, but by living. They dressed as Arabs, lived as Arabs, did only good works, and were resolved not to preach the gospel for a hundred years—a century which has not yet by any means expired.'

Somebody asked me why they are called 'White Fathers'.

'Because,' I replied, 'they wear the white burnous of a Moroccan. You will notice that its hood hangs across their shoulders, and it is not to be confused with the very different cowl of a monk's habit. They wear a rosary round the neck, as desert Moslems do, and they have adopted the red tarbush for their head-dress. These fathers must not be confused with the Dominicans, who also wear white, but whose dress is very different.' I added that wine from the White Fathers' vineyards in Morocco is used for altar wine all over the Catholic world.

The Church of St. Anne is a lovely building, a perfect example of

Crusader architecture. Only at Abu Ghosh have I seen anything approaching it in grace and dignity. It is so well preserved because Saladin appointed it as a college for the study of the Koran and did not destroy it as he did many other churches the Crusaders had built. We could see over its doorway the plaque of Arabic lettering which Saladin placed there. A Benedictine convent stood here in the days of the Christian Kingdom and it was here that Baldwin I, who had married Arda, an Armenian princess, and then repudiated her as his wife, compelled her to become a nun. I told the members of my party how the Turks offered the church to England in 1840 after we had bombarded Acre, but it was refused. It would have made a fine cathedral for the first Anglican Bishop who, two years afterwards, settled in Jerusalem. It was finally presented to the French in 1854 as part of their reward for aiding the Turks in the Crimean War. It has been French property since then, except when the Moslems used it during the last war.

We entered the church and stood staring up at its lofty roof and the smooth lines of its square-cut pillars. The only thing to mar its majesty was the canopied altar standing out in the nave at the east end. How perfect the whole interior would have been if a simple altar had been retained in its original position within the apse. Apart from that, the church is unspoiled. An architect friend of mine once pointed out to me the tiny irregularities in the building. Not one feature is exactly symmetrical, yet the whole is perfectly balanced. The early craftsmen desired to give a tiny twist to the nave in order to represent our Lord's body hanging on the Cross. We found it very cool and shady under those great arches.

We went down some steps to see the grotto which is the reputed birthplace of the Virgin Mary. It contained a tawdry altar with many gewgaws all round. The notion that the traditional parents of Mary, Anna and Joachim, lived here, is a curious one. Apparently it is due to a confusion of Bezetha, which means 'suburb', with Bethesda, which means 'house of grace', which in its turn became Beth Hanna, 'house of Anna'. The grandmother was quite an important person in medieval Italy, and pictures of the Holy Family of that period often show St. Anne standing by Mary and Joseph and the Babe.

Across the compound we entered the excavations of the Pool of Bethesda. These were apparently incomplete, but had ceased for the time being. We descended into the remains of a Byzantine church crypt, that of St. Mary in Probatica, and passed a none-too-pleasing modern chapel with locked glass doors which enabled us to see a lot of blue-and-white tiles in a small area round an altar. This marks the supposed location of the healing of the paralytic. A church was known to be at the Five Porches in the fourth century. It was destroyed, of course, and rebuilt, and then lost in debris. It was only by descending some slippery steps deep into the earth that we were able to see the pool—a rectangular stretch of water under a high-arched vault with a number of fat goldfish swimming in it, put there probably to prevent malarial mosquitoes from breeding. The original colonnades and porticoes have been fairly well reconstructed in plans displayed at the excavations.

There was no sign of the waters being troubled. The text of John v. 4 is, of course, omitted from the Revised Version, so we need not accept the idea that the pool was disturbed by an angel. It is very likely that there was an intermittent bubbling from a spring here, however, that would have been ascribed to supernatural agencies and to possess therefore miraculous powers. The pool at Gihon—a name which means 'gushing'—now known as the Virgin's Fountain, manifests a certain intermittent overflow even to-day, due probably to some subterranean irregularity which in earlier times might have affected Bethesda also. There is no doubt that Bethesda is here. We know that it was near the Sheep-gate, which was north of the Temple. The pool must have been outside the city wall when Jesus visited it.

I have never had a very high opinion of the character of the man who was healed here. I do not believe he wanted to be cured. He certainly gave no affirmative answer when Jesus asked if that was his desire. Instead, he gave his professional beggar's whine about having nobody to put him into the pool. Even when he walked through the streets of Jerusalem on the Shabbat with his palliasse under his arm, he did not do so proudly, but cravenly put the blame for this 'sin' upon Jesus. No wonder when Jesus met him in the Sanctuary He had occasion to remind him of his cure and to tell him to sin no more.

The dear old White Father at the entrance to the Pool was over eighty, and he sat there every day presiding over a tray of photographs and curios. Some of the men bought ancient coins which have been found amongst the ruins, carefully divided into their appropriate periods by the monks. I am, as I have said elsewhere, the proud possessor of two 'widow's mites' of the period of Herod which were found there.

The museum by St. Anne's is not usually opened on Sundays, but I had previously secured permission to take my party into it as Sunday was normally the only opportunity for the men to visit this place. The Fathers had kindly waived the usual charge of a shilling for each one who entered. We were led round it by a dignified and bearded White Father whose only speech—apart from his Arabic and Latin—was French. All the exhibits had labels in French also, which was not too easy for us. But I had seen the museum before, and was familiar with many of its possessions, so my imperfect French, combined with my knowledge of the exhibits, made me a tolerably successful interpreter.

The Fathers had the idea of collecting a specimen of everything mentioned in the Bible, which they have assembled with very little order in very little space; and although they have accumulated a lot of rubbish, there are also some very interesting things there. I simply have not room to describe all the things we looked at that afternoon. It was bewildering and fascinating. There were coins and weights and measures, including an immense stone 'talent'; there was a flute, harp, sackbut, psaltery, dulcimer; in fact, all kinds of musick! There was one of each of the jewels of the Holy City of the Apocalypse; there were seals, slings, earrings, hairpins, cosmetics; baskets, loaves, and fishes; locusts and wild honey; gold and frankincense and myrrh; stuffed birds of all kinds, the skeleton of behemoth, a crocodile, a serpent's egg; manna, virgins' lamps, a grain of mustard seed; a figure of the Aaronic high-priest in all his robes and jewelled breastplates; phylacteries and rolls of scripture; scale models of Rome and Jerusalem; a model of a rock-cut tomb with a little stone that could be rolled away; and instruments of the Passion: nails and spear, a scourge, and a crown of thorns. These and many other strange objects gathered from near and far over many years taught us many lessons as they lay mutely in their cases. One could return again and again to that motley assortment of curios and find something new and fascinating. I had no idea, for instance, that a talent was a weight of 40 kilograms, that an alabaster vessel looked like that, so slender and tapering, that 'husks that the swine did eat' were such very unpleasant-looking rations. . . .

We dragged ourselves away at last. It had been one of the most interesting of our excursions. Before we left the Old City, however, we looked in at the Cotton Bazaar along the street that passes the Temple Area. It is deserted now, its high, shady roof silent where once, 500 years ago, it echoed with the cries of vendors of cloth from the Orient, fine cotton and silk from Damascus and Baghdad. It was the Black Death which finally stopped the commerce by the overland route which formerly made this bazaar so prosperous. We wanted to peep into the 400-year-old Turkish bath that still functions in that gloomy bazaar, and to see the Byzantine church font that graces its 'cooling-room' as a great goldfish bowl. I had penetrated its steamy interior, though not to remain long there, on former occasions, and the men wanted to see it. The amiable proprietor, whose ancestors have stoked the fires under its waterpipes for generations, was standing at the door, however, and regretted that he could not admit us. Sunday was the day when Arab ladies occupied the baths. He would be pleased to show us round another time. As we came away we saw several fine cars drawn up at the entrance. The ancient Oriental luxury of a Turkish bath was accompanied by the best of modern means of transport. Here was another example of the incongruous juxta-position of East and West. A Rolls-Royce carries a veiled Moslem woman to the steamy heat and cool sherbet of a Turkish bath in the old Jerusalem Cotton Bazaar.

CHAPTER IV

WAY OF SORROWS

How great is thy glory, O exalted rock, wherein was set the cross whereby mankind was redeemed!

SOPHRONIUS, A.D. 637.

WHEN I first explored Jerusalem I expected to find a street called the Via Dolorosa, the traditional way along which Jesus carried His Cross. I discovered, however, that this is the name given by Christians to a route through the city which follows several narrow streets in an uphill and downhill zigzag course between the site of Antonia Palace and the Holy Sepulchre. Without a guide, it is difficult to follow, for indications are scanty, and in one way I was glad, because I had feared that I would be led along a Holy Way preserved for pilgrims and adorned with ecclesiastical ornaments. But the Stations of the Cross in any Roman Catholic church are more easily to be seen than the veritable places on the way that He is believed to have trod. The fact that the Via Dolorosa consists of one or two of the dirty winding streets of the Old City helped me to realize, and the hundreds of troops I afterwards led along it at different times, that the Crucifixion was a casual, everyday affair, when it was nothing unusual for criminals to be driven along busy streets to their execution. The stage was not specially set at that time, nor is to-day, fortunately. Men gambling, a potter's workshop, and a crowded bazaar, provide a characteristic setting, for it was past such Eastern scenes as these that Jesus went on His last journey. Like all the great dramas of life and death, His tragedy was enacted within sight and sound of the commonplace and normal.

There is no record before the thirteenth century of the Via Dolorosa. It was located in 1294 by Ricoldus of Monte Croce, who went to Jerusalem, as he says, 'in order that the memory of Christ's sufferings might impress itself deeper on the mind, and that the blood of Christ, shed for our salvation, might become unto me strength and support, to enable me to preach and die for Him who by His death gave life to me'. Apparently he mapped out the most probable course from what was thought to be Pilate's Judgement Hall to Golgotha, and decided where the various events took place *en route*, some mentioned in the Gospels and some legendary. As a matter of fact, if, as seems likely, the Antonia Palace was the place where Jesus was condemned and Calvary is where tradition has placed it, then His way must have lain somewhere along the course

followed by the present Via Dolorosa. Naturally, it passed outside
the walls of that time for part of the way, and the present streets are
very much higher than the ground level 2,000 years ago—indeed,
anything from 10 to 20 feet higher. So although it is difficult to say
'this is the way the Master went', none the less for centuries it has
been an aid to devotion for millions of faithful pilgrims to follow
this route round its sharp corners and under dark arches. The
Byzantine Way of Sorrows followed quite a different course,
beginning at the House of Caiaphas on Mount Zion.

I shall discuss in my chapter on the Garden Tomb the authenticity
of the Holy Sepulchre, so all I need say here is that I believe the
most likely place of the Crucifixion and Resurrection of Jesus is
where that church now stands. I am not quite so sure about the
beginning of the Via Dolorosa, however. It is taken for granted
that the Antonia fortress to the north of the Temple Area was
where Pilate set up his throne of judgement at a place called Gabbatha, the Pavement (John xix. 13), and certainly a large area of
Roman pavement has been found there, marked with the games of
Roman soldiers, which is exactly at the spot where the Via Dolorosa
begins. Without doubt a praetorium was there, but it has never
been proved that Pilate used it as his judgement court. Josephus says
that Gessius Florus used Herod's palace, where the Citadel is now,
for his headquarters when he was Governor, and Pilate might
have done the same. This would accord with the fact that his
wife was with him—it is unlikely that the Governor and his wife
would be quartered in the troops' barracks at Antonia—he was near
to Herod for a sending to and fro of this Prisoner, and the knoll in
Joseph of Arimathea's garden was a convenient place for execution
nearby. Professor Dalman thought that the Citadel was the more
likely place at which to locate Gabbatha, but the overwhelming
bulk of authority and tradition places it at Antonia. The fact that
Pilate and Herod had been at enmity between themselves would
scarcely cause the Roman to stay elsewhere when he was in Jerusalem! But there is no tradition whatever for the Citadel as the scene
of the judgement, and all this is purely speculative. At the time of
Passover tension, Pilate might have functioned at Antonia. It is not
likely that the Scala Sancta in Rome, which Helena is supposed to
have brought from Pilate's Judgement Hall in Jerusalem in A.D. 326,
came from the Citadel. It might have been part of the Antonia
Praetorium, or from another now discredited location of the court,
somewhere in the valley beside the Temple. Its authenticity is
doubtful. It was erected in Rome in A.D. 845. The fact that the
Gospel writer records a Herodian place-name, Gabbatha, would

E

perhaps be a good reason for accepting the traditional site, for local names probably persisted much later. It is interesting to realize that we have at least six local names mentioned in the New Testament as aids to the early identification of places round Jerusalem. They are: Siloam, Bethesda, Gethsemane, Akeldama, Gabbatha, and Golgotha.

The military power in Jerusalem has occupied successive buildings on the site of Antonia Fortress without a break since Roman times. Turkish barracks were there, and during the 'Troubles' a few years ago troops of the Black Watch used it as a garrison. To-day it is a police station with a high flat roof, on to which I received permission to take parties of troops in order to get the magnificent view of the Temple Area which is only possible from that spot, and indeed from that eminence to survey the Mount of Olives on the one hand, and the Old City on the other, a picturesque tumble of little domes and tapering minarets and narrow, twisted streets. Not only did I take a party there at least once a week, but on our Sunday afternoon outings the Wednesday Fellowship would occasionally tour the Way of Sorrows, starting from that point. We could realize the proximity of the Temple to the fortress in which probably Jesus was confined and from which He began the journey to the Cross. Away amid the huddle of houses the dark dome of the Holy Sepulchre arose to point the direction we should take. It was possible to discern the twin square towers of the Citadel on the northern horizon of the city, which in the days of Jesus marked the corner of the northern wall, which ran directly across the city from where we were standing. Antonia Fortress covered a much larger area then than the police station does to-day. The Franciscan Convent of the Flagellation next door is on part of the site, and so, of course, is the Convent of Ecce Homo, of the Sisters of Zion, the basilica of which was immediately beside us. We gathered there one Sunday afternoon, about twenty of us, men of the Army and the R.A.F., to see again the view which had become so familiar to most of us, but of which we never seemed to tire. I pointed out again to them the principal landmarks and reminded them that it was to this place Paul was taken upon his arrest in the Temple Area, and from its steps he addressed the crowd, as it is related in Acts xxi. 40. We descended the many old stone stairs to the roadway and knocked at the door of Ecce Homo Convent.

This church and the beautifully preserved Pavement in the crypt is one of the most delightful places in Jerusalem. It stands over the part of the castle courtyard where it is believed that Jesus was loaded with the Cross, and the kindly sisters who maintain it spend many hours every day in leading groups of visitors round it and telling over and over again the story of the condemnation of our Lord. The church decorations are very simple and the whole atmosphere is one of grace and piety. Invariably the troops on leave whom I took there, many with but the scantiest familiarity with churches and often suspicious and awkward with nuns and priests, were impressed by the spirit of the place and the friendly hospitality of the sisters. Here there is none of the garish crudity of the Holy Sepulchre, nor division according to the interest of various factions. Yet, as Mother Mary so often told the men, it belongs to Christendom, and the faithful of any Church are invited to enter and to pray. When I was first introduced to her as a Methodist chaplain, the good soul declared that she had always admired Methodists as a very pious people. I felt that we did not altogether deserve her admiration, but we always tried to maintain the high standard she expected of us. Invariably she invited me to lead the men in prayer when we went down to tread on the actual flagstones of the Via Dolorosa.

An arch curves across the street outside the convent and passes through its wall to continue inside the church across the altar. It is known as the Ecce Homo Arch, and dates from Hadrian's time, which is old enough in all conscience, but not quite old enough to be the arch under which the people stood crying 'Crucify Him!' when Pilate told them to 'Behold the Man', as it was formerly believed. Under it in the outside wall is a tablet:

VIA DOLOROSA

AD ARCUM ECCE HOMO
UBI PONTIUS PILATUS
CHRISTUM
JUDAIS TRADIDIT UT CRUCIFIGERETUR

'To the Ecce Homo Arch, where Pontius Pilate delivered Christ to the Jews in order that He might be crucified.'

A French sister admitted us and, after we had waited awhile, clanged a deafening bell to summon Mother Mary, who gave us her usual welcome and led us into the church. We passed a nun seated in a tiny courtyard working busily at a sewing-machine, its mild whirr adding to the general atmosphere of peace. Here was a domestic touch in a holy place, another of the incongruities of the Holy City. Above the place where Jesus had been mocked and scourged by brutal soldiers a black-robed sister was treading a

Singer sewing-machine. Besides the preservation of the Pavement here, and their acts of devotion in the church over it, the Sisters of Zion, who are mostly of French origin, have in their convent a school for girls and an orphanage. It was founded by a Jew, Father Ratisbonne, who had been converted to the Roman Catholic faith by a vision of the Virgin in Rome in 1842. As reparation for the deeds of his people, he spent his wealth on excavations on this site and the establishment of the church and orphanage.

We sat in the pews of the church while Mother Mary told us a little of the history of the place, and pointed out the words in Latin across the altar, 'Father, forgive them, they know not what they do', a reminder that it was a Jew who had built it. A fine thorn-crowned figure of Christ stands above the Roman arch, and under its curving masonry is the altar, built of paving-stones from the Via Dolorosa. We were led down a flight of steps to the excavated courtyard itself, in a long low-ceilinged chamber beneath the church. Mother Mary slowly walked ahead of us.

'This is a pilgrimage,' she said as she walked. 'We are treading on the very stones our Lord Jesus Christ trod when they mocked Him and scourged Him and loaded Him with His Cross.'

We felt that, too. The soldiers with me were tiptoeing in their heavy Army boots over those ancient flagstones, and we were all hushed and reverent. The Mother rolled back a piece of rush matting and we saw crude outlines scratched in the stone.

'The Roman soldiers were great gamblers,' she said, 'and this is one of their games. It is called the game of the crown and the spear. The winner was called "king" for a day, and a prisoner was slain in place of the loser. We have found many such games here.' She went on to tell us that one theory is that the soldiers got the idea of dressing Jesus in mock-royal robes and hailing Him as 'king' from this game that they were playing, since He was charged with declaring Himself King of the Jews. The fuel for their fires was dry bramble, called *zizyphus*, and it may be that they used some of it from a pile nearby to plait a crown of thorns for this King who was the object of their mirth and cruelty.

Slowly we followed her black-robed figure to the end of the courtyard before a mosaic mural picture of Christ carrying the Cross. At the top of the wall a grating showed the ground level of the present public thoroughfare of the Via Dolorosa. Beneath our feet the old stones, polished with the traffic of ages, were grooved to prevent horses from slipping, with here and there a gutter to carry away the rain. It was certainly a roadway in Roman times, passing through the courtyard and out to the road beyond the city wall. Undoubtedly if Pilate's praetorium was here, then the feet of Jesus had trod this way.

Here was 'Gabbatha' of John xix, and here we all knelt in prayer while the Mother moved quietly away. I lifted up my voice to the Saviour who had suffered there for us. We confessed that it was sins like ours that burdened Him with the Cross. We gave thanks for His great love that endured so much to lead us into life eternal. We prayed for faithfulness to follow our own way of sorrows for the joy set before us. And we prayed that the world which was crucifying Him afresh in these days of war should learn of Him the things that belong unto peace.

Before we left the sanctuary we were shown a piece of linen stretched upon the wall with a light behind it, which we were told was a replica of the Shroud of Turin, believed to be the veritable cloth in which the body of Christ had been wrapped in the tomb, and bearing the outline of His form and features. It showed a face, bearded in the traditional manner, and stained with pain and sorrow. It is not genuine, of course, although the original linen may have once covered a corpse which by some chemical action affected the cloth. I forbore to remind the gentle Mother that Pope Clement VII in a papal bull forbade the exhibition of the Turin shroud as an authentic relic. It meant much to her, and was an appropriate decoration for that holy place. Round the walls were inscribed the names of individuals and Army units who had paid for a tablet to be affixed there for them. A light was switched on to enable us to peer down to subterranean chambers with the stilly water of a great pool, once presumably the water supply for the fortress. At least two tunnels lead away from here in the direction of the Temple Area. It was a pity that there was no access to them for us, for we should have loved to explore those ancient passages which linked the Temple environs with the castle in the days of Jesus and Paul.

Upstairs once more we bought articles of needlework made by the orphans, and books and photographs, and we gave a grateful farewell to Mother Mary and the aged nun who acted as doorkeeper. The simple and beautiful shrine they maintain had helped us to understand as never before the reality of the great events of Holy Week. We should all leave Jerusalem with precious memories of the place where Jesus began His Way of Sorrows.

Down the street we passed the Hospice for Greek pilgrims, on the site of what they believe is the actual prison of Christ. It is true that there are some old rock-cut chambers under it, but the stocks they display there are of much later date, and there is nothing to indicate that they had anything to do with Jesus and His imprisonment. Solomon Street goes across the bottom of the rise, the continuation of the old Valley Lane that once ran along the bottom of the chasm dividing the Temple from the Upper City. We turned to the left along it, away from the direction of the Damascus Gate. At this corner is the location of the third station of the Cross, where Jesus fell for the first time, and a little beyond it we entered the gate of the Armenian Catholic Convent of the Spasm, a fine though little-known church which stands over the fourth station, where the Mother of Jesus fainted when she saw Him pass. Like other places, there is no historical warrant for this happening. An old woman who spoke only French, besides Armenian, opened a door for us which led down to the crypt, and we descended to a floor of mosaic which by the varying sizes of the little pieces of stone suggested that it was a composite production of different centuries. There was little design except at the oldest part in the centre, where the smallest stones are. There we saw the black outlines of a tiny pair of shoes. Here, we were told, is the actual place where Mary stood to watch her Son carry the Cross, and swooned to see His sorrow. The shoes were scarcely large enough for a child, but it was interesting to see this example of early Christian naïveté.

The fifth station, where Simon of Cyrene was compelled to take up the Cross, is marked by a chapel at the corner of a street which goes steeply uphill under the famous half-arches renowned as a view of the Via Dolorosa. In the wall is set an old stone with a rough imprint in it, stained dark with the hands that have been pressed upon it. It is said to be where Jesus leaned against the wall as He paused on His weary pilgrimage, and the soldiers seized Simon to assist Him. One of the members of the party had seen a picture in Khartoum Cathedral representing Simon bearing the Cross, in which he was depicted as a black man. 'Was he black?' he wanted to know.

We examined the evidence. It is tempting to missionaries appealing to natives of Africa to say that Simon was a negro because he is described as 'of Cyrene' in Mark xv. 21, and, of course, negroes and not Arabs were in North Africa at that time. But Cyrene was certainly a Roman settlement then—indeed, the Romans occupied the whole of the Mediterranean basin—and it is well known that Jews lived in most of the principal Roman cities. There were more Jews outside Palestine than in it even in the days of the New Testament, and many made special journeys to be in the city of their fathers at the great feasts, especially Passover. Simon is a Jewish name, so it is possible that he was a Jew from North Africa. It is very unlikely that he was a Roman proselyte to the Jewish faith, for the troops would scarcely have seized him for this task if that had been so. It is not impossible that he was a black proselyte, like the Ethiopian eunuch who was converted by the preaching of Philip, and he had taken a Jewish name; and because he was a strong native he was loaded with the heavy timber. But the great probability is that he was a Jew. It is likely that he became a Christian, for Mark says that he was the father of Alexander and Rufus, obviously known to the early Christian community who were Mark's readers. Possibly the Rufus and his mother mentioned by Paul in Romans xvi. 13 belonged to the same family, which would suggest that not only Simon but his wife and whole household accepted the Christian faith. The last chapter of the Epistle to the Romans is generally believed to have been intended for the church at Ephesus, whither Simon might later have migrated. He seems to have been a traveller, perhaps a merchant through the cities of the Empire.

Simon is, however, described as 'coming from the country', or 'the fields', which might suggest that he was a farmer coming in from his land. It would indicate that the Via Dolorosa led to a main road into Jerusalem from the countryside. An interesting suggestion is that he did not come from Cyrene at all, but from Kyrenia in Cyprus, which was an important town in those days and has a local legend that it was the home of Simon. That there were Jews from Cyprus who owned land in Palestine is proved by the account in Acts iv. 37 of Joseph Barnabas, who was a Cypriot. It is significant that the first missionary journey was to Cyprus, possibly because in the Antioch Christian community were those who came from that island (Acts xiii. 1). We know that Mark, who gives us the names of Simon's sons, went to Cyprus with Paul, and he might have met Alexander and Rufus there and quoted them in his Gospel as his authorities for that particular incident. Actually Simon is of even greater importance than appears at first sight, for surely he is the eye-witness who is the Gospel writer's authority for the events of the Via Dolorosa up to Mark xv. 32. Luke's reference to Simon being compelled to take up the Cross after Jesus may imply that he did not carry the whole of it, but assisted Him. Perhaps the erect post was already in position, and it was the cross-beam that was being carried. Like many another in these days imagining himself to be a mere onlooker of the sufferings of the world, Simon had been constrained to share in those sufferings; and he, like all those who have followed Christ on the Way of Sorrows, was sharing in the task of man's redemption.

The sixth station of the Cross is marked by a Melkite chapel half-way up the hill. It commemorates the legendary story of a Roman woman, Berenice, who took pity on Jesus as He toiled past her house, and wiped His face with her handkerchief. In gratitude, He left upon the linen an impression of His face. It is said to exist still, and copies of it are popular holy pictures. St. Veronica, as she came to be called, probably derives her name from *vera ikon*, 'true image', which it was customary to write upon so-called authentic pictures of Christ in early times, which thus were called *veronicae*. The present house of St. Veronica is about 300 years old, but its cellar is the crypt of an early church.

Before we continued up under some overhanging arches into what the Crusaders used to call the Street of Bad Cookery, and which does not smell very sweet to-day, we entered the workshop of a potter who sat at his wheel, and we watched him building up the wet clay into a tall bowl as it whirled beneath his hands. His craft was an ancient industry in the days of Jeremiah, and he still uses the old method of working a pedal to twirl a wheel between his knees. It is a fascinating thing to watch a potter at work, and there were plenty of lessons I could have imparted to the members of my party as we stood watching him, but we had to move on quickly. We went past the seventh station, a tall, grimy chapel in the busy market, marking where Jesus fell for the second time, and past the stone in the wall of this boundary of the Holy Sepulchre which is station number eight, where Jesus rebuked the women, the daughters of Jerusalem, for bewailing His end, and told them to weep for themselves. The ninth station, where He fell for the third time, is above the steps leading to the roof of the Holy Sepulchre, where is the Coptic community and the quaint huddle of little huts which is the Abyssinian village. We went up to look at it.

In the centre of a wide, flagged courtyard rose the dome, with windows round it, of the Chapel of St. Helena within the church below. Once the Abyssinians had possessed that chapel, but during a plague in 1838 it had been possible for the Armenians to seize it, and they have held it ever since. So these poor black Christians took up their abode amid the ruins of the cloisters of the Augustinian Canons of the Middle Ages, around the chapel dome. They have a little chapel of their own there, but at the special feasts they erect a magnificent pavilion in a corner of the wall and set up their altar in it, and parade round the dome in gorgeous robes of barbaric colours, wearing crowns of gold and silver. They possess a fine cathedral outside the Old City, however, a great-domed structure near the Street of the Prophets. About eighty black Christians dwell on the roof of the Holy Sepulchre, behind rickety doors roughly marked with big crosses in blue chalk.

A few silent Abyssinians in long robes stood by as we walked through the village to see their own holy place: wooden palings, cobwebbed and neglected, surrounding a young olive-bush which they say, quite regardless of the facts of history and geography, is the veritable thicket in which the ram was caught when Abraham was about to offer up Isaac. As we stood looking about us, a black man in a dirty robe came out of a doorway with a brazier, at which he squatted, and proceeded to cook some primitive dish. Like the British, who transplant what they can of the Old Country to the remotest parts of far-off continents where they may be compelled to live, these exiles from the land of Ethiopia endeavoured to reproduce the atmosphere of home. Not many months before I had seen natives such as he sitting by similar fires in villages among the hills of Abyssinia. He was making himself at home amid the graceful arches of medieval culture. Where a thousand years ago had trod solemn abbots and learned canons from the West, now crouched a swarthy Abyssinian over a brazier such as he knew in the heart of distant Africa.

I led my party downstairs again to the bazaar and we went in to see the Russian excavations before reaching the main—indeed, only —door into the Church of the Holy Sepulchre. We passed what was known to the Crusaders as the Street of the Palmers because here pilgrims purchased the palms which they took home as attestation of the success of their pilgrimage. Later the Moslems had an evil-smelling tannery here, beside the Christian shrine, in order to give offence, in the same way as they had a shambles near to the Jewish quarter. To-day, when they are angry, they refer to the church, not by its correct Arabic name of El Kiyama, 'Resurrection', but as El Kimama, a similar word which means 'dunghill'. El Khenkeh, 'hospice', is their name for a tall minaret they have built at the corner of Francis Street and Christian Street, in order to overshadow the Holy Sepulchre.

The Russian Hospice was built just before the 1914–18 war, and in process of its erection some ruins were disclosed of an old Roman gateway and some ancient wall-stones. The gateway may belong to an entrance to a market of those days, or to a praetorium that was by the city wall. Some pillars and blocks of stone almost certainly are part of Constantine's Church of the Anastasis, or Resurrection, which covered a larger area than the present building. According to the Madeba mosaic map of sixth-century Jerusalem, his church had a grand entrance on the main thoroughfare through the ancient city, and these pillars were part of the colonnade shown on that map. There are some steps leading to a rock platform, and the Russians believe that they have found here the actual stage upon which Jesus was tried before Pilate. This means that the Orthodox Church does not regard the Ecce Homo Convent as being on the site of the Pavement, but believe that Jesus was condemned here, quite close to Calvary, and the Way of Sorrows was therefore a very brief route to the mound outside the wall.

A Russian nun admitted us and showed us the way through some well-furnished apartments to the excavations. We saw a wide flight of stone stairs leading down beside a Roman arch—part of the praetorium—and over a piece of the floor of the rocky platform was a glass covering, marking where it is believed the feet of Christ touched it as He stood before Pilate. A few of the customary lamps hung burning over it, but there was little of the tawdry ecclesiasticism of older places of Orthodox pilgrimage. Behind a huge crucifix we found massive blocks of masonry rising in a great wall. This is not, as some people formerly imagined, part of the original northern wall of the city, but it dates from about A.D. 335, when the Holy Sepulchre was dedicated, and probably is part of that church. The flight of steps they have now restored led no doubt up to its main entrance. The great platform, however, which would have been below Constantine's church was almost certainly a strong point in the Second Wall that Josephus described, running in a general line from north to south in this corner of the city. We saw that in the wall-blocks was a series of holes apparently made to receive copper clamps which secured slabs of marble formerly covering the stone. An immense picture of the Christ carrying His Cross was stretched across the top of the steps, and all around the great hall were paintings of the various events of the Passion. They were quite modern and pleasing pictures, unlike the typical Byzantine style of art. We were able to gain access to the little church on the platform itself and we went through it to see a modest museum of articles of antiquity found on the site.

When we left the Russian Hospice we passed the huge white Lutheran Church of the Redeemer, now closed, of course, which was built on the site of the Crusader Church of St. Mary of the Latins, and which followed its design. One doorway retains the twelfth-century stonework, but the rest is new, built at the end of last century when the Kaiser presented the land to his own nationals. The area here is known as the Muristan, which is Arabic for 'madhouse'. Apparently Saladin established a lunatic asylum here after the Crusades. We walked in front of the shops which are built all round the area of the Holy Sepulchre church and which effectively hide it on every side. Once, in Constantine's day, the church on this place was an immense and magnificent edifice, so impressive that it was called the New Jerusalem, and early Christian pictures of heaven often depicted a series of buildings corresponding to the Church of the Holy Sepulchre. There is still to be seen in Rome a fifth-century mosaic of New Jerusalem which is an obvious reproduction of this church and indeed it has enabled scholars to reconstruct some of its features. The Crusader church which was its medieval successor was also an imposing structure, more rambling but not so grand as Constantine's, and the shell of it still remains, but it is impossible to appreciate its architecture. It is hemmed in on every side with houses and shops. Only at the entrance can one perceive what must once have been graceful lines of stone. But even there iron stanchions shore up the walls, weakened as they were in the earthquake of 1927. While we were in Jerusalem we saw the ugly and cumbersome timbers removed, to be replaced with stronger but not less ugly metal girders. And the fine French Crusader carving over its entrance has for safety been removed to the Archaeological Museum. Characteristic Crusader arches and square tower remain, however, and the whole façade dates from that period. Broken columns of stone stand in the courtyard, relics of a noble atrium that once was there, and beside the door is the tomb-stone of an Englishman, Sir Philip d'Aubigny, who died in the Holy Land in 1236 as he wished to do, according to his epitaph, after living there for fourteen years. We stood looking at the still-legible coat of arms engraved on the stone. That crest is to be seen in Wells Cathedral, and on seals in the Channel Islands, where he was Governor. He had been tutor to King Henry III, and was one of the signatories of Magna Charta. Scholar and warrior and resister of tyranny, he rested at last near the place where they laid the body of his Lord.

This courtyard has seen some strange sights. I describe later, in my Easter diary, how I was caught in a mad rush of people who stormed the doors in order to see the Holy Fire on Easter Eve, a scene which is repeated every year, in former times to the accompaniment of much bloodshed. Curzon, who visited Jerusalem in 1835, describes in *Monasteries of the Levant* how he saw over 300 bodies carried out of the church and laid here, wrapped in the shrouds they had brought to measure against the Stone of Unction. Many more were injured in that Holy Fire stampede, mostly by trampling. In the seventeenth century there was an outbreak of persecution, and Franciscan monks were burnt here. To this spot came the first Crusaders on July 14th, 1099, after their thirty-seven-day siege of the city. Godfrey de Bouillon led this army of 20,000 men upon a dreadful slaughter of the population. Probably 100,000 Moslems and Jews were massacred, men and women and children, and even some Christians who were unrecognized until one of their priests lifted a roughly made cross as they cowered in a corner of this courtyard. The Crusaders carried with them a mixture of faith and frenzy which did not forbid their leaders even upon this holy errand

> to wade through slaughter to a throne,
> And shut the gates of mercy on mankind.

Shall we ever understand how they could stride into the Holy Sepulchre, their bodies splashed with blood, 'red from the wine-press of the Lord', and fall upon their knees to give thanks to God for His great mercies? Two million Crusaders died in the effort to gain the *Terra Sancta* for Christendom, and the Holy Sepulchre was the centre of their intention. Often the last words they gasped were: 'Save us, Holy Sepulchre!'

I always warned the men I took to see this church for the first time to be prepared to be disappointed. They would see no

> green hill far away,
> Without a city wall,

but a gloomy church propped up with stanchions, to keep it from collapse. They would see no rocky tomb with the stone rolled away from its opening, but a bizarre marble chapel under a giant rotunda with its once-blue ceiling now discoloured and peeling. They would find different sections of it owned by different communities, for six separate Christian Churches possess various chapels in it and claim rights and interests. Yet all this is inevitable in view of its history. The Turkish authorities sometimes favoured one community and sometimes another, and the present division of the whole place was a Moslem solution of the subsequent difficulties. It is true that they sometimes get in one another's way, and squabbles ensue, but they are Oriental Christians for the most part, excitable like children, and they are very earnest to protect their holy places. Mr. C. N. Johns has reminded me of what Mr. Midshipman Easy was told when he complained about the swearing on board ship: 'It is zeal, Mr. Easy, zeal in the King's service.' And the accumulation of church ornaments is most repellent to an Englishman. Gaudy lamps and candles and pieces of ribbon are all over the place, besides crude pictures and tasteless sculptures in marble. But again we should remember, I used to warn the troops, that these folk are like

children, and it is their idea of respect to decorate their altars in such
lavish fashion. Pretty coloured balls and gold and tinsel are their
toys, and I am sure that their Father understands them and likes to
see their playthings and the games they enjoy with bright clothes
and processions and the swinging of incense. After all, some of
these ancient churches have kept unbroken a tradition of worship
that goes back to Byzantine times and perhaps even earlier, and
they have maintained it in face of trial and temptation through
centuries of Moslem rule and persecution. It is not surprising that
they have lost some evangelistic enthusiasm. It is surprising that they
exist at all.

Inside the great wooden door we saw to the left the broad divan
which is the seat of the Moslem doorkeeper. He is a member of
one of the oldest families in Jerusalem, the Nusaibeh, which has held
this post by heredity since the thirteenth century. The Moslem
division of the church into areas controlled by different Churches
is called the 'minute system', which necessitated a neutral to keep the
peace, and the old tradition has been maintained. He and his friends
are very obliging and friendly nowadays, and he uses his right to be
present at the major Church ceremonies. The Government has
several times considered 'buying him out', as his presence is no
longer necessary.

The small area at the entrance, with the Stone of Unction before
us, flanked by giant candles, was dark and dismal. High overhead
the bare stone vault looked most insecure. Big criss-cross timbers
filled the space between walls beyond, and the whole had an air of
dilapidation. Yet there was a strange atmosphere about the place
that was attractive. I cannot describe it, but I always felt it. Surely
there is some accumulation of piety about a place which has been
the fervent object of pilgrimage for over 1,600 years?

Upstairs to our right we found the Calvary Chapel. It stands on
a platform some 14 feet above ground-level, built on solid rock, as
is proved by a section of it carefully preserved under a sheet of glass.
For the rest, the floor is a duplication of Crusader tessellated paving.
All the interior architecture of the Holy Sepulchre Church dates
from the early part of the nineteenth century, after the great fire
which broke out in the Armenian Chapel on the night of October
12th, 1808, and consumed all but the outer walls and some inner
pillars. That was the worst possible period imaginable from the
point of view of architecture, and to make matters still worse the
Greeks were in the ascendancy at that time, and they were able to
dictate the form of the rebuilding. An unknown Greek designer was
in charge, and he built the hideous marble kiosk which now stands

over the Tomb. 'Profiting by the embarrassment caused by the Napoleonic wars going on in Europe', writes L-H. Vincent in *Jerusalem Nouvelle*, 'in March, 1809, the Greeks obtained a *firman* from the Sultan Mahmoud II authorizing them to restore the basilica of the Holy Sepulchre.' All round the Calvary Chapel is an unpleasing balustrade of stone, with narrow steps leading up on either side.

There was a low arched roof above us of gilt mosaic which was illuminated for our benefit by concealed lighting, switched on by a brown-robed Franciscan, bringing us suddenly from gloom into light. We were standing at the tenth station of the Cross, where they stripped Jesus of His garments. Before us was the Roman Catholic altar on Calvary, which is their eleventh station, with a large modern mosaic in the wall above it depicting the event it commemorates, the Nailing to the Cross. This was the Latin side of Calvary, separated from the Greek by several large pillars. Through a window to our right we looked into the Chapel of the Agony of the Virgin, bright with coloured glass windows, which marks the place where it is believed that Mary stood when Jesus committed her to the care of John, the beloved disciple. In the stained-glass window, a Roman soldier is shown in Crusader uniform.

We walked slowly forward to see the three altars which stand on the traditional Golgotha: the Roman Catholic Altar of the Nailing to the Cross; the Stabat Mater, a glass case containing an image of the Virgin with her heart pierced by a jewelled sword and surrounded by a garish cluster of votive offerings of pilgrims: gold and jewels of every kind amounting to quite £3,000,000 in value; and the Orthodox altar over Calvary itself, surmounted by a life-size crucifix of silver with painted wooden face and arms and flanked by similar figures of Mary and John. Jewels were glistening and lamps hung in dozens from the ceiling, whilst an intricate golden candelabra was pendent in the centre. We peeped under the altar to see a hole which is supposed to be where the Cross went in the ground, and two similar holes at the back where were the thieves' crosses. A rent in the rock, caused, they say, by the earthquake at the time of the Crucifixion, could be seen to the right. It runs down to the Chapel of Adam underneath where it is thought that Adam was buried. A legend declares that the blood of Christ flowed down the cleft and touched the skull of Adam, bringing him to life again, obviously a story from the Pauline dictum, 'as in Adam all die, so in Christ shall all be made alive'.

There is no happening at Golgotha without its appropriate shrine, which later came to be believed to be the exact location of it. It is impossible to be sure where the Cross was erected, not to mention the other events at the time, but it was an aid to faith in early times to mark them by an altar. Only the most credulous believe to-day that the actual locations are the ones shown. There are, for instance, shrines marking the place where the women stood afar off, beholding; where Mary Magdalene mistook the Risen Lord for the gardener; where He was derided; where the soldiers cast lots for His garments; and other events real and imaginary. There is even an altar to St. Longinus, believed to be the Roman soldier who pierced the side of Jesus with a spear. He is thought to have been blind in one eye and the blood and water which came from the side of the Lord touched his eye and healed it, and later he was converted to the Faith.

It was very difficult for us to imagine the scene when this low mound stood outside the wall of the city and three crosses on it were silhouetted against the sky. It was the turning-point of history when Christ hung there, the God who knew the agony of man. It was a garden then, with flowers trampled underfoot, and death where life had been. They took a tree, a thing of beauty, and nailed the Son of God upon it. The Cross is the sign of what man has done to God. But it is more than that. It is the sign of what God has done for man. It is the emblem, not of defeat, but of victory. Man has striven and still strives against God, and the Cross is the worst that man can do. But he cannot conquer love. Love was eternally triumphant on this hilltop, as on all the Calvaries of human life. Love conquered the last enemy. There is an empty tomb not far away.

Down the stairs again we looked at the Stone of Unction, an oblong piece of brown limestone, on which it is said the body of Jesus was prepared for the burial. Actually there is no warrant in the Gospel record for the existence of such a stone, but the faithful have revered it for centuries. This is the third or fourth stone to lay in this place, its predecessors having been worn away by kissing! It was a common custom to bring one's shroud to be cut to the size of the Stone of Unction.

Through more bastions of wood, we found ourselves under the wide rotunda of the Tomb itself, an impressive place in spite of the garish Edicule which covered the centre. Many men used to declare it was incredible to them that the Tomb could be so near to Golgotha, and they would suggest that the two places had been placed under one roof for convenience. But John's account suggests that they really were not very far apart, both tomb and place of execution being in Joseph of Arimathea's garden. It is 135 feet from the Calvary altar to the Tomb. Constantine's builders left the mound outside their church, a simple monument surmounted by an immense cross. It was the Crusaders' predecessors who put a roof over Calvary when they constructed their church in the eleventh century.

How is it, men would ask me, that the Tomb of Jesus to-day is under a marble chapel when it was originally a rock-cut chamber? I used to reply that from the records we have of the building of Constantine's church in A.D. 335, we can imagine how the workmen pared away the hillside, leaving a rocky monument round the tomb to preserve it, which became the chief centre of Christian veneration. Hadrian had built a temple to Venus on this site, possibly because it was central and possibly, though less probably, because it was a Christian shrine. It had been there for 200 years when the Christian Emperor gave orders to search for the tomb of Christ. It is no wonder that, when they found it, following the tradition that Jesus had been buried on this site, they declared that it had been found against all hope. From the researches of students—Williams, Vincent, Jeffrey, Duckworth, Pierotti, Wilson, and others I have read on this subject—it seems certain that there is not only a solitary and distinctive rich man's tomb of the Herodian period here under the marble, recorded by eye-witnesses at the restoration after the fire in 1808, but that it closely corresponds with both the evidence of the earliest pilgrims who described the tomb, and with the details given us in the Gospel records.

We must remember that 300 years after it was built the church and especially the Tomb was deliberately destroyed by the Persians, in A.D. 614. It was rebuilt in 629, only to be smashed again by the mad Khalif Hakim in 1008, after which it lay waste for thirty years. Several times it has been rebuilt. The rock has also suffered at the hands of devout pilgrims, who chipped off pieces of it as souvenirs; and in 1603 there was actually an attempt to steal the Tomb by Italians, who even began operations on it! The present marble covering does not pretend to be the veritable bench on which the body of Jesus lay. It protects vestiges of original rock, with probably a side opening in which the body was placed, and not a trough-shape as some believe it to be. All this was within a rock-cut chamber, scarcely any part of which now remains. The Edicule stands where once was a monument carved out of the hillside.

Both architect and masons of the Byzantine church were accustomed to building heathen Roman temples. It was doubtless the first Christian sanctuary they had built, and they followed their former style and methods. Perhaps they cut a bizarre ornamentation on the Tomb, rather like the work of the rock artists of Roman times that we can see to-day at Petra. It may have been semicircular in plan, with the rotunda surrounding it of the same shape. It was in the open air originally, with the great Church of the Martyrion, or 'Witness', to the west of it, where the Greek Catholicon now stands. Indeed, in the dome above it there was an aperture open to the sky until its last rebuilding, if old engravings are to be believed. The present covering dome, with windows at the top, was put there in 1868, and appears not to have been repainted since.

We filed into the Chapel of the Angels, which is an ante-room for the Tomb itself, a mass of marble scrolls all round us, and in the centre we saw a pedestal containing what is thought to be a genuine piece of the original rolling stone on which the angel sat. It is a portion of white limestone about a foot square, smoothed by kisses. One by one, we filed into the tomb-chamber itself, bending low to enter, and found room for about four of us before the slab of marble which covers the grave from which Jesus rose from the dead. The bench fills half the space in that tiny room, and across it there is a deep crack, caused, they say, deliberately, to prevent the Turkish authorities from appropriating such a fine piece of marble. Clusters of lamps hung above it, belonging to different Churches, and the wall was completely covered by holy pictures, carvings, and ecclesiastical ornaments. I opened a little door in the wall covered by a picture of Mary holding a jar of burial perfume, and disclosed some chipped rock which may be part of the original interior of the tomb. We crept out again and allowed others to follow us in.

The Greek Catholicon, before the entrance to the Tomb, is almost completely hidden by the wooden bastions crossing its walls, as indeed they fill the spaces between the pillars round the rotunda itself. It is not a very large church, or, rather, cathedral, and is a poor successor of the glorious Byzantine church that once was here. In its centre stood a pedestal round which we gathered. It has a metal cross sunk in the top to mark the Centre of the Earth, the relic of an idea that persisted until recent times that the earth was flat, that Jerusalem was its centre, and, of course, the Holy Sepulchre marked the very heart of it.

The other things we visited before we left that amazing church, with its dark corridors and mysterious passages and rambling series of chapels and shrines, were: the Rabboni Chapel of the Roman Catholics, with great marble stars in the floor to mark both where Mary Magdalene stood and her Master when she met Him on Easter morning; the Chapel of the Apparition, a little place newly built which is at the legendary place of the house of Joseph of Arimathea and where Catholics believe that the Risen Jesus appeared

F

to His mother, although there is no Gospel record of such an appearance; a part of the Column of Flagellation preserved in an altar in that chapel, and the sword and spurs of Godfrey de Bouillon, first Crusader ruler of Jerusalem, in the Franciscan sacristy; the old rock-hewn tombs in the Syrian Chapel off the rotunda, now called those of Nicodemus and Joseph of Arimathea, and certainly of Jewish origin, showing that here was a burial place, and thus the site was outside the city wall; the Chapels of the Parting of the Raiment and of the Derision, in a gloomy ambulatory; and the Chapel of St. Helena, down a widening stairway with little rough crosses cut in its walls. Here St. Helena, the mother of Constantine, is said to have sat while workmen, obeying her dream, unearthed a cistern and found three crosses in it, one of which, by miraculously curing a sick woman, was proved to be the True Cross.

We thought this last place very interesting. It had been newly renovated and simple altars stood in the place of unpleasing former erections. One is to St. Helena and the other is dedicated to the Penitent Thief, with a grille in the wall hiding a cavity which once, they say, opened into hell itself. It was filled up because sensitive souls could not bear to hear the cries of those in torment below! The Armenians found a fine old Crusader stone altar here, and it would have been ideal to put it into use again, but they preferred to cover it with a modern one. A flight of stone steps led down into darkness to the Chapel of the Invention of the Cross, and we descended it, walking where pilgrims for centuries had worn the stone. We needed a candle or two and electric torches to see where we were, and found that it was a rocky cavern almost under Calvary itself, certainly under the ridge of which the site of the Crucifixion is a part. An early writer describes holes for buckets in the roof here, and it may have been a cistern when the place was a garden.

I know nothing of the authenticity of the crosses that were found here. The contemporary records say nothing of it, although later writers declared that their discovery led to the location of the Tomb. The True Cross for which Heraclius fought, which the Persians carried away with them, splinters of which are now scattered over Christendom, was doubtless the timber that was dug from this cistern. Later, there are records of the possession of such things as the sponge, the reed, the spear, and the title which was over the Cross. A story dating from about A.D. 440 tells how Helena sent the Holy Nails to Constantine, who had them made into a helmet and horsebits (there must have been a great deal of metal in them) to fulfil the prophecy of Zechariah xiv. 20 which, from the Greek, reads: 'There shall be upon the horses' bits, Holy to the Lord

Almighty.' St. Helena's Chapel dates from about the tenth century, but the four great columns were probably part of Constantine's original building. We could see the characteristic Byzantine basketwork carved in their capitals. They must have been originally in another part of the church, for they do not fit very well the arches resting on them.

The many little crosses in the stone blocks of the wall are often thought to have been cut by Crusaders, but they were probably made by later, fourteenth-century pilgrims, when, as their custom was, they spent their first night in Jerusalem in the Church of the Holy Sepulchre. The newly-found manuscript of Margery Kempe describes how she spent all night in the church.

My party peeped into the Chapel of Adam, under Calvary, before we left. It is a small chamber noted not only for the legend of the skull of Adam I have mentioned, the supposed resting-place of which can be seen in its little apse, but for the fact that for long it was believed that Melchizedek was buried here. It is certain that at least two Crusader kings had their tombs here, and possibly two others. The tombs of Godfrey de Bouillon and his brother, Baldwin I, were here, with Latin inscriptions, until the 1808 fire. I have seen a copy of an old engraving showing their elaborate cenotaphs. But the Greeks, who hated anything Latin, took the opportunity to cast out the tombstones and the bones under them when they built the church after the fire. Now the places have benches where we gratefully rested after our pilgrimage. Through a door leading from it we could see the offices, complete with desk, telephone and filing cabinets, of the Orthodox priests. Incongruities indeed to find in a room under Mount Calvary!

It was not easy to be in prayerful mood in the Holy Sepulchre. Although the stalls selling beads and crosses and other objects of piety are no longer at its doors, giving justification to charges of 'commercialization', it is all still very much of a show-place, which, of course, is inevitable, since nearly every Christian visitor to Jerusalem makes his way there some time before he leaves; and the constant stream of visitors, together with the darkness of the church and its state of bad repair, combine to give it a strange, awesome air quite foreign to the spirit of devotion. On Friday afternoons there were processions of singing choirs of Catholics and Armenians and Greeks, besides the daily services, but it was always hard for me, and for most to whom I spoke, to gain the true atmosphere of worship. It is a vast museum piece, public property and yet inscrutably aloof from the world, and the strange atmosphere I mentioned earlier was invariably noticeable to me: an odour of age, and long-dead superstitions, and frantic zeal expressed in crude forms, and lingering prayers which ascended here long ago. I cannot explain it. But I loved to visit the Holy Sepulchre. It had a weird fascination always for me. It is unfortunate that the various interests concerned cannot agree about the rebuilding of the place. The administration arbitrates, but there is an ancient rule that still persists, to the effect that the party which repairs a roof or a wall owns it, and he who sweeps a floor obviously is sweeping no floor but his own. So each is anxious to provide the funds for repairing the church, to prevent the other claiming it as his own. None the less, there is admirable co-operation between the Churches in the Holy Sepulchre, noticeably at Easter, when the ceremonies might clash. Rivalry in the holy places is not here, where there is complete understanding about traditional rights. Rather is it in the establishment of a rival site for Calvary and the Tomb on the part of the adherents of Gordon's Calvary and the Garden Tomb, providing alternatives that have scanty authority and serve only to confuse the simple soldier and to disgust him with the rival claims concerning the Tomb of Jesus. I deal with this subject in a later chapter.

But sometimes there are misunderstandings. A certain famous Anglican bishop in Jerusalem once prevented a conflict between two of the factions in the Holy Sepulchre. His old friend the Coptic bishop visited him to ask his advice. A newly-appointed Coptic priest had inadvertently censed a whole pillar instead of the half of it which the Copts owned. The Latins, who owned the other half of the pillar, were furious at this violation of their rights. They revenged the insult by sending a servant, carrying a tray of food, to walk through the congregation standing before the Coptic altar early next morning during Mass. It stands by a technical right of way. He thus intruded into the Coptic solemnities.

'What,' said the Coptic bishop, 'shall we do about it?'

'I suppose you want to be one up on the Latins?' said the Anglican bishop.

'We certainly do.'

'Well, I imagine that they are awaiting your next move and are wondering what it will be.'

The Copt agreed that this was so.

'Well,' said the Anglican, 'I will tell you what to do. They don't know what form your retaliation will take or when it will be. Let them remain uncertain. Keep them in suspense.'

The Coptic bishop was delighted with this novel idea, and it was duly carried out. The weary old church was saved yet another conflict and the aggressor had coals of fire heaped upon his head.

CHAPTER V

TEMPLE

At the dawn, when the light of the sun first strikes on the Cupola, and the Drum catches the rays; then is this edifice a marvellous sight to behold and one such that in all Islam I have never seen its equal; neither have I heard tell of ought built in pagan times that did rival in grace this Dome of the Rock.

MUKADDASI, A.D. 985.

A CENTRE of interest for every pilgrim to Jerusalem is the great space known as the Temple Area, to the east of the Old City. When I say 'every pilgrim', I am being accurate, for not only Christians but Jews and Moslems reverence it and come to the Holy City specially to see it. Jews, however, can only go as far as the Wailing Wall. The Temple Area itself is in the possession of the Moslems, who at special times allow anybody but a Jew to enter. The Orthodox Jews say they do not want to go in, anyway, because they believe that the Ark of the Covenant and other treasures of the ancient Temple are buried there, maybe under the floor of the cavern of the Rock, and they do not wish to add to its desecration. The nearest they will go to the Temple Area is the lofty stretch of its wall that remains against the Old City, and there, at the holiest place the Jews possess, they mourn in their extravagant fashion for the loss of the Temple and pray for its restoration. When Rothschild visited Jerusalem, many years ago now, he was carried over the ground of the Temple Area, lest his foot should desecrate holy things.

Normally a charge of 200 mils (4s.) was made for non-Moslem sightseers, who could enter the Haram es Sherif (the 'Noble Sanctuary', as the Arabs call it) on any morning except Fridays, provided that they left the place by 11.30 a.m. But the Supreme Moslem Council had agreed to issue permits allowing members of H.M. Forces in to the Area without charge. So the troops' leave hostels organized parties to go there nearly every day. The Temple Area and the Holy Sepulchre were the two places that every visiting soldier was advised to see first. So I soon found that I was often in demand as a guide to the Temple Area. To equip oneself for this task was no light matter. I had to do a lot of reading and exploring. The great space, occupying a quarter of the total area of the Old City of Jerusalem, is a vast museum. It has associations going back through the centuries to the time of Abraham. Before I plucked up enough courage to take a party of soldiers round it and explain things to them, and, worst of all, answer their questions, I made quite half a dozen visits to it, and listened to various guides, some Christian, some Moslem. I knew I could never emulate their air of omniscience and speed of utterance, but it seemed to me that the average soldier might learn even from an amateur guide like myself something that was more worth while than the bare recounting of facts and dates. I discovered a charm and a romance about that incredibly ancient sanctuary that I resolved to try to pass on to others. It was necessary, of course, to relate a number of facts of Biblical and later history, as it is in Sunday school, but only as a background to another story: that of man's search for God and God's search for man. So it came about that after some months of constant tours of it, I was almost as familiar with the Temple Area as Caiaphas must have been!

It looked very different in his day, of course. Instead of an Arabic dome, the House of the Lord lifted its head nobly above surrounding walls and courtyards, and gleamed with white and gold in the sunshine, whilst colonnades encircled its boundary, and the smoke of the burnt offering on the altar in the open air spiralled up to heaven as a sweet-smelling savour to Yahveh. Now part of the surrounding space is rubble and weeds, but a large paved area, bordered with occasional slender Saracenic arches, has in its centre the famous Dome of the Rock, the oldest and most beautiful Moslem building in the world.

I was keen to include this place in the visits that I made to the local historic sites with the members of the Wednesday Fellowship, but it was difficult to do so because admission was only possible for us in the morning, when the men were busy at their daily duties. Other places we could see on Sunday afternoons. On Sunday mornings many of the men were free, but I was not, for I had always one and often two services to conduct at that time. But it was important that the men who dwelt in Jerusalem should have an opportunity of visiting the Temple, and one Sunday I found that I was able to arrange with a colleague to take my service and I was free to conduct a party of Methodist lads on a pilgrimage to the place that Jesus knew and where He worshipped.

We met at the Jaffa Gate one bright spring morning, and pushed through the jostling throng in the narrow steep street called David Street. We did not turn to the left along Christian Street, which leads to the Holy Sepulchre, and where on Sunday all the shop shutters were closed, as befits the Christian quarter of the Old City. We continued along the busy market, dodging laden donkeys and twisting around the shouting Arabs, swarthy men and veiled women who were buying and selling under the crumbling Crusader arches, until we found the Street of the Chain that led us to the quaint arabesques of the entrance to the Area. We went downhill all the way, as the ancient Jews must have done along this very street, which was a viaduct over the valley. Yet they always said that they went 'up' to the Temple, so holy was it to them.

An Arab with a huge black moustache and a red tarbush stopped us at the gate and I presented our pass. It was written in Arabic characters unintelligible to me, but apparently it related the correct number of men to be admitted, and we mounted the wide steps of the sanctuary, to encounter several important looking officials at the top, who demanded piastres from each of us for the loan of slippers. We could walk about the outer paving without covering on our shoes, but not under the Dome or in the Mosque el Aksa, to the south of the Area. The same applied to the use of cameras. We could take snaps outside, but not inside the buildings. I warned the men that smoking was forbidden anywhere within the Area. I took my party aside in the shadow of a wall to our right, and answered their questions. Before us rose the stately curves of the Dome, dominating the view, and a few smaller domes and pillars stood around us. The walls of the main building were covered with bright blue tiles, placed there by Suleiman the Magnificent in the sixteenth century, and above it bulged the huge cupola itself, surmounted by the crescent of Islam. Behind, against the sky, was the familiar outline of the Mount of Olives across the Kedron Valley.

'Is this the Temple?' inquired somebody.

'No,' I said. 'It is not. The temples which have stood here have all been destroyed. This is the Dome that a certain Khalif of Damascus, Abd el Melik by name, built in the year of our Lord 691. The latest theory is that it stands over the site of the Holy of Holies of the Jewish Temple. The altar was in the open air to the east of it. Do you know why it was placed there?'

Nobody did. I told them.

'David had captured the city of the Jebusites,' I explained. 'Down there to the south of the present city wall, and then the Jews were threatened with a plague which the angel of the Lord stopped at the threshing-floor of a man named Araunah the Jebusite. You can read all about it in 2 Samuel xxiv. So David bought the threshing-floor and put an altar there to the Lord, and that was the beginning of the worship that has gone on here in one way or another ever since.'

'What was the date of David's reign?'

'About 1066 B.C.,' I replied.

'Did he build the Temple?'

'No, actually he didn't. According to the account in 1 Chronicles (chapter xxii, verse 8) he was not considered worthy to do so because he was a man of blood, and his son Solomon built it. It was a fine building, and there are a good many chapters in the Old Testament describing its materials and workmanship. It was known as Solomon's Temple for centuries.'

'Half a minute,' said one of the soldiers. 'How do you know that this is where the threshing-floor was?'

I knew that one, too. 'In 2 Chronicles iii. 1 the site of the Temple is definitely associated, not only with Araunah's threshing-floor, but with Mount Moriah, where Abraham tried to offer up Isaac, but sacrificed eventually the ram that was caught in a thicket. Over in the courtyard of the Holy Sepulchre the credulous Greeks will show the visitor the very thicket—an olive bush—and on the roof of the church the Abyssinians display another, which they declare is the true one. Incidentally, the boundary between Benjamin and Judah is believed to have crossed the area of the Temple, some say between the House of the Lord and the altar.'

'How many temples have stood here, then?' I was asked.

'Three, all on the same site,' I said. 'Solomon's Temple lasted until 586 B.C., when Nebuchadnezzar captured Jerusalem and took the leading Jews away to Babylon. It was in ruins until they were able to return, and a man named Zerubbabel rebuilt it in 516 B.C. Then, in the second century B.C., the Greek ruler of this part of the world, Antiochus Epiphanes by name, annoyed the Jews very much by polluting the Temple by sacrificing swine on the altar, and that resulted in a rebellion led by Judas Maccabeus which eventually proved successful, and he restored the Temple. Then when Herod the Great became a sort of puppet king under the Romans he thought he would please the Jews by building them a fine new Temple. He started it about 17 B.C., taking down the rebuilt Zerubbabel's Temple stone by stone, and enlarging the whole area. It was not completely finished when Jesus came to Jerusalem, and it was not fated to last very long. When Titus destroyed the city in A.D. 70 after a siege of three months, the Temple was burnt down, although he had hoped to preserve it. The Jews fought with such fury here that he could not prevent its destruction by his troops. As a matter of fact, he was so curious about it that he tried to enter himself into the Holy of Holies, but he was driven out by the smoke.'

'What happened after that?'

'After that the Roman Emperor Hadrian built a brand new city

in A.D. 135, which he called Aelia Capitolina, and he used this place
as a site for a temple to Jupiter. When the Byzantine Empire became
Christian, most of this area was left desolate. People used to think
that Justinian's great Church of the Theotokos (the Mother of God)
was here, where the Mosque el Aksa now stands, but they were
wrong. That church was probably on the other side of Jerusalem,
across the Tyropean Valley. The Moslem invasion of Jerusalem
under the Khalif Omar was in 637, and this Dome was put up
about fifty years afterwards.'

'Why is it called the Mosque of Omar?'

'I'm not quite sure. It certainly isn't the Mosque of Omar, which
is that old place with a minaret opposite the entrance to the Holy
Sepulchre. I suppose people got a little confused. The correct
name for it is the Dome of the Rock. It was Omar who led the
Moslem invaders into Jerusalem and who located the Temple Area
as the Prophet's jumping-off place for heaven. He found the site
piled with rubbish, as apparently the site of Jewish sacrifices was
abominable to the Christians of that time, and they neglected it
completely. In the old Madeba mosaic map of sixth-century
Jerusalem most of the area of the Temple is completely ignored.'

One of the men asked me why the Moslems reverence the place.
I explained that Mohammed collected a lot of odds and ends of
various religions he encountered in his travels, such as the Persian
faith, Judaism, and Christianity, and put them all together with the
Arab's own tribal religion, and produced Islam. That means that
many of the Jewish heroes are included among the Moslem 'prophets', and they respect Jesus also. Mohammed said his prayers
facing Jerusalem for a year or so, until, say the Moslems, he asked
Allah's permission to pray towards his native city of Mecca, and it
was granted. Moslems have prayed in that direction ever since.
Still, Jerusalem is regarded by them as the third holy place, Mecca and
Medina only being more important, and the faithful have valued a
pilgrimage to the Dome of the Rock ever since it was built by Abd
el Melik. He had some sort of a disagreement with the people at
Mecca, and put up the Dome in order to attract people to Jerusalem
instead. It is distinguished not only for its beauty—he took the
columns for it from churches and fine buildings all over the city—
but for the fact that it was the first building to contain every necessity
for Moslem worship: niches or mihrabs facing towards Mecca,
indications of the proper times for prayer, a pulpit for the leader,
and so on. They have a legend that the Prophet Mohammed
ascended to heaven from the Rock, so that is why it is specially
holy to them. In A.D. 1047 a Moslem pilgrim wrote that a prayer

said in Jerusalem has an effect equivalent to 25,000 prayers said elsewhere; Medina prayers have twice that value, and a prayer said in the city of Mecca is worth 100,000.

'Why didn't the Crusaders destroy it?' I was asked.

'They thought it was *Templum Domini*, the Temple of the Lord. They carefully preserved it and erected buildings all round. They put up a great cross over it where the crescent is now and built a high altar on the Rock itself, where they believed the ancient Jewish sacrifices were made. The perfumes that Saladin used later to wash away the defilements of the Crusaders could not obliterate the steps they cut in the rock or the marks of their picks, which can still be seen. The faithful point to them as the marks of the Angel Gabriel when he pushed the Rock back as it was trying to follow the Prophet to heaven.'

'How long were the Crusaders here?'

'Less than a hundred years, from 1099 to 1187, although they lingered in other parts of Palestine, such as Acre, until 1291. The Order of Knights Templar was founded here and, of course, the octagonal shape of the building was copied for the Temple Churches in Europe, notably in London and Cambridge. Chippings from the Rock, by the way, were sold by the Crusaders to pilgrims for their weight in gold.'

'And it has been a Moslem place ever since?'

'Yes, Saladin renovated it, and so have various Turkish rulers since his time. Almost every square yard has some Moslem legend attached to it. It is rather interesting to realize that the *muezzin*, the imam's call to prayer that echoes regularly across these flagstones from one of the minarets in a far corner, is very similar to an ancient prayer that was heard here in the days of the Hebrew Temple. The Moslem cries, "Allah is One! Allah is most great! There is no Allah but Allah!" That is strangely like the *Shema* of the Jews: "Hear, O Israel, the Lord our God is one Lord." '

We walked across the doorway where between two pillars squatted an old Arab who had a pile of tattered slippers which he proceeded to tie on over our shoes. As he did so, we looked at the two designs resembling birds to the right of the entrance. The legend is that they were magpies which were turned to stone by Solomon.

Inside the doors we had to stand blinking a little in order to accustom our eyes to the gloom after the bright sunshine outside. Beneath our feet were soft red carpets, and to our right a grandfather clock with Arabic numerals and the name of a famous London clockmaker on its dial. Apart from that incongruity, we had stepped straight into the world of *The Arabian Nights*. The circling wall, 180 feet in circumference, enclosed a forest of pillars, each standing in orderly relation to the others to support the vast cupola which loomed above our heads. Not one column was exactly like another, for they had all done duty elsewhere in various buildings before they were gathered here well over 1,000 years ago. The great tie-beams that linked their massive capitals under a succession of regular arches were elaborately ornamented with fantastic Oriental tracery, as was every square foot of space on walls and roof. The many windows under pointed arches stained the sunbeams with the most gorgeous hues of rich crimson and blues and greens and yellows.

We were very interested in those windows. Their designs were cast in plaster, and admitted the light only in direct rays through little tunnels that led to the coloured glass so that the marvellous intricacy of their patterns could only be appreciated if we stood right in front of them. Nothing at all could be seen at an angle, which accounted for the prevailing gloom of the place.

Our rough leather slippers made no sound on the covered floor as we passed between the columns round a screen of fine wrought iron that encloses the Rock in the centre. This screen is the only surviving relic of the Crusaders in that place. It is about 10 feet high and encloses the whole of the inner area under the Dome, and is a wonderful example of medieval craftsmanship. We passed an occasional Koran student, with a broad white band round his red tarbush, squatting before the holy book on an X-shaped stand and reading from it in a low monotone. Strings of little vessels of olive-oil were hung between the columns. Near the entrance to the cave beneath the Rock I pointed out a black scar in the marble under the screen.

'What do you think that is?' I asked.

'It looks like a bullet-hole,' said somebody.

'You are right,' I said. 'These people are normally friendly, but they don't like to be laughed at. A few years ago two girls were being shown round with some English visitors, and were giggling together at some private joke. One of these earnest brothers thought they were laughing at him or at his religion, so he produced a revolver and wounded one of the girls. This is one of the bullet marks. He was a fanatic, of course, but it is prudent as well as courteous to respect the holy things of others.'

There is a story about the projection that looks like a tongue over the entrance to the cave. When the Khalif Omar arrived here after his conquest of Jerusalem it is said that this tongue gave him the customary Arabic greeting, 'Peace be on you!' to which of course he gave the appropriate reply.

We descended the marble steps into the twilight under the Rock and found ourselves in a dark cavern some 20 by 15 feet in area and the rocky roof nearly touching our heads. Two bearded imams stood at the bottom of the steps and provided us with candles, with which we explored the cave. We were standing in one of the holiest places of the Moslem world, under the Rock which every follower of the Prophet believes is the centre of the earth. A Moslem's idea of reverence, however, is very different from ours. Apart from the rich ornamentation of the Dome itself, he leaves everything in bare simplicity, which is perhaps fortunate, although he will not allow any disturbance by archaeological excavations. But the two custodians used no hushed voice or reverent mien. I was a familiar visitor of theirs, and they hailed me with loud greetings. They invariably gave me a warm welcome, perhaps because they knew that I never brought a party into the Dome without giving them 50 mils, the equivalent of an English shilling. I had discovered the wisdom of that policy. If no *baksheesh* were forthcoming, they would be inconveniently missing when I arrived with my next party of sightseers, and there would be endless difficulties in gaining admittance.

'We shall call you the Mosque Padre soon,' said one. They both laughed.

I made a polite and quite truthful reply about being totally unfitted for such a post, and asked them to point out to the men the significance of the place in which we were. One of them dutifully stamped on the floor to demonstrate its hollowness. It is supposed to lead to the source of all rivers, but probably it is a drain by which rain-water flowed away from the Temple buildings. We lifted our candles and saw a wide hole in the roof. Then with a lighthearted disregard of history, he pointed out round the walls the praying-places of Abraham, Solomon, David, Mohammed and Elijah. Most of the niches were rough indentations in the rock wall, but Elijah had a grand shrine of his own supported by a slender marble column which stood upside down with its capital of Romanesque workmanship on the ground. Our friend informed us that St. George had worshipped here. One of the men was a little startled at this, and wanted to know whether the Moslems reverenced St. George.

The imam was quick in explanation.

'Moslem say St. George and Elijah same man. Christian say they are two men.'

Later I explained to them this interesting example of the confusion of the identity of two local heroes. That almost legendary third-century figure, St. George, a native of Lydda, is known as the Ever-green One, the fountain of youth, and the Moslems know him as the Sheikh el Khidr, meaning 'green', which is their name for Elijah. Every year in the cave under Mount Carmel where Elijah is supposed to have lived, mothers bring their babies to be dedicated to him, not only Catholics, but often also Orthodox and Moslem women, and the Carmelite father sprinkles holy water on them all; Moslem children, too, bring a lock of their hair for Sheikh el Khidr.

Before we left that strange grotto I pointed out the indentation in the roof above the crude prayer niche that Mohammed is said to have used. The legend is that he rose to his feet without sufficient care and his head encountered the rock. Obligingly, however, the stone yielded to the shape of his head as though it was butter, so he was unharmed.

What secrets had that cavern known in the long-dead past? What priests of some ancient cult had used it in their fantastic rites? Had any of those great Biblical figures ever entered it? Had it been the scene of mysteries in the dim days of Melchizedek? Or did the Jebusites use it as a dwelling, or Araunah as a store for his grain? Were the Ark of the Covenant and the Temple treasure still buried here? We shall probably never know. Perhaps it was a Canaanite high place which the Israelites adapted for Yahveh-worship, and the niche inside the cave on the left contained an effigy before which blood poured through the hole from an altar above. In that case, the area was never a threshing-floor. Maybe the reference to Araunah was an insertion by later priests to hide the fact that their Altar of Sacrifice stood where idolatory had once been practised.

We surrendered our candles, put a shilling into the waiting hand, and mounted the steps into the fresher air under the Dome.

Inside the screen, when we stood upon a marble ledge with our backs to it, we were able to appreciate the marvellous decoration of mosaic which covers the walls supporting the cupola. There, and all over the interior of the Dome, are the most intricate designs in lovely gold and blue, always without representation of man or beast, and consisting chiefly of passages from the Koran in elaborate lettering. The origin of 'arabesques' was, of course, in the necessity of avoiding 'images'. A Cufic inscription running round the lower wall proclaimed that it had been built by one Abdullah el Mamun. He, however, was a later ruler, a son of Haroun el Rashid, of *Arabian Nights* fame and friend of Charlemagne, and he had altered the inscription, putting his name in place of that of the true builder, Abd el Melik, but forgetting to alter the original date! The verses from the Koran are from the *sura* 'Mary', which describes Jesus as the son of Mary, the Word of truth, and gives a warning against the doctrine of the Trinity. I am told that the end of the encircling inscription meets the beginning in the middle of a sentence, its decorative character being presumably more important than its sense.

We could see the uneven surface of the ancient Rock itself, still with the marks of the Crusader masons. In a way it is fortunate that the Moslems have had the custody of it, for had the Christians been enabled to do so, they would of course have covered it with altars, lamps, crosses, and ikons, as in the Holy Sepulchre, so that its true nature could not be discerned.

Although we need not believe, with the Moslems, that it has been suspended in space since it was pushed down by Gabriel when it sought to follow the Prophet to heaven, yet we might consider the fact that this sacred, rugged rock, some 60 by 40 feet in dimension, is thought to be the peak of Mount Moriah, where Abraham made an altar on which to offer up his son. The Moslems, not surprisingly in view of the Arab's reputed ancestry, declare that Ishmael was the intended victim, and say that this is the Foundation Stone of the World. Here the Holy of Holies of Yahveh stood for centuries. Near it was the altar, the scene of the special sacrifices at the feasts and of the daily offerings. The time of the evening sacrifice, for instance, the ninth hour, about three o'clock in the afternoon, must have been most impressive, when a lamb was slain, and there were chanted prayers with the tinkling of cymbals and the singing of psalms, whilst every worshipper prostrated himself.

Jesus worshipped at the Temple. He did not condemn the sacrificial system of worship. Indeed, He said that the altar sanctified the gift upon it. But He insisted on sincerity and a loving spirit, that a man should first be reconciled to his brother before offering his gift. He compared a self-righteous Pharisee with a humble publican who stood in an outer court, not deeming himself worthy to be admitted near to the altar. Jesus not only worshipped at this place, as was obligatory upon all adult pilgrims to Jerusalem at the three great feasts, but no doubt He slew His Passover lamb here beside the great altar, and bore it home for the Passover meal with His disciples.

In John's Gospel, chapter vii, we are told that on the last and great day of the feast, which would be the Feast of Tabernacles, Jesus cried: 'If any man thirst, let him come unto Me and drink.'

This would very likely be when the priest had returned from the Pool of Siloam in solemn procession bearing a golden pitcher of water, and after elaborate ceremony and to the sound of silver trumpets, the people moved seven times round the altar and the High Priest raised his hands and solemnly poured water on to it. As the robed and bearded figure let fall that cascade, the people heard the words of Jesus. Only on that occasion, in the sevenfold circuit of the altar, would Jesus, a layman, be permitted to pass between the altar and the House of the Lord. We were looking at the site of the Holy of Holies, the Shekinah, the place that for the Jews was the Presence of God. We were standing where Jesus was not permitted to enter.

But none the less, He superseded the High Priest who entered the Holy of Holies once a year to sprinkle the blood of atonement for the people. As a writer to Hebrew Christians said only a few decades later, 'Christ entered not into a holy place made with hands . . . but into heaven itself', and we can follow Him with boldness, 'by the way which He dedicated for us, a fresh and living way'.

In a corner of the painted wooden fence enclosing the Rock we examined a towering casket which is said to contain two hairs from the beard of Mohammed. We saw a veiled Moslem woman insert her hand into an aperture beneath it, and when she had gone we did the same, to feel the outline of what is believed to be the footprint the Prophet made when he went up to heaven.

The fact that the Moslems remove their shoes in their sanctuaries reminded us of that Old Testament sign of reverence: 'Put off thy shoes from off thy feet, for the place whereon thou standest is holy ground.' No dust from travel was permitted to fall anywhere within the great Temple Area in the days of the Jews, and the cautious would leave their shoes at the gate. Doubtless Jesus did the same when He came into the surrounding colonnades to teach the people. The Levites who officiated within the Inner Temple did so bare-footed. This was no doubt the origin of the practice in Islam. The slippers covering our shoes were removed at the doorway, and we stepped out into the brilliant sunshine.

The late Dr. Schick declared that the Holy of Holies stood over a place where a few cypress trees rise at the foot of some stairs leading down directly from the west of the Dome of the Rock. Dr. Hollis, however, in his recent researches, has located it over the Rock itself. This confirms the ancient Jewish tradition. The wall enclosing the Inner Temple ran in a great rectangle in the centre of the whole sanctuary area, and the House of the Lord, with the Holy of Holies in the leg of its T-shape, was to the west of the altar in the centre. East of the altar lay the lesser grades of holiness, the Levites' Court, the Court of the Women, and so on. The Court of the Gentiles was outside the boundary of the Inner Sanctuary, and tablets have been found that came from the wall, bearing a Greek inscription which reads:

'No stranger should enter the limit and enclosure of the Sanctuary. He who is caught will carry the guilt on himself, because death will follow.'

We had seen a plaster cast of one of the tablets in the wall of the Quiet Room in the Newman School of Missions.

Its careful wording suggests that no legal execution could be expected, but that possibly mob-law would be justifiable. Certainly that threatened Paul, when he was falsely accused of taking Trophimus the Ephesian into the Inner Sanctuary. We could see in the far north-west corner the Antonia Fortress where he was taken by the Roman troops, and from the steps of which he addressed the throng. The place has been a stronghold for soldiers of the occupying power in Jerusalem ever since. Turkish troops used to be billeted there, and to-day it acts as barracks for the Palestine Police.

The Treasury, I pointed out, where Jesus saw a rich man ostentatiously making a large gift and a poor widow dropping in two mites, or half-farthings, was probably by the Court of the Women. That title, by the way, did not mean that men were excluded, but that women could normally go no farther. I took from my pocket and showed the men two 'mites' of the time of Pontius Pilate which I had obtained from one of the White Fathers at the Pool of Bethesda, where they were found. Were either of these tiny pieces of copper one of the very gifts which that poor woman made? It is an exciting possibility. Her great merit lay, of course, in the fact that she put two coins into the trumpet-shaped chest when she could have put in only one, though the two were all she had.

In those days there were many grades of holiness, which could only be traversed by those who were ceremonially clean. Indeed the grades reached over the city itself and beyond it, so that there were regulations as to behaviour and various ceremonies to be observed as a pilgrim approached the far environs of Jerusalem. Judaism was a very exclusive religion. Only a very few could get to its centre. Jesus reversed all that. Now no barriers of birth nor hindrances of ritual prevent the human soul from access to the Father in His all-inclusive love.

To the east of the Dome there is a much smaller one, with no

[Photo by C. J. Rawlings.

THE DOME OF THE ROCK.

[Photo by J Melhuish.

THE TEMPLE AREA VIEWED FROM THE ROOF OF ANTONIA FORTRESS

circling walls to conceal its pillars, and we stood under it. Just above our heads hung a piece of rusty chain from the centre of the cupola. The legend is that a chain from heaven once hung here which nobody could grasp if he was telling a lie, so it was found very convenient for testing legal witnesses. A man accused of robbery, however, cheated it by hiding the stolen money in a stick, which he gave his accuser to hold. The thief was thus able to hold the chain whilst he declared that his accuser had the money in his possession! At any rate, this smaller replica of the great Dome, and probably built as a model for it, is now known as the Dome of the Chain. The Dome of the Rock probably had no wall originally, but was open at the sides like this smaller dome. For all I know there may be some connection of this with the golden chain presented to Agrippa by the Emperor Caligula, and which according to Josephus was hung up over the Treasury chamber in the Sanctuary. Certainly some chain or other has persisted in Jerusalem's memory. The Street of the Chain is the main thoroughfare leading to the Temple. The Crusaders called this little dome the Chapel of the Presentation. Mary would have brought her Infant to a place farther east, between the Court of the Women and the altar.

We trod the old flagstones, many with grass between them, which cover the main area of the Haram, as the Arabs call it. Some workmen were filling big black skins with water from an opening down to one of the several conduits running round the Dome. When the skins were full they filled out to the shape of the goat from which they were made, with stumps for legs and head, and were hung over the backs of the water-carriers. The delicate arches which stood at the top of the stairs leading up on all four sides of this wide paved platform are called the 'Balances', because the Moslems say that the scales on the Day of Judgement will hang from them.

There are names for all the little domes we could see standing about the area. For instance, the tiny cupola on slender columns in the north-west corner was the Dome el Khidr (Elijah and/or St. George!) and that larger one farther away was the Dome of the Spirits, where the ghosts of Moslem saints come to worship after dark. The broad octagon yonder was the Dome of Gabriel or Mohammed's Ascension. One of these domes is almost certainly a Crusader baptistery.

Towards the north could be seen the tomb of Mohammed Ali, the Indian Moslem leader, who died at the Round Table Conference in London about ten years previously. It was a tremendous honour for his body to be brought from London to El Kuds, Jerusalem the Holy, and laid in this sacred place. The tomb to the west is that of

Husain, friend of Lawrence of Arabia and father of King Feisal of Iraq.

What a wonderful sight the Temple must have been when Jesus walked here. His disciples marvelled at the immensity of its stones. The earliest remains discernible to-day are of Herod's walls, and the largest stones are over 33 feet long. If Josephus was accurate, there were larger ones in his day. It is not often realized that Herod's Jerusalem was one of the finest cities in the Roman Empire, and the Temple, round which the city centred, stood in an area measuring 1,000 feet by 1,600 feet, more than twice as large as the famous Altis at Olympia or the Acropolis at Athens, although perhaps in Herod's time the boundary was not quite so far north as it is to-day. It had a colonnade running all round its boundaries, and above the wall of the Inner Temple rose the white stone House of the Lord with its face of beaten gold towards the east, the 'gold of the Temple' by which, Jesus said, men were wont to swear. When the morning sun was on it, it must have presented a wonderful view from the top of the Mount of Olives, causing Jesus to weep that, with all its sacred rites and symbols, Jerusalem did not know the things that belong unto peace.

'Where did Jesus drive out the money-changers?' I was asked, a question asked of every guide in the Temple Area each time he conducts a party round it. Some of the guides are vague, and others draw too much upon the resources of their imagination. I had studied the writings of Professor G. Dalman on this as on many other questions of location of holy sites. He points out that Herod had built a tremendous three-aisled basilica along the south end of the Area, where the Mosque el Aksa now stands, and an old double gate under it now maybe marks the spot where stood the early church that was dedicated to the driving out of the traders. This is very likely the place, with a popular entry and a roomy shelter, where the influential Sadducees, modernist and materialist, would permit money-changers to set up their tables; for the Temple tax, half shekels (Exodus xxx. 13) or didrachma, had to be paid in exact coinage before the Passover feast. Jesus did not object to this tax, for He paid it Himself, but He rebelled against the hypocrisy of using the sanctuary for trading, and, according to His allegation, dishonest trading. This would also be a suitable place for the sale of pigeons for women after childbirth and the poor to bring for their sacrifices. Dalman thinks that John's reference to oxen and sheep may be a later addition to the story.

Holy places always provide opportunities for 'commercialization', and Jerusalem in earlier times became notorious for that tendency chiefly because of the curio shops permitted in the Holy Sepulchre. But they have long ago been banished, and in spite of the popular idea to the contrary, the Christian holy places are not commercialized. There is no trading within them, and no charge is made for admission to them. Moslems demand payment, as a rule, but to every authentic holy place kept by Christians all the time I was in Jerusalem, my parties of visitors were admitted without any charge. I could enlarge upon this subject, for it cannot be too strongly emphasized that visitors come to the Holy City expecting to find 'commercialization' and ready to be offended by it, but can only perceive it in the clamouring for *baksheesh* of urchins in the street, or in the collection plate that awaits any gifts in the churches, as it does in our churches at home.

My party and I went to see the famous mosque which has stood since the middle of the eleventh century over the scene of Jesus' anger with the traders. It is called El Aksa, or 'the most distant place', because it is believed that this is the farthest place from Mecca to which Allah brought Mohammed. He arrived here in twenty-four hours on his winged horse, El Burak, 'Lightning'. The fountain outside, with stone seats for the faithful to use while they wash their head and hands and feet before entering to pray (head, behind the ears; hands to the elbows; feet to the ankles;) probably connects with a conduit which goes back to Solomon's day.

We admired the series of arches before the entrance. We could see their similarity to the entry to the Holy Sepulchre church, the façade of which is of Crusader origin. This impressive building is a mixture of Crusader and Arab architecture. Apparently the Crusaders found a mosque there, with some tall arcades round its dome dating from the early ninth century, before it had been enlarged. They utilized the building as a kind of headquarters, and built various chapels along its east wall, most of which have now been destroyed, particularly in recent renovations. Only one piece of Crusader wall now remains, with a great rose window, badly smashed. The Moslems restored the place as a mosque when they drove out the Crusaders. Immense new marble pillars were put in the great basilica while we were in Jerusalem.

We donned overslippers again, and went in, past the new white columns on which Arabs were working, and walked up the long aisle to the southern end, facing Mecca, so nobly decorated with mosaic over walls and dome. The men with me were very interested in two pillars, quite close together, but worn away by generations of men who had squeezed between them. The theory is, I explained, that nobody can enter heaven who cannot pass between those

pillars. Moslems allow that a rich man can enter, provided
that he is not also a fat man. Because, however, in 1881 a stout
gentleman died between the pillars as he strove frantically to pass
between them, a bar was placed there to prevent further tragedies.
That has now been removed, and visitors can once more try the
'columns of ordeal'. One of the men insisted upon stepping through,
which he did easily, only to find the imam standing at the other side
smilingly holding out his hand for *baksheesh*.

We looked at the amazing pulpit of cedar wood inlaid with
mother-of-pearl which Saladin brought from Ascalon and placed
here in 1187. An inscription on it says that it was made in Aleppo,
to the north of Syria, in 1168. We could see the piece of wood
chipped away some years ago by an Army officer, which caused the
mosque to be closed to visitors for some months, and nearly resulted
in the culprit being cashiered from the Army. The imam pointed
out the twin *mihrabs*, or prayer-niches, of Jesus and Mohammed, and
some weird formations in the grain of the wall-marble; and then he
opened a long window to enable us to see the southern view. We
all crowded round and I pointed out the trees round the Pool of
Siloam; the village of Silwan across the Kedron Valley; and above
it the Benedictine Convent for Syrian Catholics on the Mount of
Offence, where Solomon is said to have made pagan sacrifices to
please his foreign wives. The southern hill of Jerusalem, stretching
away from the wall below us, and now dotted with dirty hovels
amid fields of rubble or occasional crops, was once enclosed within
the city walls, and was a part of the city familiar to Jesus. Here it
was that the Jebusites held their stronghold of Ophel which David
captured, and the modern theory is that his Zion was in this south-
east corner, and not farther west, as was formerly believed. Far
below us, in the hillside, was where Hezekiah made his famous
tunnel, and I promised to take my party there on another day.

We shed our slippers again outside and walked through piles of
builders' rubbish towards the so-called Solomon's Stables, in the
far corner of the Area. Some steps led down under the mosque, but
repairs prevented us from descending. It is where the great Double
Entrance led up into the Temple. There is a tale told, probably
legendary, that the graves of two of the murderers of Thomas à
Becket, sent to the Holy Land to do penance, lie there. There are
certainly some immense pillars of early cloisters, exactly as Josephus
describes them, as wide in circumference as three men with out-
stretched arms. The half-quarried column lying in the courtyard
before the Russian Cathedral, to the north-west of the Old City, is
reminiscent of them.

Across in the south-eastern corner we found a little doorway guarded by a large-moustached custodian who saluted me and gave us a broad smile. He also knew that I never took a party down those steps without handing him a 50-mil piece, lest the door be locked and he mysteriously absent when next I came. The narrow stairs down greeted us with a musty smell, and the odour was no fresher in the dingy space with discoloured walls which is the reputed house of Simeon, whither the Infant Jesus was brought. It was the crypt of an early church, which contained a wooden cradle in 1165. On the ground, under a hideous and rotting wooden four-posted canopy, lay the alleged 'Cradle of Christ'. It is obviously a Moslem prayer-niche lying on its back.

We did not waste much time over that, but descended some broader steps into the high, cavernous arches known as 'Solomon's Stables'. It is not possible to say what was there in Solomon's time, but certainly Herodian stone has been used for the giant bases of the curving arches. We could distinguish their characteristic margined shape by the dim light that entered through the high southern windows. The latest theory is that these underground supports were constructed when the first mosque, in pre-Crusader times, was built along the southern wall of the area. The Crusaders probably used the spaces for stables, for the holes for tethering their beasts could still be seen through the corners of the stones. No doubt great ramps ran down from openings in the wall, which have now been bricked up. We wandered through them for a while, and noticed how accumulated debris of centuries had raised the level of the ground. It was chilly and damp in there, and we were glad to mount the steps into the sunshine.

That corner with its underground chamber leading to the stables is interesting, however, inasmuch as the outer Herodian stonework suggests that there was a specially strong foundation here for a tower that raised its head 170 feet above the surrounding colonnades and Temple Area. We had only to mount the wall, which we did at that point, to realize that the Kedron Valley lay sheer below us there, which from the top of the tower would appear to be of great and precipitous depth. Was this the Temple 'wing', as the R.V. margin renders 'pinnacle' in Matthew iv, from which Jesus was tempted to cast Himself down? Undoubtedly, here was the Byzantine Church of the Pinnacle, to be seen on the Madeba map. One could imagine the young working-man leaning on its balustrade at the top of the tower and staring at the throng of priests and people gathered below on a feast day. What an unutterable temptation it must have been to Him, knowing all that He did of

Himself and His Father, to display to the callous gaze of the crowd the power that was at His command, proving that He was more than a carpenter-preacher! He could demonstrate the Psalmist's promise of protection for the Messiah, and rally them to Him by jumping down unharmed. We shall never understand the agony of mind and heart that Jesus endured on that tower, and then came down to go the way of His Father, leading men into the Kingdom one by one in sacrificial fellowship. We do not understand the power of God sufficiently, as Jesus did, to be tempted to put Him to the test like that. Only One who could turn stones into bread would be tempted to do so. His were the sort of temptations we should have had if we had been in His place. How human was that desire to cast Himself down. He was tempted in all points as we are, yet without sin.

We followed the precarious path long the battlements until we could all get a good view of the Kedron Valley, directly below the eastern original wall of the Temple Area. I pointed out the now concrete-lined watercourse of the Kedron, and the three landmarks on its opposite bank which must have been familiar to Jesus, not only when he looked down from that tower, but when He crossed the Brook Kedron to Gethsemane. The road to Bethany traversed the Mount of Olives rising before us, its slopes covered with tombstones.

One of these landmarks, the one shaped like an inverted trumpet to our left, is known as Absalom's Pillar, although it cannot possibly be the one which that rebellious son put up, for it is, like the other two, of Greco-Roman style and dates from about 100 years before Jesus saw it. It contains several tombs and is probably the mausoleum of a Maccabean ruler of the city, possibly Alexander Jannaeus, who died in 78 B.C. It stands approximately where David fled over the Mount of Olives, weeping with indecision. The Jews are said to throw stones into its opening whenever they pass it. A little way to the right we could see some columns at the entrance to a rock-hewn tomb. Some epitaph inscriptions in Hebrew dating from about 10 B.C., have been found within it, though it is now known as the Grotto of St. James. It is believed that the Lord's brother hid there when Jesus was arrested. That is possible, of course, as the cave was there when Jesus was taken past it to the house of the High Priest on Mount Zion in the south part of the old city. The other tomb, cut from the solid rock in pyramid style, and commonly thought to be the tomb of the prophet Zechariah, is of similar origin.

Both Moslems and Jews believe that this Valley of Jehoshaphat between the Temple and the Mount of Olives, will be the scene of the dramatic events of the Last Day. The slope of Olivet is a desirable place for a Jew to be buried, therefore; while Moslem graves cover the steep slope immediately below us, and olive groves fill the fertile bottom of the valley. The Moslems say that when the Last Judgement takes place Mohammed will sit on a protruding column in the wall of the Temple Area, while Jesus will be on the top of the Mount of Olives. A hair-fine bridge will join them, over which every one will pass. The good ones will be upheld by angels, but the evil ones will be left to topple into perdition. The Prophet will assist the 'weaker brethren' to cross, however. He will turn them into fleas and himself into a sheep, and carry them across clinging to his fleece!

As we looked at the sea of white, flat stones marking ancient Jewish graves, we thought of what Jesus had to say about whited sepulchres. We made out the age-old olive trees in the Latin Garden of Gethsemane beside the new Church of All Nations, its mosaic shining in a huge triangle of gold. Farther up the hillside are the onion-shaped domes of St. Mary Magdalene, the Russian church, rising out of a green cloud of firs and cypresses, and on the summit of Olivet the tapering point of the tall Russian tower and the minaret in the foreground which stands where the ancients located the Ascension. The view was superb.

Before we left we went along the eastern wall to look at the Golden Gate, the old stone structure that stands near the site of the Gate Beautiful. It is possible that Jesus used this entrance to the Temple when He entered it on the first Palm Sunday. Peter and John entered by it when the crippled beggar was healed. The Turks blocked up this entrance to prevent Jesus from entering it in triumph at His second coming, as it was thought from Ezekiel's prophecy that the Messiah will use this gate. One writer suggests that General Allenby should have been advised to enter by this gate as a symbol of divine mission, especially since his name could be transliterated into 'Allah en Nebi': the prophet of God. But even if Allenby had thought of it, it was not a gesture of which that good man would have been capable. Now it is a dusty and forlorn relic of a glory that is past and theories that are obsolete. There is a fine hall of Byzantine columns between the great doors, but admission was barred to us at that time.

Not far from it is a double-domed little building by the wall called the Throne of Solomon. It is said that the king was found dead there, but his body remained supported by his staff for forty years, until the stick rotted away and he fell forward. Only then did the devils know that they were freed from the power of his wisdom. Probably here was the northern limit of Herod's Temple.

We walked back across the Temple Area. We were not allowed
to remain there after half-past eleven, and it was nearly time to go.
We paused, however, to mark the spot where long ago a vaulted
gallery with a double row of columns ran along the eastern wall.
In the days of Jesus it bore an inscription, 'The Hall of Solomon',
and it was then possibly thought to date from the original building
of the Temple. It can at the earliest have been but a remnant of
Zerubbabel's Temple. Here it probably was, with the unsheltered
side facing the Inner Temple, that Jesus sat to teach, and where no
doubt He had stood to hear the teachers when He was twelve years
old. Later, that colonnade would be where the Apostles also taught.
It would have been a good place, in full view of the altar past the
Court of the Women, for those to gather who wished to hear the
daily prayers in the Sanctuary, but whose lack of ceremonial purity
forbade them to enter the Inner Temple.

Here, where only broken pieces of stone lie about, and where an
occasional party of sightseers like ourselves might pass, were
uttered some of the greatest truths that ever came from the lips of
man. And from this prominent platform of the Temple we could
see to the west the dark semicircle over the Holy Sepulchre and the
smaller dome covering Calvary. How simple it was for the priests
in the sanctuary to stand and watch the Cross raised up on that little
mound, and to give the gibe which was also a testimony: 'He saved
others; Himself He cannot save.'

They were answered by an earthquake. It rent the great curtain
of fine linen, blue and scarlet and purple, which veiled the Holy
Place. What awesome symbolism was this? The everlasting doors
were lifted up, and the King of Glory entered in.

CHAPTER VI

ROUND ABOUT JERUSALEM

Walk about Zion, and go round about her: tell the towers thereof.
Mark ye well her bulwarks, consider her palaces; that ye may tell it
to the generation following.

PSALM xlviii. 12–13.

JERUSALEM has shifted slightly northwards in the course of the
centuries, and where the City of David once stood is now a wide
plateau south of the present city wall, for the most part uninhabited
and covered with heaps of rubble and miserable Arab shacks amid
a few cultivated fields. Dust and stones have been allowed to
accumulate to a height of over 30 feet in places—even 60 feet in the
valley—and unless he wishes to explore that ancient site and get
himself covered with white dust, a visitor avoids the area beyond the
south wall. Occasionally a group of Arabs trudge along the path,
usually with a few well-laden donkeys, but for the most part the
place is desolate. It is an undulating stretch of ground, sloping down
towards the Pool of Siloam among some trees in its south-east
corner, and is roughly in the form of a crescent with a vague sort of
valley dividing an eastern ridge from one to the west. All the way
round this wide piece of land, almost as large as the present city,
are precipitous slopes down to the valleys surrounding it, and one
can understand why the ancient city had the reputation for being
impregnable, especially when one visualizes the wall that towered
above the chasms on every side. It was not until nearly 1,000 years
after Christ that the southern boundary of Jerusalem was finally
formed in its present line, leaving Zion and Ophel, as these two hills
were called, outside the city wall.

The only exception to this desolation is the high western ridge,
which is covered with a number of buildings, churches for the most
part, which commemorate historic sites on what was believed as
early as the Byzantine period to be Mount Zion. It is still called by
that name locally and most professional guides inform pilgrims that
it is the location of the City of David. But in recent years archaeologists have explored the whole area, tracing the course of the
original wall and finding in particular a piece of what might be the
wall from which the Jebusites taunted David as his army approached
it, and the tower built in its breach after the conquest. It is now
generally accepted that Zion was the name of the hill commonly

called Ophel, to the direct south of the Temple Area, the lesser eastern ridge of this desolate plateau. Here it was, where straggling crops grow and cactus hedges line dusty paths, that David built his city on the precipice above the Kedron and which up till New Testament days was the heart of the Holy City, spread by that time over surrounding hills. So the neighbouring hill where the churches stand to-day is not, strictly speaking, Mount Zion, but without doubt it was covered by a residential district in the days of Jesus.

On that hill the early Christians located the house of the Last Supper, the house of John Mark, the house of the High Priest to which Jesus was taken immediately after his arrest, and the house in which His mother died. From the fourth century onwards the meeting place of the disciples after the Resurrection and at the time of Pentecost was believed to be on this high ground, and there is little doubt that it was somewhere near there. Later, in the sixth century, a church was built over the place where the Last Supper was believed to have been held, and Justinian's great basilica of St. Mary covered the whole area, including within it the place of the institution of the Lord's Supper, the Pentecost room, the deathplace of the Virgin Mary, and the Column of Flagellation, whilst the site of Caiaphas' house became the first Christian hospice for pilgrims in Jerusalem.

In those days the city wall enclosed that area, but about 100 years before the Crusades we find that pilgrims began to describe the Church of St. Mary of Zion as being outside the wall, and that fits in with some evidence discovered while we were in Jerusalem, as I shall tell later in this chapter. The magnificent buildings on 'Zion' suffered the vicissitudes of holy places in Palestine, and although the Franciscans built a monastery there in 1342 the Moslems took possession of what remained of it in the sixteenth century, and they still hold it. The Franciscans, under the protection of the Venetian Republic, used this monastery as the headquarters for their duties as 'Custodians of the Holy Land'. The site of Caiaphas' house is now in Armenian hands and the Latins possess the reputed place where the Virgin 'fell asleep'. Their Church of the Dormition, or the 'Falling Asleep', as they call it, built during the last thirty years, has an immense cone and a tower which vies with the Y.M.C.A. building as the most distinctive feature of the Jerusalem skyline. There are, besides these churches and surrounding dwellings, the famous Bishop Gobat's School on the western edge of the hill, and several walled cemeteries: Armenian, Orthodox, and Latin; and the British cemetery with its fir trees and cypresses is on the lower slopes.

Needless to say, the members of the Wednesday Fellowship often wandered about the old sites in this part of Jerusalem, and I organized several Sunday afternoon visits to it. One Sunday a party of us were the guests of the Headmaster of Bishop Gobat's School, which provides such fine opportunities for education for Arab boys—and some Jewish lads also—and which was the fruit of the labours of perhaps the best-known of all the Anglican bishops in Jerusalem. It is a rambling old building built on to the original escarpment of the Old Testament wall and, as necessity demanded, rooms have been added in the course of years and very recently a new annex for classrooms. We wandered along its old passages and labyrinthine stairways and saw that the side of one narrow corridor was the rough face of the rock itself, the foundation cut by Nehemiah's masons when they were rebuilding the walls of the city. And down by the British cemetery we found ancient cisterns in the rock and pieces of the ancient wall itself. When Sir Flinders Petrie was laid to rest in that cemetery in July, 1942, an acquaintance of mine picked up two pieces of Roman mosaic from the graveside and showed them to me afterwards. The ground there is full of the remains of antiquity. How fitting it is that the greatest archaeologist of all time should lie amongst the relics of the past.

I had given an address to the schoolboys, many of them Moslems, one Sunday evening in their chapel, and made the acquaintance of a few of them. One boy, a lad of about eighteen, was the son of the sheikh in charge of the Coenaculum—the Last Supper Room—and the Headmaster arranged with him to secure admittance for us on several occasions. The Moslems normally make a charge to admit people into their building, but this was waived in our favour, and the lad acted as our guide. At the time of which I am thinking there was a crowd of about twenty of us who met my Arab friend at the top of the rise leading up outside the city from the Jaffa Gate towards the Zion Gate in the south wall, and he conducted us along a cobbled street to the Coenaculum. A notice board announced that here was the Room of the Last Supper.

We mounted steep stone steps and passed through an anteroom into what was obviously part of a medieval monastery, with gothic arches and heavy columns, the curving roof covering an area not very much bigger than a very large room. Two principal columns stood in the centre. Rugs covering the floor were the only ornamentation in the place, except for fourteenth-century carving in the heads of the columns and a grille protecting most of the space. This might have been the refectory of the Franciscan monastery which stood here centuries ago. It certainly was not the 'upper room' we read of in the Gospels, although the space between the two central pillars is pointed to as the very situation of the Table of the Last Supper. We had not expected to see the original room, of course, for we all knew very well that all Jerusalem had been laid waste by Titus in A.D. 70, but it was a matter of interest to us to see the present place of pilgrimage. A dais at one side is said to be where the Feet-washing took place.

Although crowds of Christians visit the Coenaculum at Easter, especially on Maundy Thursday, it is on the Feast of Pentecost that the place is officially opened by the Moslem keepers, by special and long-standing agreement, for the Christians to enter in solemn procession. It is an ancient tradition that the scene of the Last Supper was at the place where later the Pentecostal fire fell upon the Apostles, although there is no evidence for that in the New Testament. I have described in an earlier chapter the theory that the house of John Mark, where we know the disciples met together and where they might have been given the Pentecostal experience, was where the Syrian Church of St. Mark stands in the Old City.

It is most likely that because of the traitor amongst the Twelve and the danger that threatened Him on that last night, Jesus would find a place for the Passover meal that was remote from His friends' house, so that they should not be embarrassed by impending events. The Gospel record implies in Matthew xxvi. 18 that Jesus had arranged for the use of a special room to which He sent disciples to prepare this meal. Such a procedure was not at all an uncommon one, with the city crowded with visitors needing Passover accommodation. Nobody can be sure where it was. It was probably somewhere on this high residential district of Jerusalem, and not far away was the house of John Mark, just over the present city wall maybe, where the Syrian church is, or nearer to this traditional site; and if not in that house at any rate in one near it took place the Resurrection appearances of Jesus and the dramatic events of that Pentecost.

It is interesting to realize that the archaeologist Weill discovered in 1914 not far away from this site some cisterns and steps with an inscription in Greek describing a synagogue there built by one Theodotos, which is a Greek name. So before A.D. 70 Greek-speaking Jewry had a synagogue in Jerusalem near this very place. Was it that of the 'Libertines' mentioned in Acts vi. 9, members of which opposed Stephen and caused his arrest and death?

It was not really likely that the very place at which we were looking was the exact location of the last meal that Jesus had with His friends, but it is where for centuries Christians have commemorated it, and we set our thoughts upon that scene in the Upper Room and tried to understand something of the mystery of the sacrament we had inherited.

They reclined round the table, probably a low circular one with cushions beside it on the floor, for the rule was that even the poorest at that supper must take his ease. The bread that was broken and eaten with special solemnity was the unleavened 'bread of affliction', and the 'cup of blessing' was the third cup, commonly associated with the saving power of the blood of the passover lamb. Jesus' reference to the new covenant of Jeremiah xxxi was a significant addition to its symbolism. The hymn they sung would be the Hallel psalm. There used to be an Aramaic proverb: 'Even if the Passover is only as big as an olive, the Hallel cracks the roof.' The Hallel is Psalms cxv-cxviii.

The cup that was used at that Last Supper has been the object of quest and poesy through the ages. The Holy Grail, derived from *sang real*, 'holy blood', became an emblem in ancient chivalry of the attainment of the noblest and the best. S. L. Caiger, in *Archaeology and the New Testament*, tells us that there exist to-day about half a dozen glass bowls that were common then and might have been used at a Passover. The Weigand Cups, as they are called, all have a Greek inscription round their rims:

EPH'O PAREI; EUPHRAINOU.

That is the best way I can write it without using Greek letters. It means: 'What are you here for? Cheer up!'

Dr. Deissmann, who after the 1914–18 War sent his Weigand Cup to Dr. Rendel Harris (only, incidentally, to get it smashed in the post, although a course of 'invisible mending' repaired it perfectly), suggested that the words of Jesus in Matthew xxvi. 50 are from this inscription. They are *'Hetaire, eph'o parei'*: literally, 'Comrade, what are you here for?' It is possible that Jesus was reminding Judas of the 'cup of kindness' they had shared only that evening. The cups are wide beakers without handles or stem, and quite different from the conventional Communion cup. Deissmann's suggestion is a far-fetched one, but not altogether impossible. Such a glass cup, though without an inscription, has been found in Jerusalem, and is now in the Rockefeller Museum.

The lad who conducted us into the Coenaculum permitted us to pass round the edge of the carpet floor into the Moslem shrine and beyond. He will be sheikh one day, for the post of head of a Moslem holy place is an hereditary one. This place is sacred to the Moslems, not because Jesus is believed to have eaten here with His disciples, but because they believe that David was buried here! In the room beyond the Last Supper Room we saw the green-draped cenotaph which marks King David's Tomb far below.

It is known that David was buried in the 'City of David', which was formerly thought to be here, but is now known to have been on the opposite hill of Ophel; and the tomb was to be seen when Peter harangued the people at Pentecost, for he referred to it as being 'with us to this day'. Perhaps the mention of this site in connection with Pentecost caused confusion in official Arab minds. It is extremely unlikely that a dwelling-house would be where David's Tomb was situated. A Jew named Benjamin of Tudela, who saw Jerusalem in A.D. 1163, described how a few years earlier workmen repairing a church wall broke into a cave. It was a large hall, they reported, with marble pillars encrusted with gold and silver, a table with a great crown and sceptre on it, and large chests all round. A blast of wind drove them out, they said, and they were full of fear. The local patriarch consulted with the Rabbi Abraham, and they decided it was the sepulchre of David and Solomon, so it was duly walled up. That legend is why the Moslems later appropriated the place, for David is a great prophet in Islam. It would be interesting to dig hereabouts to find what basis of fact lies in that old story from the Middle Ages, but excavations are not permitted near Moslem shrines.

We peeped into a beautiful little chapel adjacent to the Coenaculum. In their desire to obtain a place as near as possible to the Last Supper Room, the Franciscans negotiated, through a third party, for the possession of an old Arab house next to it. It was thirty years before it came into their hands, and the chapel, up a flight of stone steps, was consecrated in 1936. The long, low room, ceiled with smooth arches, would make a lovely college chapel.

Whilst we were upon 'Mount Zion' we visited the House of Caiaphas and the Dormition Church. These two, with the Coenaculum, must lie in the whole area covered by the early pilgrims' hospice and the Byzantine Church of St. Mary, but high walls now separate them and they appear to have nothing in common. Why the early Christians should have imagined that the High Priest dwelt so near to the disciples I cannot imagine. Perhaps it was because that apparently unlikely thing was the actual fact, which is not impossible. Epiphanius Hagiopolita, in his *Life of the Blessed Virgin*, says that James and John sold the property of their old father, Zebedee, and bought this land on Zion; and that is why John was known at the High Priest's house: because he lived next door, so to speak. That is a more likely explanation than another I have heard:

that John was known at Caiaphas' house because he delivered Galilean fish there! Epiphanius goes on to say that John took the Virgin into his house on Zion, where she died, being buried at Gethsemane.

Another theory points out that there might have arisen a confusion of identity in early times between Mary the mother of Jesus, who dwelt with John, and Mary the mother of John Mark (Acts xii. 12), who, it is said, lived in a house here which was the meeting-place of the Apostles. Mark's mother was the Mary who died on Zion and was buried in Gethsemane close to the Grotto of the Passion, this theory suggests, because the family owned the cave with the oil-press which Jesus used as a retreat for prayer, because it belonged to His friends.

'The House of Caiaphas' is an ornate little Armenian chapel within a quaint arched courtyard hanging with vines like a corner of old Italy, with a plenitude of patriarchs' tombstones for pavings. We pushed our way into the confined space within its doors and found very little of interest. The apse contained an altar covered with blue tiles, under which, a bearded deacon told us, was the rolling-stone which had sealed the Tomb of Christ. In a tiny cupboard to the right of the altar lined with similar blue tiles and with room only for one man to stand upright, was the site of what is called the Prison of Christ, where they believe that Jesus was confined immediately after His arrest. On the wall of the church were some crude paintings, and one of them, arranged like a child's puzzle to show three different pictures according to the angle of vision, was pointed to by the custodian of the church as the most interesting object of all.

We were glad to get out into the fresh air, and we inspected the mosaics which have lately been revealed in the surrounding grounds. They possess the characteristic twisted border design of Byzantine work, and undoubtedly an early church stood on this site, probably that of St. Peter, of which there are records, built as a memorial of his denial of Jesus in the house of the High Priest. Again, an ornate tomb of some Armenian nobleman of last century was the principal object to which the venerable brother sought our attention, wondering, I imagine, what interest we found in broken sections of old pavement when that beautiful piece of sculpture was there for us to see!

The Church of the Dormition which we visited before we finished that day's excursion is a Benedictine establishment and of considerable proportions. The Kaiser bought the land in 1898 and presented it to German members of the Benedictine Order for a church which, with its separate tower, has stood, white and immense, for thirty years now. A diminutive German brother in a black habit opened the door to our knock and invited us to enter. He was a pleasant little man, full of smiles all the time he was with us, a worthy representative of an ancient Order noted for its hospitality. The dome, like a flattened cone, covered a circular church with intricate designs of the Zodiac and other mystic symbols in its marble floor and elaborate mosaics in the apse, with the beginning of the Magnificat in Latin around the rim of the dome. On the altar was a shrine containing some relics of St. Martin, the soldier-saint who is the patron of the Benedictines, and altars to various saints stood around the walls, each an object of interest because of its decoration. The whole effect was reminiscent somehow of the ornate character of Westminster Cathedral. The little brother was more kindly than scholarly. When I saw the design of a labarum under my feet, the ☧ which is the first two letters of the Greek word *Christos*, an early Christian sign, I began to explain its origin and meaning to the men who gathered round me. He listened for a while and then gently rebuked me.

'You are mistaken,' he said. 'That is a P and an X, standing for the Latin word Pax, the motto of the Benedictines.'

I thanked him for this new version of an old symbol and remarked that here was an interesting example of Greek letters gathering quite a different Latin significance. Another illustration of the same thing, of course, is in the I.H.S. which often decorates the front of an English pulpit. Originally these were the first three letters of the Greek word for Jesus, but later were made to stand for the Latin, *Jesus Hominum Salvator*: 'Jesus the Saviour of men'. Even the word 'Bible', as a matter of fact, suffered in a similar way, for we do not use it in the plural, whereas the Greek word *biblia* means 'books'. In the Latin form, however, it is in the singular, and so we have come to refer to our library of sacred books as though it was one book.

Down a spiralling stairway to the crypt, we went to see the place of the 'Falling Asleep' of the Virgin Mary. It was a most impressive shrine in the form of a lifesize, recumbent figure of the Virgin cut in marble, with her hands pressed together in prayer. A balustrade with pillars encircled it, where a black-robed monk knelt in prayer, and the dim light from lamps gave it an air of solemnity and devotion. We tiptoed towards a chapel to the east of the crypt with an altar to the Holy Ghost that stood beneath a symbolic dove and descending beams of gold to denote the fire.

We did not leave the church without ascending to the gallery that runs round its mighty dome, giving us a glorious view of Jerusalem

THE JEBUSITE WALL ABOVE THE VIRGIN'S FOUNTAIN.

At the bottom left is Gihon, and high above it is Millo and the broken masonry of the wall where the Jebusites jeered at David. The watercourse up which Joab and the mighty men climbed is a vertical shaft within the cave, which is also at one end of Hezekiah's tunnel.

[See page 119

THE GARDEN TOMB.

The plant in the foreground blossoms so rarely that it is called the Century
Flower. For the Moslems it is a symbol of resurrection.

[See page 159.

and the Mount of Olives. We could see the white Government House amid its green trees on a hill to the south, and even glimpse some blue of the Dead Sea beyond the yellow hills eastwards under the Mountains of Moab. I stood on this vantage-point with the men some months later on Whit-Sunday afternoon when the devout of Jerusalem gathered on Mount Zion, and we watched crowds of people assembling in the Orthodox and Armenian cemeteries immediately below us. The Eastern Churches have some Whitsun ceremonies in their graveyards, but we were, unhappily, unable to remain to watch them. We did see, however, the Rite of Benediction in the Dormition Church that afternoon, when the high altar was covered with fiery red and the priests and choirboys were in robes of red, and their antiphonal chanting raised praises for the gift of Pentecostal fire at the place where it fell from heaven.

Catholics do not believe that the Virgin Mary died, but that she fell asleep and her body was placed in the tomb which is marked in the Valley of Gethsemane. Some days afterwards disciples entered her tomb and found only a sweet savour and her body gone, taken into heaven. The Assumption of the Blessed Virgin, as this is called, is not commemorated by the Latins at the tomb of the Virgin, however, for that is in the hands of the Orthodox Church. The Latins possess the reputed birthplace of Mary, at the Pool of Bethesda, and this Church of the Dormition, where she fell asleep.

I took a party of troops one afternoon to see some archaeological excavations on Mount Ophel, and on our way round the southern wall of the city over Mount Zion, we turned aside to see the Church of St. Pierre in Gallicante, which, like the Dormition, is a modern one; but it has some interesting remains beneath it. We turned down a drive that led through very extensive grounds to a monastery that resembled the worse type of Army barracks, tall like a riverside warehouse, but mercifully hidden from the view by a corner of the hill. Beside it, on the eastern slope of the traditional Mount Zion, stands a bright, garish church with a large dome surmounted by the figure of a cock. This place is in the care of Augustinian Fathers of the Assumption: French monks who wear black habits rather like the Benedictines; and they are very proud of their church and very sure of the historicity of its site. It is built, they say, on the location of the house of Caiaphas, and here it was that Peter denied his Lord. The Crusaders called a church on this site after St. Peter 'in Gallicantus', hence it is commonly known in Jerusalem as the Church of the Cock-crowing.

It is possible, however, that the Crusaders built it merely to

H

commemorate Peter's repentance, when he went out and wept bitterly after Jesus had turned and looked upon him. There can be little doubt that not only in the Byzantine era, but in the days of the Crusaders, the actual site of the High Priest's house, and of Peter's denial, was believed to lie where the Armenian 'Caiaphas' House' now stands. However, the Assumptionist Fathers have decided that the reports of the early pilgrims refer to their site and not the Armenian one, although I understand that other Roman Catholic orders—the learned Dominicans, for instance—do not agree with them. Be that as it may, the church was an interesting place to visit, and we explored it.

I have rarely seen so much mosaic concentrated in one place. There is far too much of it: pictures in primary colours and of elementary drawing all over the circular walls and looking down on us from the ceiling, and mosaic texts in French everywhere, written in large letters. The whole effect, to me at any rate, was gaudy and overwhelming. It is quite new—the church was consecrated in 1931—so one cannot hope that the brightness of its walls will yet become time-mellowed. How the Crusader builders would shudder if they could see this specimen of twentieth-century architecture!—as, of course, with all their cruel butchery, they would be aghast at our modern warfare.

The crypt of the church, however, is simpler and more pleasant, and we saw formations of rock that were supposed to mark the courtyard where Peter stood warming himself with the men about the brazier, and denied with curses his connection with Jesus. Peter not only denied his Lord; he denied himself. His declaration was that he was not a disciple of Jesus. I suggested to the men who were with me that we should try to visualize the scene. It probably did not actually happen here, but that mattered not. It was a place dedicated to the memory of that dark night—and a cold night too apparently, although I noted particularly at the season of the Passover the year I was in Jerusalem that it was quite warm even at night. But residents told me it was an exceptionally warm spring and often at Easter the nights are cold. Cocks crow at all hours of the night in Jerusalem, as I often found to my discomfort.

Poor Peter, his heart was cold and his spirit heavy, and all that a fire of charcoal could give him was sufficient courage to utter his denials. It is significant that at that very moment Annas was asking two questions of Jesus.

'The High Priest therefore asked Jesus of His disciples, and of His teaching.'

Jesus answered one of those questions readily enough: about His teaching. But He had nothing to say about His disciples. What could He say? Judas had betrayed Him; the others had forsaken Him and fled; Peter was at that moment in the courtyard declaring that he had never known Him. The weak place in the position of Jesus, which Annas was so skilfully probing, lay, as it always does lie, in His disciples. His teaching stands up to all criticism. His foes are, as ever, they of His own household.

Under the crypt were still deeper caverns excavated in 1889 from the hillside on which the church stands and upon which the Assumptionists base their principal claims. We descended a little catacomb of caves, one of them quite extensive with minor caverns all round it. This, one father had on a previous occasion informed me, was a prison in the palace of the High Priest. And he pointed to holes cut through corners of rock where he said captives had been shackled. One arch was without a supporting column, and he had told me that there, they believe, stood the column to which Jesus was tied when He was scourged, and part of which is now the Column of Flagellation in the Apparition Chapel of the Holy Sepulchre. Also it was probably the column known to have been exhibited in the Byzanitne Church of St. Peter. The fact is there is no record that Jesus was scourged anywhere but in Pilate's Judgement Hall. Luke xxii. 63 cannot mean a beating of this kind. The monk stood and showed me how the victim was tied and received thirteen strokes each on his chest, his left side and his right side—forty stripes save one. The holes in the wall, I may say, resembled very closely the horses' hitching places in Solomon's Stables, and when we saw, a little way beyond, a treading-place for a donkey and its stable, I was more than ever sure that these caves had housed animals, but probably not men since prehistoric troglodytes dwelt in them. It is not at all unlikely, I think, that cavemen lived here in the dim long ago.

Deeper yet into the depths of the earth we went, and found a pit which originally had only a circular opening in the top, about 2 feet across. In this cavern stands an altar with a quotation from the Psalms in Latin (Psalm lxxxviii. 6). It is believed that Jesus was lowered into this pit, the 'condemned cell', on the night of His arrest, in the same way as Jeremiah was let down with cords into a dungeon (Jeremiah xxxviii. 6). There is no evidence for this except the presence of a few Byzantine crosses painted on the rocky wall, which could mean that here was an early Christian burial-place. Nor could the palace of Caiaphas be regarded as the 'public ward' of Acts v. 18, so we cannot even say that the apostles were confined in these depths. In fact, the association of those events with this place was altogether conjectural, and due to some rather faulty reasoning. It was all very interesting, though, and we mounted the steps, turned out the electric light, and went outside to see the old stone steps the Fathers had unearthed.

These may be of Jewish date and were probably part of a steep road that led to the Upper City from the Kedron side of old Jerusalem. It is possible that Jesus trod them: wide slabs of stone set in the hillside, when houses and shops were on either side; and it is not impossible that He mounted them, as these monks say He did, after His arrest. Round this corner of the Temple, across the Kedron, would be the shortest way to the High Priest's house from Gethsemane, whether it lay on this site or higher up the hill. So this may be a Scala Sancta more authentic than the one ascended with so many prayers and kisses at St. John Lateran in Rome. We trod the old stones with reverence. It might have been the way the Master went.

The excavations to which we found our way from the Church of the Cock-crowing consisted of diggings to reveal a sewer in order to effect certain repairs to it. The drain running along the length of the Tyropean Valley which cuts the city in two is now far below ground level, and diggings to various sections of it had revealed the fact that it was a channel that ran down the centre of a Roman street. The main sewer of Jerusalem in this year of grace 1942 was a drain constructed by Roman workmen nearly 2,000 years earlier! The most interesting thing about it was the fact that the Roman pavement on either side of the drain, which was covered with flagstones, could be seen in an excellent state of preservation. Its length had been traced from the Damascus Gate in the north wall to the Pool of Siloam away to the south. It was 30 feet in width and ran along the valley under the Street of the Chain, which was then a viaduct across it. Almost certainly it is one of the main roads through Jerusalem, lined with columns, which is a distinctive feature of the sixth-century mosaic Madeba map of the Holy City. To-day it lies for most of its course under debris and accumulated earth, which has risen to a height of over 30 feet. But as the level of the city was gradually raised, connection was still maintained with the original sewer for drainage purposes.

We stood on the brink of a wide pit and could see clearly the Roman paving stones and the channel uncovered in its centre. The workmen were building a wide brick chimney up to the present ground level for ventilation. This particular digging was just outside the Dung Gate, and revealed for us some ancient wall foundations. Although Hadrian's city, Aelia Capitolina, was on much the same line as the present city, the later Byzantine Jerusalem extended much farther to the south, so this old road runs under the southern plateau I described at the beginning of this chapter. The Empress Eudoxia, the pious Byzantine queen, had the city wall extended to enclose Siloam to protect the church she had built there. The fact that the lowest courses of the present wall are of pre-Crusader Arab workmanship—we could see the characteristic stonework corresponding to a section of tenth-century Arab work in the wall above us—confirms exactly the testimony of pilgrims who, as I have said, described St. Mary of Zion as inside the city wall until the tenth century, after which they said it was outside the city. About that time, perhaps to concentrate the defences of Jerusalem, the Moslem rulers had shortened its boundary to its present size, which was found by the Crusaders who arrived about a century later.

We saw, rising quite 12 feet high, the foundations of a tower which protruded from the wall in those days. It was built right across the Roman pavement, which became a disused road outside the city and lay neglected under debris until its discovery while we happened to be there.

We had time to traverse a dusty footpath or two to the ten-year-old excavations of Professor Macalister above the brink of the slope of Ophel leading down to the Kedron Valley. Here are the remains of a Jebusite wall, without doubt where stood a wall that David assaulted and overcame. It is a pile of rounded stones set in the hillside with a section of newer stronger stonework at one side of it. This rough stone rampart has been identified by Professor R. A. S. Macalister with the tower Millo that Solomon built in David's breach of the wall, described in 1 Kings xi. 27. It was to us a most satisfactory archaeological find, for it consists not of vague foundation stones in the ground, but is a veritable wall facing the chasm of the Kedron as it might have done when David besieged it 3,000 years ago.

This must have been the very place where the Jebusites taunted David because they thought their city, Jebus, was so well fortified that it could be defended by cripples.

'And the inhabitants of the land . . . spake unto David, saying, Except thou take away the blind and the lame, thou shalt not come in hither.'

It looked impregnable to us, too, because the cliff dropped sheer away under the wall. But in 2 Samuel v. 8 there is a mysterious reference to a watercourse, up which David sent warriors; 1 Chronicles xi. 6 suggests that their leader was Joab. As one of the men remarked, they were like an early detachment of Commandos.

In recent years this watercourse has been located. It was a natural fissure of rock descending from just within this very place to the spring which is now known as the Virgin's Fountain, far below. Apparently buckets were lowered to what must have been the Jebusites' only water supply. They had in fact what Hezekiah centuries afterwards constructed: access to that same spring from within the city in case of siege. Another day we stood within it and looked up. It appears to be a perilous climb, and Joab was indeed a 'mighty man' to take the city from within in that way.

Across the valley are the flat-topped houses of the village of Silwan on the slopes of the Mount of Offence, crowned by the square white lines of the Benedictine convent. The holes of many rock-cut tombs in that hillside could be seen from where we were, acting now for cellars under the native dwellings. One rock-cut mausoleum is called 'the Tomb of Pharaoh's Daughter' because of its Egyptian design. But it is of much later date than Solomon's wife.

A broad stretch of flat rock immediately opposite us is called in Arabic Es Zehweleh, 'the Landslide', and this led Charles Clermont-Ganneau, a scholar who was attached to the French consulate in Jerusalem in 1870, to identify it with the rock Zoheleth of 1 Kings i. 9. Adonijah thought that he would be king after David, so while the king was on his deathbed he gave a feast by the stone of Zoheleth. Bathsheba, however, gained the promise of the crown for her son Solomon, and David ordered him to be crowned immediately at Gihon. The point about this story in connection with this rock is that Gihon is undoubtedly the Virgin's Fountain, which springs far below where we were standing, at the entrance to the tunnel which Hezekiah built from Gihon to Siloam. And if one reads carefully the first chapter of 1 Kings one realizes that it is impossible that Zoheleth could be so near to Gihon, for Adonijah knew nothing of Solomon's coronation until it was all over and there was loud rejoicing in the city. If he was on yonder ledge of rock he would have seen all that happened in the light of flares just below him. With Zoheleth located opposite this point, the spring En-Rogel, mentioned as near it, was thought to be the Virgin's Fountain. But that is impossible. We know that it is Gihon.

Zoheleth, 'the serpent's stone', was probably a sacred rock much farther down the valley by 'Job's Well', possibly 'Joab's Well', which would therefore be En-Rogel. Perhaps an earthquake has upset the watercourses, so that the latter is now no longer a spring. Old fullers' vats have been found there, and En-Rogel probably means 'the fuller's spring'. Nevertheless, guide-books blithely tell us that the rock at Silwan is Zoheleth, and at the same time say that the Virgin's Fountain is ancient Gihon, ignoring the incongruity of these two statements. Even the erudite Canon Hanauer falls into this error.

We had walked on holy ground and on historic ground that afternoon, and we were a trifle exhausted and ready for our tea. Our route to the canteen was through the Dung Gate and across the Old City along David Street to the Jaffa Gate.

Our next exploration to the south of the Old City was by moonlight, and we went on donkeys. We wanted to go through Hezekiah's Tunnel, and it was kinder as well as more romantic to go through by night rather than in the daytime, when our feet would stir up the mud in the water flowing out to the women washing clothes or collecting it in water pots and petrol tins at the Pool of Siloam. We decided to descend to Gehenna, the lonely valley skirting the extreme south of ancient Ophel, and make our way thence to Siloam to enter the tunnel from that end. Our donkey-boys would then await us at the Virgin's Fountain when we emerged from the hillside, to take us on round the city.

Accordingly, on Thursday night just after Whitsun, 1942, when the moon was full, we set off at about nine o'clock, clad in shorts that could be rolled higher up our legs, and armed with candles and torches. We sat our unaccustomed steeds with difficulty, but the donkeys went placidly forward with the Arab boys shouting and smacking them with sticks. We rounded the Birket es Sultan, the 'King's Pool', as the Moslems call it, which lies in the western valley outside Jerusalem and dates from the Middle Ages. It is a green and silent stretch of water, often with a pathetic group of black goats beside it, but in that glamorous light it was a silent mirror for the moon. There is a post-war scheme afoot to create a swimming-pool here, with gardens leading up the opposite slope to the windmill on St. Julian's Way. I doubt if it will shock the orthodox Jews to-day as did the Greek stadium in Jerusalem. This is not the 'King's Pool' of Nehemiah ii. 14. That was in the low-lying ground near Siloam, to the east.

We were thankful that we were riding and not walking on that stony dusty path that took us along the bottom of Gehenna. It is desolate now except for sparse olive-trees, but in the days of Jesus it was the refuse-tip of the city, where carcases rotted and rubbish was always being burned—'where the worm dieth not and the fire is not quenched'—used for such a purpose because of the abominations it had known in the days of the Moloch-worship of Solomon. A lad in the detention barracks once opened his Testament at the passage I have just quoted and asked me what it meant. I led him to the window and pointed down this valley and told him of Jesus' teaching that to become useless is to be in hell, and it is better to make sacrifices and find true life than to end up on a rubbish-heap, no good.

At the end of the Valley of Gehenna we could make out the outline of the Orthodox monastery that stands on Akeldama, the field of blood. We had, of course, been there previously on a Sunday afternoon and examined the grisly collection of skulls and other human bones in the old Crusader charnel-house. Apparently in the Middle Ages the tradition was followed of burying strangers at Akeldama, as it says in Matthew xxvii. 7, and here was the burial place for patients who died in the medieval Hospital of St. John, in the Holy City. As early as the fourth century it was used for the same purpose, the bodies being cast down holes from above. There was an idea current that the soil there had the property of preserving corpses. But, earlier than that, Papias said that the smell of decay there was so great that nobody could pass it without holding his nose!

When we explored it we found many rock-hewn tombs around it—indeed, all along the hillside—and vines growing over the Crusader chambers full of bones. A Greek church incorporates a cavern where a hermit is thought to have dwelt, and a wall-picture of him is exhibited, clad only in a long beard. He is St. Onuphrius, a hermit who actually never visited Palestine! Inscriptions suggest that this was the tomb of Annas, the High Priest who was the principal opponent of Jesus. It is mentioned by Josephus.

There is a pathetic convent of Greeks in this desolate spot, and the 'Field of Blood' is located beside it, and even the tree from which Judas hanged himself. According to Matthew xxvii. 5, though, the hanging took place before the field was bought; and in Acts i. 18 it was Judas who obtained the field, and he fell headlong, as though he cast himself from the precipice there.

The Fountain Gate which Nehemiah found when he circled the walls of Jerusalem was discovered some years ago. It is at this extremity of the valley. He, like us, had made the journey 'on a beast', by night. Rounding the jutting hillside, we presently came to the Pool of Siloam, looking eerie and darkly shadowed in contrast with the white moonlight all around us. We were certainly 'by cool Siloam's shady rill', although in the light of day it is far from pleasant and its effluvia is remote from the sweetness of the lily. It is an astonishing fact that many of the troops who came to

Jerusalem seemed to regard hymns familiar to them as having an authority equal to that of the Bible, and I have heard some assert that their religious faith was shaken by the sight of Siloam as it is, because they had been told that it was a shady rill with sweet lilies growing beside it. And the credence placed by some of them on the authenticity of 'There is a green hill far away' was pathetic. All the evidence of history and archaeology could scarcely persuade them that the Holy Sepulchre was right and Mrs. Alexander was wrong. She had probably come under the nineteenth-century influence of Gordon's incredible notions.

Stone steps lead down to a rectangular pit about 30 feet by 12 feet which contains all that is left of the ancient Pool of Siloam. A few broken columns show that a Byzantine church stood here, and the shallow stream emerges from the dark crevice and drains away to the south. The Moslems put up a minaret close by the pool when the remains of a church were discovered, in order to mark it as their holy place and prevent the Christians from building a new church. Somewhere near here stood the Tower of Siloam, the fall of which was described by Jesus. It could not have been on the site of the present Silwan across the valley, which was a cemetery in New Testament days.

We flashed our torches on its ghostly depths, and assembled on the stone bank of the pool to remove our shoes and stockings. The donkey-boys thought us crazy to enter a dark tunnel full of rats and bats and—who knows?—djinns. We banished the lads, however, and prepared to enter the hillside. How different was the scene here which the blind man beheld, when at the word of Jesus he tapped his way down to the pool and wiped off the clay covering his eyes. Then he had seen a wide, busy pool within the city, not a gloomy pit like this with the ground-level far overhead.

One of the members of my party, a burly corporal in the Ordnance Corps, told me that he had read about Hezekiah's Tunnel.

'It was discovered,' he said, 'some years ago by two schoolboys who were playing in the valley and managed to crawl through it.'

'You've learned your lesson well, corporal,' I said, 'but unfortunately you have been misinformed. I suspect that you have been reading a certain popular book on Palestine which was written by a well-known journalist. This tunnel has been known for centuries —I have seen a reference to it by an eighteenth-century traveller— and it was surveyed by Sir Charles Warren in 1867. It was cleared just before the 1914-18 War. But the story about the two boys is that about fifty years ago two lads from Bishop Gobat's School were exploring it and one of them slipped when he was a little way inside it from this end. His hand encountered a carved inscription in the rock wall, and we shall see the place where it used to be. An unscrupulous Greek tried to remove the tablet, but he was apprehended. The inscription is now in Istanbul, and it is, except for the Moabite Stone, the earliest specimen of Hebrew writing we possess, unless we count the proto-Hebraic script of the Sinai inscriptions found by Sir Flinders Petrie in 1904. And a lot of early pen writing in Hebrew has been found at Lachish.'

Later, I showed the men a copy of the inscription. Professor A. H. Sayce has translated it. It reads:

'Behold, this is the history of the excavation. While the excavators were still lifting up the pick, each towards his neighbour, and while there were yet three cubits to excavate, there was heard the voice of one man calling to his neighbour; for there was an excess of rock to the right hand. And when on the day of excavation the excavators had struck pick against pick, one against the other, the waters flowed from the spring to the pool, a distance of 1,200 cubits.'

We were shortly to see the overlap of the tunnel described on this tablet, when workmen from this end heard the voices of the men who dug from the Gihon spring, and who were three cubits to their right. A cubit is about 20 inches, or the distance between a man's elbow and fingertip, and the overlap actually is about a couple of yards, as the inscription describes. There is no mystery about the winding character of the tunnel. Obviously it followed a fissure in the rock which probably already gave a trickle of water, and was widened where necessary. That would account for the great height of the tunnel in places, for it is low only where it has been hewn out, and for the fact that voices were heard, as they would not be through solid rock.

This is the conduit which Hezekiah made in the seventh century B.C. so that the beseiged city should be fed with water when the Assyrian invaders arrived, who, on the other hand, would be robbed of a water-supply. The Bible account of it is to be found in 2 Kings xx. 20 and 2 Chronicles xxxii. 2–4. As it happened, the invaders were conquered by disease, but this remarkable piece of engineering remains as evidence of the historicity of the Bible narrative. Did the disease spread because they were short of water?

With our footwear in haversacks over our shoulders and legs bared as high as possible, we slowly waded through the water that rose to just above our knees. I led the way with a candle held aloft in a tobacco-tin. The stones were sharp, but some of us wore canvas shoes and soon we were treading on a thin film of yielding mud on the bed of the scarcely moving stream. The width of the tunnel was nowhere wider than 1 cubit, and often we brushed the rocky wall, wet in places as we passed. We saw the cavity from which the inscription had been removed, and as the roof got lower we could see the rough pick-marks of Hezekiah's labourers as they hacked hastily away into the cliff to finish their task before the Assyrians arrived. I held my candle high and scared away any number of bats which hung upside down from the roof. They appeared to screw up their wizened little faces and blink their eyes for a moment before deciding to fly away from its brightness.

The journey seemed a long one—it was rather more than a quarter of a mile—and it was uneventful. The men behind me started to sing 'Onward! Christian soldiers' and some of Charles Wesley's hymns. I am sure that was the first time those weird rock-hewn walls had echoed to the tune 'Rimington'!

Rounding the overlap referred to in the inscription and bending low as the roof descended almost to the water-level, we found the bottom of the watercourse which David's men used, and we knew we were near to the Virgin's Fountain. There happened our first misadventure. The basin of the pool where it opens to the fresh air was deeper than the tunnel, and as I stepped down into it the water rose to my waist. I called on the following party to halt and considered the problem.

There was no shallow crossing for about 3 yards, but there was no need for every one to get soaked. I was already wet and could ferry them all across, pick-a-back fashion. I put my candle on the far steps and returned, and one by one I carried each man across. There was a good deal of hilarity during this operation, especially when I hoisted up the large corporal I mentioned earlier. I am not slightly built, but he was a little too much for me. I trod on a sharp stone, and sat down suddenly with him on top of me. This seemed to amuse everybody else.

Once out in the moonlight all was well, however, for it was a warm night and well-wrung clothes, though damp, did us no harm. We were immediately below the cliffside surmounted by the Jebusite wall.

For some reason Mary is believed to have washed her Child's clothes at this spring, hence its name, although the Moslems call it the Fount of the Mother of Steps, because so many steps lead down to it. It is a dark cavern at all times, and one could imagine it at Solomon's midnight coronation. Gihon means 'gushing', and there is an intermittent flow even to-day, so that in early days it would be regarded as of supernatural origin. The Arabs say that a dragon dwells in it. Here, where a mysterious spring gushed forth from a cave, was a setting for the sacred rites of kingship, and incidentally the only occasion in the Bible of an heir to the throne being crowned before the death of the king.

Above us shone candlelight from a window as an Arab rose to see who disturbed the night. The dogs of Silwan barked and our donkeys clattered as we ascended the path that runs along the Kedron Valley. It is dry now for the most of the year, and has a modern concrete bed a yard or so wide to restrain it in the rainy season. High on either side of us were the pale outlines of the mountain-sides, to our left the battlements of Jerusalem with the bricked-up Golden Gate, and to our right the myriad of white Jewish graves on the Mount of Olives. We passed the rock-cut landmarks known as the Tomb of Zechariah and the Pillar of Absalom, which were standing there on that moonlit night when Jesus crossed the Kedron to go to Gethsemane to pray; and they saw Him return later that night escorted by the mob with swords and staves.

Past Gethsemane we went, and the Tomb of the Virgin, then uphill round the northern wall to arrive at our starting-point, weary and content, a little before midnight.

The Damascus Gate is probably the most famous gate in Jerusalem's wall. It faces north, and when the water-melon sellers and cloth merchants have their colourful wares exhibited in early morning under the graceful Saracenic arch it is a memorable picture. The Arabs call it the Gate of the Column, and nobody knew why until the mosaic map of Byzantine Jerusalem was found in Madeba about fifty years ago. In it there could be seen within this gate a quadrant with a big column in the centre, possibly to hold a statue. Some say that it marked the centre of the world: an honour it shares with the Dome of the Rock and the Holy Sepulchre. Perhaps it was a sort of London Stone, from which distances were measured to other towns in Palestine. The fact that the name had persisted in Arabic through all those centuries proves the value of local names for identification of historic places.

The Madeba Mosaic is a very interesting map. A copy of the whole of it, showing all Palestine and a little beyond, formed a fine wall decoration at the Y.M.C.A. hostel in the Old City. And at the main entrance to the Central Y.M.C.A. building a famous mosaic artist has set a copy of the Jerusalem part of it in the pavement. When once I was looking at it, a passing Arab youth stopped and told me that he was a native of Madeba, a place in Transjordan near Heshbon, and was familiar with the original mosaic. It was found, he said, in 1896, in the floor of a Byzantine Church. People had not realized its significance and a lot of it had been damaged, but the section showing Jerusalem was the best preserved. It dates from the fifth or sixth century and gives valuable evidence of what the Byzantine Holy City looked like. Different churches can be identified, with other landmarks, and there are pictorial representations of such places as Bethlehem, the Jordan with fishes in it, the Lake with men rowing on it, and the whole map duly decorated with animals and trees in their appropriate colours.

We were familiar with the Damascus Gate, of course, but often when I passed that way with a party I would pause to show them to the left the top of one arch of the Roman gateway, now protected by railings, its top level with the present height of the ground. Each party would include at least one who would not have seen it before.

Excavations were made along this northern wall by the Department of Antiquities in 1937-8. The archaeologists found a block of stone above its archway with some letters of an inscription which appears to have contained the name of Hadrian's city, Aelia Capitolina. If this is so, then it is a triumphal arch dating from A.D. 135. The lowest courses of the adjoining wall are later, about fourth-century. It is not certain that the arch was part of the city wall when it was first built, although that is possible. All we could see was the curve of its top built into the masonry. On the other side of the gate, too, the archaeologists had left a shaft to reveal the lower stones of the wall.

We went along the road a little way in order to explore the famous Solomon's Quarries. They open at the cliff under the wall and lead below the city. A large red S outside the cave announced that here was a public air raid shelter, and no more efficient one can be imagined. It is said that this mighty cavern goes right across to the other side of the city—with what truth I cannot say—and that some solemn rites of the Freemasons take place there. The principal design on the white stone objects arrayed for sale within the cave was the familiar rule and dividers of the Mason's badge.

Armed with torches, we descended the steep slope of the cave and saw that the rock around us was creamy white in colour. There is no evidence for it, but it is possible that here were hewn the blocks of stone for Solomon's Temple, cut in these depths so that, as it says in 1 Kings vi. 7, no sound of work could be heard in the House. It is very likely that Herod's Temple was built from rock quarried from here. Josephus describes its whiteness, which he called marble, but which might have been this fine stone. We could see the signs of quarrying all around the walls. Canon Hanauer says that a Babylonian *graffito*, or cave-drawing, was found here, dating from the fifth century B.C., as well as niches for masons' lamps. 'Jeremiah's Grotto', on the other side of the road, is really a continuation of these diggings.

We did not remain in the quarries for long, but emerged into the sunlight and went along the Nablus Road to see St. Stephen's Convent beyond the Garden Tomb. St. Stephen's is the home of the Dominican Fathers in Jerusalem, their centre of archaeological and Biblical study. I was privileged once to be shown their library, and to wander amongst its treasures. For those who imagine that there is any restriction placed upon the range and scope of the reading of these cloistered monks a survey of that library is a revelation. In various languages and from the pens of widely differing scholars were books on every conceivable aspect of Biblical and theological study. All the classical reference books were there, of course, and I found some of the most recent wartime publications of the Oxford University Press and other leading authorities. *Formgeschichte* and other strange modern subjects were rubbing covers with orthodox Catholic literature. I was not surprised to espy the names of prominent Methodist scholars under titles on some of the books. No longer are the Dominicans the *Domini canes*, 'dogs of the Lord', pursuing heresy with direst penalties, but in Palestine their black hoods are exchanged for white, and their pursuit is the gentle one of learning.

The men were charmed with the courtyard before the church, and we sat in the shade of the cloisters, where a window of many-coloured glass stained the sunlight. In the centre of the square is a stone figure of the youthful St. Stephen, and around its edge a series of simple arches that have been built in modern times on Byzantine foundations. Some old flagstones in the *atrium* were there when the Empress Eudoxia built her great church here in A.D. 450 to mark the place where St. Stephen was stoned. This location, called also by the Jews 'the place of stoning' since ancient times, was for some reason almost ignored by the Crusaders, perhaps because stables were all over this area then, and they decided that the first Christian martyr had died in the Valley of Jehoshaphat. The place is marked now by a Greek shrine outside St. Stephen's Gate.

It is true that the mob acted with haste in doing Stephen to death, but none the less they would scarcely have slain him so close to the Temple. Stoning should be at least 2,000 cubits from the

Sanctuary, and there were regulations about how it should be done. The victim should be pushed over a bank that was 'two men high', and stoned from the top. Even in their haste they would hurry Stephen to the regular stoning-place. The oldest tradition places it at this spot. The nearby Gordon's Calvary cannot claim this as additional evidence for its authenticity. The Roman place of execution would not be near the Jewish one. The Crusaders built a little chapel here near the roadside and left untouched the Byzantine remains, which was fortunate for the Dominican excavators who came here about fifty years ago. They unearthed the foundations of the church and its attached monastery, including some very interesting rock-cut tombs and a series of fine mosaic floors.

One of the fathers came out to us and led us round the peaceful colonnades and into the spacious gardens to show us the tombs.

This monastery was in Byzantine days a home for deacons who officiated at the Holy Sepulchre, which was called the Church of the Holy Anastasis, or Resurrection, at that time, and tomb inscriptions announcing this fact have been found here. We saw some of them, and entered the tombs cut in chambers leading from one to another, each with three benches round the walls and some provided with little headrests for the bodies, a unique feature among Palestine tombs. It was possible to trace Greek inscriptions with passages from the Psalms over some doors, and the names of Holy Sepulchre deacons, such names as Nonnus Onesimus, Euthymius Pindiris, Michael, were plainly inscribed. In the far corner of the garden was the principal group of tombs, an underground *hypogeum*, as it is called, and the monk unlocked the door for us to descend.

It is doubtful if this cemetery was originally Jewish. It was probably made for these Byzantine deacons and used again, in one place at any rate, by a Crusader, for whose body a special excavation was made. It was rather eerie in those sepulchral depths by the light of the candles we carried. The caverns are being used to-day as a burial-place by the local fraternity of Dominicans. It was only when we were outside again and looked about us that we realized that the Garden Tomb was immediately over the garden wall from this spot, and is exactly 2 metres from the nearest of these tombs. As the wall is modern and the tomb almost identical with those we had seen, it appeared obvious to us that it was a tomb that had belonged to this Byzantine cemetery. Indeed, its trough-shaped graves give it rather a later date than most of them.

The church itself we found to be a large one—it follows the proportions of Eudoxia's church—although its style is modern and not altogether in keeping with its history. What fascinated us most was the beautiful mosaic floor, great sections of which were wonderfully preserved, and we could imagine the fine carpet of colour that was under the feet of the early Christian worshippers. There were no pictures in its design of complex interweaving lines; and the subtle blues and reds and yellows of the tiny pieces of stone had remained unfaded through 1,500 years. I am the proud possessor of an early example of nineteenth-century colour-printing, a reproduction of this variegated pattern, which hangs on the wall before me now as I write. It was the gift of one of the Dominican fathers when first I made their acquaintance in my explorations of Jerusalem.

In the centre of the church before the high altar was a sanctuary down a few steps. This, in the early church, marked the site of Stephen's stoning, and although its authenticity cannot be guaranteed, it is respected again to-day as a holy place. Within the shrine until recently was a golden casket containing supposed relics of St. Stephen, but it was stolen from the church a few years ago.

Before we departed I took my party round to the outside of the east end of the church to point out to them how the early builders had excavated a hill in order to make a level space for the building. The hill remained with this section cut away, as we could see by the quarrying in the rock. Why had they done this? Obviously to ensure that the church surrounded what they thought was Stephen's stoning-place, where the shrine is now. This is precisely what the early records say that Constantine's builders did, a hundred years earlier than this, at the Holy Sepulchre. Here was an illustration of the process employed, to cut away the hill around a sacred place within it, and surround it by a church.

We went down the Nablus Road and rounded the corner into the Street of the Prophets in order to find the Armenian mosaics. We had had our fill of ancient mosaic floors for one afternoon and we did not stay long, for there was little to see.

Some Moslem workmen when building one of the many huddled houses in this area had discovered a floor, some 12 feet by 20 feet, covered with mosaic flowers and birds, with Armenian lettering. They asked whether the Armenians wished to buy the ground, as it was presumably a relic of one of their monasteries which had flourished 1,000 years ago. They agreed to do so, and have preserved it as a memorial to the many Armenians who have perished in their sad and long history of persecutions. It is in a rickety basement with dirty houses all round, and is so hidden in an alley that it was an achievement for us to find it. The custodian was delighted to display its beauties to us. The design is more formal in character than the well-known Tabgha mosaics, having its birds within the circling branches of a vine that appears to sprout in conventional Armenian fashion from an ornate flowerpot. Peacocks are there, and pheasants—indeed, birds great and small of many kinds and in the brightest of colours; and one little bird is depicted as a prisoner in a cage, hanging among the grapes of the vine.

We each dropped a small coin into the box as we came out. It is a queer little backwater of Jerusalem ignored by guide-books, and seldom visited; but in this dirty slum lies unsuspected beauty, a patch of loveliness hidden by squalor. I felt that there was a sermon somewhere in those tiny coloured stones for those who could read it.

There is a castle from fairy-land in a valley near Jerusalem. When first I saw it I thought immediately of the medieval battlements that illustrated the story books of my childhood, when a wimpled maiden leaned from a mullioned window to bid farewell to her knight in armour, who rode a trusty charger, attended by his squire. She was his ladye fayre and he, her very parfait gentil knight, was off to fight dragons for her.

Never have I seen so romantic a sight as the Convent of the Cross. Wide buttresses uphold a wall of dizzy height, whilst mysterious towers and pinnacles project above the slits for archers in the stone-work. A cluster of green trees, dark cypresses and lighter olives surround it, and on either side rise the rocky slopes of brown-and-white hills. Once it was a mile and a half from Jerusalem; but from the Jaffa Gate have slowly crept in modern days the streets of a new Jerusalem, a city of square bungalows or towering mansion-flats or stone villas in neat gardens, so that to-day the houses are on the brink of the overlooking hill, and the story-book castle is no longer in seclusion, although it remains remote from the life of the city.

We liked to wander in that direction sometimes on a Sunday afternoon, and to clamber down the hillside to it for a visit as we passed. The last time I went with the members of my Fellowship my foot slipped as I descended, I remember, and a sharp rock removed some of the skin from my hand and arm. This seemed to amuse my companions, and it was the Secretary's principal entry in the week's diary. When he read it the following Wednesday at the meeting he related how the Padre fell on stony ground and arose with such a speed that he must also have fallen among thorns. I retaliated that at any rate I didn't spring up and choke him.

We had to bend low in order to go into the compound, as the doorway was designed more to prevent people from entering than to facilitate their entrance in the stormy days of not so long ago.

I

Since the seventh century a church has stood here without a city wall, so its own defences were strong. The legendary founder of it was Miriam, the Christian King of the Iberians who died in A.D. 342. There are records of a monastery here in the sixth century, destroyed by Samaritans and rebuilt by Justinian. Until 1850 it was a monastery for Iberian monks, or Georgians as they are more commonly called because of their attachment to our own patron saint. It was the last of the many establishments they possessed in Palestine. It is now in the hands of the Orthodox Church and was their theological college for a long time. We found many Greek refugees living there. Once I paid a visit with a friend to the Convent of the Cross and met a Greek from the United States who told a sad story of unemployment and hardship. We asked him what work he could do. He was a man of fifty.

'I kin cook and I kin drive,' he told us in fluent transatlantic English. 'I'll do anything.'

Next day my friend was asked, of all unusual things, for a cook-chauffeur. The Greek started work the same day, delighted to be in the activity of the world instead of being secluded in this picturesque but I fear rather unhygienic turreted castle.

The church itself within the centre of these defences we found to be an interesting place. It is reputed to be the restoration of a late Byzantine sanctuary. Certainly the mosaic floor is old, with traces of the usual birds and twisty border design. Whether their story is true that great purple stains on the mosaic paving were caused by the blood of martyred monks I cannot say. The story is that the Persians under Chosroes II invaded the sanctuary in A.D. 614 and slaughtered the Iberians on these stones. It is possible that they died here, but the men with me thought that the bloodstains would have vanished after all these years. I thought so too.

Georgian inscriptions were on the walls and some quaint crude paintings, many obliterated by decay. A musty atmosphere was everywhere. A big pulpit rose to one side of the quite modest-sized nave, and I was able to make out the text in Greek which ran round it.

'We only preach Christ crucified'

I read. That was a refreshing Methodist text to find in an Eastern Orthodox Church. And yet, thought I, who are we to claim a monopoly of evangelism? Were not these Christians the direct heirs of the Apostolic Church, using the very speech of St. Paul? The elements in their system which we called superstitious and corrupt were nevertheless not what they considered the heart of things.

They still preached, and they preached Christ crucified. We could not understand what they were saying when they spoke, and it might be that they were closer to us in their gospel than we realized. They were children, and out of respect for their sanctuaries they decorated them with baubles. Who were we to say that God's children must not put toys in His house? They thought us dreadfully irreverent because we did not do so, and could scarcely believe that our emphasis is upon Christ crucified, for we never made the sign of His Cross, as they were ever doing, not only in worship, but in daily life. They find it as difficult to believe in our sincerity as we do in theirs. The children in God's family vary greatly. Fortunately, He understands us all.

The church was built on this site, according to tradition, because here grew the tree from which the timber was taken to make the Cross. It was a three-fold tree, they say, its triple trunks of fir, cypress and cedar having sprung from three twigs given to Abraham by his heavenly visitors. Abraham when he fled from Sodom gave them to Lot who planted them here. Water from the Jordan was necessary to make the tree grow, and thirty-nine times Lot brought water on a donkey, only to have it stolen by the Devil. His patience was stronger than the Devil's, however, who tired eventually, and Lot was able to water the tree. It was deliberately not touched when timber was wanted for Solomon's Temple, for it was realized that the tree had a purpose in connection with man's redemption. When Christ was crucified, the planks were cut from this tree to make His Cross.

The black-robed deacon led us into a pitch-dark shrine in the wall, and by the aid of tapers we saw the marble covering of the hole where the tree grew. Round about it were recent bright-hued pictures illustrating each phase of its story. We were solemnly informed, I fear, that all these facts are recorded in the Bible! In this old-world corner we were able to catch some of the atmosphere that must have surrounded the credulous and pious pilgrims of the Middle Ages, who heard the most fantastic stories when they came to the Holy Land, when almost every stone and tree had a sacred association in their minds. One pilgrim, I read, never lifted his feet from the ground the whole time he was in the country, but proceeded in a sort of shuffling gait lest he should miss treading on any ground which had known the footsteps of his Lord. Outside, we saw a queer, twisted tree with three trunks in one, and could understand something of the rise of the legend.

We went to explore some catacombs in the nearby hillside before we departed. They were close and gloomy caves in which they say that monks sheltered when invaders came. They appeared to be natural cavities artificially enlarged, and might have been used for that purpose. An olive orchard filled the valley and the air was loud with crickets which in midsummer in Palestine haunt olives and create a tremendous din. They must have been large creatures, but we were never able to find one.

Our route back home led us over a steep hill to the edge of a Jewish suburb. All around us were the rolling heights of Judea, with the city in a basin in their midst. The Psalmist had looked at these same hills and seen a parable in them.

'As the mountains are round about Jerusalem, so the Lord is round about His people from this time forth and even for evermore.'

CHAPTER VII

MOUNT OF OLIVES

All believers in Christ flock together from all quarters of the earth, not, as of old, to behold the beauty of Jerusalem, or that they may worship in the former Temple which stood in Jerusalem, but that they may abide there, and both hear the story of Jerusalem, and also worship in the Mount of Olives over against Jerusalem, whither the glory of the Lord removed itself, leaving the earlier city. There also, according to the published record, the feet of our Lord and Saviour, who was Himself the Word, and, through it, took upon Himself human form, stood upon the Mount of Olives, near the cave which is now pointed out there.

EUSEBIUS, early fourth century.

FEW people realize how near the Mount of Olives is to Jerusalem. When I took a party of newcomers to the Temple Area or on to the roof of Antonia Palace and told them that the hill to the east was Olivet, they usually expressed surprise at its nearness to the city. We are told in the Gospels that it was a Sabbath day's journey from Jerusalem, but it is not easy for us to understand how far that is. A Sabbath day's journey was 2,000 cubits, rather less than a mile. In fact, the distance from the top of the mount across the valley of Gethsemane to the nearest point of the present wall is less than half a mile, but the New Testament reckoning was not 'as the crow flies', but as a man would walk by the winding valley path to the opposite side of the hill. Both sides of the valley are steep, rising 200 feet up to the Temple wall and on the other side 450 feet to the top of Olivet, which is 2,720 feet above sea-level. All round one side of it, from the Garden of Gethsemane on its lower slope facing Jerusalem and round to the south, are myriads of flat white tomb-stones of Jewish cemeteries, with not a vestige of green over its glaring, eye-aching expanse. But north of the Garden are grass-grown slopes with many olive trees right up to the summit. There are one or two churches on its lower grade; and on the top of it, beside an untidy Arab village, there are more churches, a Moslem mosque, and the Russian compound with an immense campanile rising 150 feet, which, with its slender, tapering roof, creates the skyline of Olivet so familiar to the modern pilgrim.

On the various occasions when I led a party of troops on excursions to the Mount of Olives we went by different routes. Sometimes we would take a bus to Bethany, about three miles from Jerusalem along the Jericho road which winds round the bottom of the hill, and we would walk back to the city along the footpath over Olivet which in the days of Jesus was the only Bethany road. In particular we followed that way on Palm Sunday, which I describe in my Easter diary. At other times we followed the shortest, steepest way from the valley directly uphill to the Ascension Chapel, sometimes by the original road and sometimes by one of its winding deviations which bring the climber to the same place at the top. It is possible also to travel by Arab bus along a very circuitous route round by the British War Cemetery and the Hebrew University, over Mount Scopus, and up to the terminus of the road in the village on Olivet. In this chapter I want to describe a climb we made on a hot Sunday afternoon up a path unfamiliar to most of the men: the way which lies across the upper part of the Valley of Gethsemane and over the high ground protruding from the Mount of Olives to the north-west, and thence to its summit.

We descended the valley from a point opposite the north-eastern corner of the Old City wall and found the slope there much easier than the sharper, steeper, more direct way farther south. We went through hay-fields and standing corn towards the rising path which leads up to the wall round the Greek Patriarch's summer residence. It was very quiet in that valley, and it seemed to us a very likely theory that this more lonely and deserted part of Gethsemane would be the place to which Jesus would retire to pray, and not to the traditional place of the Agony, which then as now was beside a main road and at feast-times would be busy and noisy. The Garden was a park of olive-trees stretching probably right up the valley. Judas, as John tells us (xviii. 2), 'knew the place', so it was apparently a quiet and secluded spot not known to every one. 'Gethsemane' means in Aramaic an 'oil-press', and many such presses, of great stone wheels, have been found along this valley. A little to our right was the Grotto of the Passion, which we visited on our way back.

As we mounted the opposite rise we felt a welcome breeze and congratulated ourselves upon our wisdom in forsaking the hot and sultry city on that summer afternoon to find the higher, cooler air of Olivet. When we entered the Patriarch's garden and sat on the low stone wall under pine trees overlooking Jerusalem we were amply rewarded for our heavy climb. There was not only a grateful shade and a gentle breeze, but a glorious view lay before us. In the sunshine it was Jerusalem the golden, its domes and minarets and towers gleaming below us within the encircling battlements. The Holy City from the Mount of Olives is an unforgettable sight. It is one of the great memories of a man's life. The Dome of the Rock, with its blue walls and cupola of dull lead, stands majestic in the

centre of the white expanse of the Temple Area. Beyond it and
around lie the clustered streets of the Old City. Against the sky are
the familiar outlines of the Dormition Church on Mount Zion, the
peak of the Y.M.C.A. building beyond, and the square mass of the
Citadel; whilst the dark dome of the Holy Sepulchre can be distinguished among the huddled houses to the right. Gleaming white
on the northern side of the city are the smooth lines of the Archaeological Museum, and behind it the 'green hill far away', Gordon's
Calvary, covered with Moslem graves. Nebi Samwil is on the far
horizon to our right, and Government House away to the left, with
the monastery on the Bethlehem road a little to its west. The
rolling yellow hills of Judea stretch away on every side.

The eminence upon which we stood has been since the sixth
century identified with the 'Galilee' of Matthew xxviii. 16, apparently because the early Christians found it difficult to associate that
particular Resurrection appearance of Jesus with the northern
province. Perhaps some similarity of the name, a 'ring of stones' or
'trysting-place', caused this early tradition. It is still known as
Galilee, as a stone-carved text in Greek at its gate testifies. The wall
towards Jerusalem bears yet the marks of bullets fired by Turkish
troops on the British in 1917—the only occasion when there was any
shooting round the Holy City. We entered the large sprawling
mansion, and a Greek nun admitted us to the Patriarch's private
chapel, kept beautifully clean, with two shrines marking places they
associate with the Resurrection. The members of my party were
interested in an aviary full of singing birds that ran along one side of
it. It was here that the World Missionary Conference gathered in
1928, and delegates camped about the grounds under its olive trees.

Mount Scopus is a hill to the north of the Mount of Olives and
attached to it by a ridge that dips only slightly in between, so that
in that direction, curving round the city a little, it forms a slight
range of hills. A road runs along the top of this ridge and we filed
on to it to turn along to the top of Olivet. Behind us was the squat
stone tower of the Augusta Victoria Palace, built by the Kaiser in
1898, some say in which to dwell when he had conquered the world,
and others that it was no more than what it pretended to be: a
Protestant hospice for German pilgrims. Inside its stately courtyard is a life-size figure of Wilhelm in the Crusader dress of the
Knights of St. John, to whose Order he belonged; and within the
chapel he and the Kaiserin are in a painting on the ceiling, surrounded by Crusader kings, Richard Lionheart, Barbarossa, and
St. Louis, beside a grand picture of the Ascension.

From a vantage-point on the eastern side of Olivet we had the glorious panorama of the chrome hills that lie eastwards, towards the Dead Sea, which was a line of deep blue in the distance, and clearly to be seen beyond it were the hills of the Land of Ammon and of Moab. It looked like a painting by Van Gogh.

In one of those folds of yellow hills north-east of Olivet lies the little village of Ain Farah, beside still waters. There are some who say that the Twenty-third Psalm was written in its cool shade, the one green spot in a dry and weary land. And there are some who declare that here it was Jeremiah came when he buried a girdle by the waterside for a parable, and later dug it up, 'and behold, the girdle was marred, it was profitable for nothing'. In Jeremiah xiii it is said that he went to Euphrates for this purpose, which has caused great difficulty to scholars, for no visit of the prophet to Babylon is otherwise recorded. But it is possible that he went to Ain Farah, not a very great distance from Anathoth, where he dwelt, in order to present his parable in dramatic form. A form of Ain Farah could look very much like Euphrates when written in Hebrew without the vowels. A very old tradition associates the place with Jeremiah, and an Orthodox chapel there to-day is dedicated to him.

To the east, Jericho lay twenty miles away behind a bare hill this side of Jordan. Most of us had been on a half-day trip there by car, to bathe in the salty waters of the great lake, to step across into Transjordania by the Allenby Bridge, to see the murky flow of the Jordan and to explore the excavations of Jericho. Truly a traveller 'goes down' from Jerusalem to Jericho. The country drops 4,000 feet in those twenty miles. On Olivet we were 2,720 feet above the level of the Mediterranean Sea, and the Dead Sea lay 1,292 feet below sea level, desolate and arid, especially in the summer, as we had discovered.

Jordan we found a trifle disappointing. We saw a muddy river of quite modest proportions—the Thames even at Richmond is much wider—with overhanging trees on either side rather like the upper reaches of the Severn. It courses at times between the cliffs of a ravine, at others beside low stony banks. The Jericho of the Old Testament, fortunately, is remote from the modern town of palm trees. The city that Jesus knew was south of old Jericho and is now no more. Professor J. Garstang has written a fascinating book about his discoveries there in which he describes the Neolithic settlements and the Bronze and Iron Age cities he has found on the site, including city walls of the fourteenth century B.C. which appear to have been toppled by an earthquake shock, and correspond remarkably with the narrative in Joshua vi.

In a remote *wadi* away to the south-east of where we were standing, lies the lonely Greek monastery of Mar Saba. My most vivid recollection of a visit to it is of a monk devoutly kissing the three skulls of seventh-century martyrs, which he kept in a wooden box!

Away to the south of the Dead Sea, in the Akabah region, Dr. Glueck of the American School of Oriental Research has unearthed the remains of great copper-mines where Solomon had some of the industries which made him wealthy. The Israelites had an early link with metal craftsmen in Tubal-Cain, and if the 'Kenite hypothesis' is right their religion was influenced by that desert clan of smiths. In Deuteronomy viii. 9 they were told that their Promised Land contained hills of copper, which must mean this area, the City of Copper referred to in 1 Chronicles iv. 12, where Solomon's immense smelting furnaces have been found. One can see slag still rich with ore; and Dr. Glueck has identified the site of Ezion-Geber nearby, Solomon's port on the Red Sea. The rich timber of this Valley of Smiths would have provided the necessary fuel for smelting. This now sandy area he describes as the Pittsburg of Palestine, and Solomon as the first 'copper king' of history.

We could not see the Good Samaritan Inn from where we stood, but on our Jericho trip we had paused at it for a moment. It is an old Arab *khan*, mostly in ruins and surrounded by a long low wall, and stands probably where a watering-place would be in New Testament times. There would have been no need for an inn before reaching Jericho, which was a day's donkey journey from Jerusalem. Jerome said that this *khan* marked the place where the man in the parable was attacked by robbers. Some say that the Good Samaritan story can be accepted as historical because Jesus or the Evangelist did not preface it by saying that it was a parable, but appears to relate it as an actual happening. But He did that on other occasions, and it is an obvious, characteristic parable of our Lord, many of which doubtless had their origin in actual happenings.

We went into the Russian Compound on the Mount of Olives, which is on the east side of the hilltop. As at Ain Karim, a community of nuns live here in great poverty, with one or two little churches and a museum beside their lofty tower. When I climbed the Mount of Olives on Ascension Day, I found the compound crowded with people, mostly Christian Arabs, who encamped in families under the shady pines and olive trees. It was a true festival, with every one in Sunday clothes and hawkers with toys and sweets and ices, the latter crying 'Eskimo!'—the name of the icecream they sold—and there were vendors of drinks and fruit amongst the shouting children, who played on hammocks slung between trees or under ragged canvas bivouacs. As I walked amongst them, never had I been so strongly reminded of Hampstead Heath on Whit-Monday. But to-day everything was quiet, and a black-coifed nun admitted us and showed us their church with the customary ikons, the museum with specimens of Byzantine tomb-lamps and Armenian mosaics, and the place where the buried head of John the Baptist had been dug up. In how many unlikely places has his head been found! When I was in Damascus I was told that it had been discovered there, and I heard a similar story at Sebastieh.

The Orthodox Church claims that the Ascension of Christ took place here. They may be right. It seemed to me that its location was more likely to be on this side of the hill than at the traditional place facing Jerusalem, because, according to Luke xxiv. 50, the event happened when they were 'towards Bethany'—that is, on the east and not the west of the hill-top. But the reference might be, of course, to the Bethany road. We were 'over against Bethany' where we stood, as we saw when we ascended the tower. It lay below us in the valley—a village of flat-topped stone houses, called by the Arabs El Azarieh, a corruption of the name Lazarus. Since the fourth century an ancient rock-tomb with several recesses has been displayed as the supposed scene of the miracle, but there is no evidence of its authenticity, nor are there any means of locating either the house of Simon the Leper or the house of Mary and Martha where Jesus lodged before crossing this hill-top for His last days in Jerusalem. There is a stone seat in the grounds of the Russian Convent at Bethany, which has a Byzantine inscription saying that it was used by Jesus. It is likely that the village lay a little farther away from the city than it does at present, for John tells us it was 15 *stadia*, or furlongs, from Jerusalem, presumably by the direct route over the hill, and dwellings would not have been where the old tomb is, as they are now. Bethphage is more difficult to locate. It was apparently on the way from Bethany, and a mound to the south-east has been given that name. Some Orthodox buildings and a church are on it.

The climb to the very top of that tower of 214 steps was an achievement for us in that weather, but, like the reward we had earlier upon mounting to the top of 'Galilee', it was worth it. I think the view from the Russian tower on the Mount of Olives is one of the finest in the world. The geography is certainly more crammed with history than anywhere else.

We gathered on the western side overlooking Jerusalem and I took my Testament from my pocket. The men stood silently looking at the view before us as I read from the Book of the Revelation: 'And I saw the holy city, new Jerusalem, coming down out of heaven from God, made ready as a bride adorned for her husband.' John the Seer's New Jerusalem was not this Jerusalem, of course; but its beauty, as it stood like a crown upon the crest of Judah's hills, was the best analogy he could summon for his dream of the world that is to be.

On the summit of the hill immediately below the tower on which we stood we could see the mosque beside the octagonal court built by Crusaders to mark its highest point, the site of the Ascension. In its centre is a modern domed chapel. It covers a slab of marble containing an indentation reputed to be a footstep that Jesus made as He left the earth. It is doubtless the one revered by Byzantine Christians, in spite of the fact that it is no bigger than a child's footprint and is in marble—no part of the original mountain. In the fourth century A.D. Queen Helena built a church on the Mount of Olives and formed the Imbomon, an open space for public worship, round the Ascension stone. The Christians before Constantine seem to have worshipped on the Mount of Olives more than anywhere else, possibly because it was an easily-located holy place and untouched by the pagans.

The Moslems have for centuries possessed the place where the early Christians believed that Christ went up to heaven, and their little minaret by its side commanding the view over the city earns them a handsome profit from visitors. They accept the story of the Ascension of Christ, but not that of His arrest and Crucifixion. They believe that He went direct from Gethsemane to the point of Ascension. To mention the death of Jesus to a Moslem elicits from him parrot-like the quotation from the Koran: 'They did not kill him, they did not crucify him, they only had his likeness.' Had Mohammed heard the legend of an obscure Syrian sect to the effect that Simon of Cyrene died in the place of Jesus? Christians are allowed to worship in this Moslem shrine on Ascension Day. I saw then candles propped against the stone, and various groups of members of the Eastern Churches round the ruins of the old Crusader columns. Priests, I am told, used to sit by the stone and cut paper patterns of the footprint for the credulous, but I did not see them when I was there.

It is naturally difficult to decide exact places associated with particular events in the life of Jesus, but of one thing we could be certain: Jesus had been on this hilltop. Here He had taught His disciples; here He had prayed; here He had seen the view: His birthplace away to the south, the scene of His baptism and His temptations in the desert to the east, northwards the sweeping line of hills over which He had tramped with His friends from Galilee; before Him the bulwarks of Jerusalem around the House of the Lord, full of erring children over whom He yearned with mother-love. Sir Flinders Petrie used to say that the path from Bethany over the Mount of Olives was the most authentic holy site in Palestine. Jewish legend declares that the olive branch which the dove carried to the Ark after the Flood came from this mount. Most of us carried away a sprig of silver olive leaf from one of its many trees to remind us, not of an old legend, but of a living truth: we stood where He stood, we prayed where He prayed.

Down the tower again and round the Moslem shrine, we found the Church of the Paternoster. It was built seventy or eighty years ago by Princess Latour d'Auvergne, on the site of a very ancient sanctuary on a hill which 1,000 years ago knew the fiery eloquence of Peter the Hermit. It is of no great interest to-day except for the panels set round the church and vestibule and under the colonnades surrounding a quiet court. On each panel is the Lord's Prayer in a different language, painted on tiles set in the wall. Every imaginable language is there, modern ones we could recognize and strange tongues we had never heard of, written in queer script. Luke xi. 1 reads as though He gave His friends the Lord's Prayer immediately after a visit Jesus made to the house of Mary and Martha, presumably at Bethany, which contrasts with Matthew's record of the Sermon on the Mount. Accordingly, from very early times the Mount of Olives was located as the place where the prayer was first spoken. A Byzantine church was on this site, over a series of caves which were believed to be where the Twelve gathered to hear the teaching of Jesus about the 'end'. It was thought that the Apostles' Creed was formulated there, and under the altar of a Crusader church on the site was inscribed a Paternoster which was believed to have been engraved by the Lord Himself. We wandered about the courtyard with its encircling tablets in many tongues, and before we left we stood in a group and quietly said together the Lord's Prayer. . . . An old Carmelite lay sister took us down to the age-old Grotto of Our Lord's Teaching, beneath the scaffolding of a new Basilica which will be completed beside the Paternoster Church after the war. Here was the Eleona Church which was destroyed by the Persians in A.D. 614, and undoubtedly was a very early Christian meeting-place. Primitive tombs are in cavities leading from it. A heavy grille separates the praying-place of the Carmelite Sisters, whose convent is connected with this place and whose Order is a closed one.

From well before the New Testament days the slope of the Mount of Olives has been considered a desirable place for Jewish burial, owing to an interpretation of the prophecy of Zechariah about the 'last things' happening there, and to the queer idea called the Gilgalim, or 'rollings': that every one will burrow from his grave to the Valley of Jehoshaphat for judgement. To be buried near the valley would necessitate but a short burrow! Not only modern cemeteries reach almost to the summit of Olivet on its southern slope, but old rock-hewn tombs line the valley. I was invited on one occasion to be present at the survey of a tomb that had been discovered by an Arab as he was digging in his garden. All Palestinians appear to be aware of the fact that every *antika* they discover must be notified to the Department of Antiquities, and the archaeologists there were duly informed of this find, and under their direction the tomb was excavated. I went along to see an archaeologist at work: separating and classifying the lamps and vessels, disposing of the human remains, clearing and measuring the rock-cut chamber and assessing its date and importance.

The tomb was half-way up the southern side of the hill, nearer to Bethany than Jerusalem, where an Arab family had built a new stone house on their land among some fig trees. They had cleared away accumulated soil from a vertical rock face and disclosed the entrance to a tomb. I looked at the assortment of earthern bowls, glass and earthenware slender phials, and small clay oil lamps that came from it. These articles enabled the date of the tomb to be ascertained. My friend the archaeologist pointed out to me the differences in the lamps and bottles which told the story of the tomb. It had been made in the first century B.C. and had been used a second time in the first century A.D., when it was sealed again, to be re-opened subsequently by some marauders, who had caused only slight damage; and then it had remained forgotten until now. That some one had violated the tomb since it was last used was proved by the fact that some earthenware water bowls were smashed and not all the pieces could be found.

I had to stoop to enter the small aperture that led into the rocky chamber. It was about 6 feet high and 10 feet square, with rock-cut benches on three sides of it for the bodies. When it was used again 100 years later—a very common practice—some cavities were made in the rock into which the bones of its first tenants were placed and duly sealed up with slabs of stone, other bones being contained in ossuaries—clay boxes about a foot long—in a corner. Other bodies were then placed on the benches and the chamber was sealed with a heavy stone slab which now lay on its side by the opening. I watched the expert marking the dimensions of its interior upon a scale plan, and when he had done he explained to me how the appearance of the tomb confirmed the evidence of the lamps and bottles in it. I asked what they were for and learned that they were ordinary household articles which were left in the tomb after use, probably because by contact with death they had become unclean, as the mourners themselves were until they had ceremonially cleansed themselves. I could see niches in the wall where lamps had stood to illumine the chamber while the body was anointed with spices. The bowls were probably used by the workers for washing their hands afterwards, and the lovely, slender bottles doubtless contained the perfumes which they had spread on the body. Curiosity shops label such phials 'tear bottles', but they were not really used to hold mourners' tears. The psalmist's reference to tears in a bottle may account for this delusion. The alabaster cruse of ointment which was broken over Jesus at Bethany would doubtless have been a costly vessel of this nature.

It was a wonderful experience to be present at the opening of a tomb near to Bethany which was used in the time of Jesus. Perhaps He had looked on it, perhaps a friend of His was buried here, perhaps . . . It was useless to speculate. By such speculations possibly many of the 'holy places' had been located. It was, my friend told me, quite a common type of grave used by first-century Jews of no great social standing. It was not a rich man's tomb. I was able to visit on another occasion a mausoleum of the same date on the other side of Jerusalem made for the Herodian family. It was a series of large chambers lined with smooth blocks of stone and with a stone cylinder in a groove which rolled in front of the entrance to cover it completely. Joseph of Arimathæa's grave would doubtless be more modest than that one, but more distinctive than the type of tomb I saw on Olivet. The latter might have been the kind from which Lazarus was raised, however.

My party turned homewards down the steep track which is the traditional Palm Sunday route that Jesus took. A tablet set in a wall told us in Latin that here Jesus saw the city and wept over it. Ruins of an old mosque on the site of a Crusader church lie beside the place, but the view is now obscured by trees at that point. In the meadow alongside it, however, there is a fine aspect of Jerusalem. It is the place where we gathered on Palm Sunday morning. That wider space would possibly be where the great multitude came out to meet Him with palms and hosannas.

We followed the path down as far as a door in the wall which opens into the grounds of the Russian Church of St. Mary Mag-

dalene, roofed with a cluster of pointed bulbs amid tapering green
cypresses, pines, and olive trees. This is often called the Russian
Gethsemane, and it was under one of its trees that I led our Maundy
Thursday evening service. Later, the Wednesday Fellowship would
sometimes come here for a little open-air service. We peeped into
the church, a nineteenth-century structure presented by Tsar
Alexander III, and were in time to see some nuns, some young and
some very old, chanting responses to a service led by a bearded and
vested priest. Above the *ikonostasis* is a great picture of Mary
Magdalene presenting an egg—a symbol of resurrection—to Pilate
as she begged for the body of Jesus.

In the wall outside the compound stands a broken column
marking the place where Judas is believed to have betrayed his
Master with a kiss. Below it lies the Latin Gethsemane with a few
hoary old olive trees propped up amid a formal garden kept by
Franciscans, always full of colour and scent. Sweet-smelling stocks,
pansies and violas, beds of lavender and tall white daisies, roses and
bougainvillea, none of these were in the Garden of Gethsemane that
Jesus knew. At that time it was an olive-orchard with a few wild
flowers in their season. But this makes a pleasant spot for meditation
to-day, with the slope from Kedron up to the Temple to be seen
across the valley. In 1925 an ornate church was built beside it, full
of Italian mosaic inside and out, to cover the supposed Rock of the
Agony. It stands where a Byzantine and later a Crusader church
once enshrined the Rock, and some of the early floor mosaic has
been preserved. It is called the Church of All Nations because the
Catholics of fourteen countries contributed to its cost, each being
responsible for a dome in its roof. Within it, we found the atmosphere most impressive, due not only to its great marble pillars and
fine paintings over the altar, but to the subdued light which entered
through the windows, which are not, as appeared, of opaque glass,
but of alabaster dyed purple. As we came out, a monk told me the
name of a flower blooming by the Garden wall. It was 'love lies
bleeding'. . . .

The Grotto of the Passion, a cave near to the Tomb of the Virgin,
was to us an interesting place. It is a little way up the Gethsemane
Valley to the north of the old Bethany road and has been revered
since very early times. There is a Latin altar within it, but it does not
spoil the place. Professor Dalman's theory is that Jesus might have
used this shelter as His place of retreat. It would not be wanted for
pressing olives for oil until the autumn; it would be warm on chilly
spring evenings; there was room for all the Twelve to gather there;
it was away from the main road, which the present location of the

place of Agony is not; three or four flat stones there could have been tables or seats. Probably Jesus went 'a stone's cast' from here up the quiet valley, and prayed in agony while Peter, James, and John were sleeping.

I have already mentioned the possibility that Mary the mother of John Mark was buried in the vicinity. Did that family own this land, and was it because this cave was their olive-press that they gave it to Jesus for a place of retreat? The ceremonial bounds of Jerusalem went as far as Bethphage, so here He would be technically within the Holy City, as pilgrims were required to be during the Feast. The Evangelist records how Jesus lodged every night in the Mount of Olives. Is this the place? Judas knew where it was and led the soldiers to it, but Jesus 'went forth' (John xviii. 4), possibly to meet them at the junction of the roads. The site of His agony does not require a rock with knee-prints in it such as we see before the altar in the Church of All Nations. It would be a secluded spot more in the direction of this cavern.

The tomb of the Virgin is a church dating from the Byzantine era, with a Crusader façade, and is, as a board outside states, the oldest church in Jerusalem. Its many steps leading down into darkness—so dark that we had to obtain candles from the Greek priest at the door—ensured that at the bottom we would be at the approximate ground-level of New Testament times. Half-way down on the left is the tomb of Queen Millicent, the turbulent Crusader Queen of Jerusalem who died in A.D. 1161. The lower part of the church is the earliest, and we groped about in the darkness until we found remains of an old tomb behind the altar. This is the supposed scene of the Assumption of the Virgin Mary, where her body was received into heaven. The Orthodox priests do not, I fear, keep this historic sanctuary in very good order. Nearby is a Moslem prayer-niche, for it is a minor holy place for Islam also. We soon ascended the wide stone steps again to the fresh air. A few years ago were found the remains of a great monastery which stood in this valley in Crusader times. The Arabs call the Kedron Vale the Valley of the Lady Mary, and St. Stephen's Gate, the only entry in the eastern wall, the Gate of the Lady Mary. They give her name also to a pool in the Moslem cemetery there, and to a Turkish bath within the gate.

We climbed up to St. Stephen's Gate past the Greek shrine to that first Christian martyr, and went through the Via Dolorosa to the other side of the Old City. We were glad of tea and a rest in the Toc H hostel. As one of the men remarked, the Padre's Jerusalem Sunday School was an exhausting business. But it was worth it.

We had traced the steps of Jesus, and had seen the view from the Mount of Olives. That was a memory we should treasure when peaceful days came and we were home once more, an experience that would enable us the more readily to respond to His leading, guiding our feet into the way of peace.

K

CHAPTER VIII

GARDEN TOMB

It is much to be regretted that a good many Protestant tourists show an inclination to make a fetish of the medieval tomb called Gordon's.

J. E. HANAUER, 1892.

UPON my ordination I was given a fine copy of the Revised Version of the Bible, a production of the Oxford University Press, which I carried with me upon my travels through the Middle East. The last pages of it contain a series of maps which I often consulted. It had never occurred to me to doubt their authenticity until I had dwelt in Jerusalem a little while. Then it was I discovered that the location these maps give of Biblical sites in the Holy City are in most cases hopelessly inaccurate. They were apparently compiled from the records of some Victorian excavator whose guesses were more erroneous than the Christian traditions about the holy places which he seemed to despise. There were many such investigators during the last century, mostly British and American, who began the difficult and long-neglected task of identifying the scenes of Biblical history in Palestine, and especially in and around Jerusalem. The general tendency was to regard the traditional sites as suspect, and the result was that sometimes the most impossible theories were put forward, which gained currency at the time, but which have long since been discredited by scholars. The most dogmatic statements were made by visitors to Palestine who had the fewest claims to scholarship, as any study of early numbers of the *Palestine Exploration Fund Quarterly Statement* will reveal. But some of these theories, especially if they were backed by a famous name, have been slow in dying, and the consequence is that, in spite of modern archaeological publications and the work of the Department of Antiquities of the Government of Palestine, many of these fallacious ideas still persist. My Bible maps, in an otherwise up-to-date production, give a completely impossible location of the Upper Pool of Gihon, identifying it with Mamillah; they place En-Rogel at the Virgin's Fountain, with Zoheleth beside it, whereas both of them are much further down the Kedron Valley; Zion is given as the name of the western ridge south of the city, instead of the eastern; Millo is placed near Hezekiah's Pool, instead of above the Virgin's Fountain, on the other side of Jerusalem; the line of northern wall in New Testament days is shown following a course which long ago was disproved;

and outside that line the cartographer has actually provided us with the location of Calvary, presumably following the theories of the late General Gordon.

Of all the popular fallacies that die hard, the identification of Calvary that is associated with the name of Gordon is the most persistent. He had far less claim to scientific knowledge than most of his contemporaries, but he was a famous soldier, the idol of the Victorian public, and the more dogmatic his statements were upon subjects of which he knew little, the more were they popularly received. He was a fundamentalist, with mystical theories tainted with rabbinicism, and like-minded people to-day still regard him as one of their prophets. He had a strong personality, the enthusiasm of a neophyte being combined with the decision of a strategist; and he left his mark upon the topography of the Holy City. A hill outside the northern wall is known as 'Gordon's Calvary'.

The good folk who maintain the pleasant garden near this hill are passionately convinced that they are custodians of the site of Our Lord's Resurrection. They have found an old tomb there, which they say is the one in which the body of Jesus was laid, and they advertise the place as 'The Garden Tomb'. The hill nearby, pitted with holes in its cliff face, has been a Moslem cemetery since the fifteenth century. It is still used as a burial place, and is covered with modern graves, and it is difficult of access. I always felt that the sight of a tomb in a garden, beside a hill outside the city wall, enabled one to understand much better the story of the Crucifixion and Resurrection, and to gain an adequate setting for that mighty drama. But at the same time I believe it is a pity that its guardians are so dogmatic about the authenticity of the place, for they can quote no authority more adequate than General Gordon.

I visited the Garden Tomb, of course, one Sunday afternoon, in company with the members of the Wednesday Fellowship, and we were impressed with the quietness and order of the place. We were shown an old wine-press, to demonstrate that it had been a garden in early times, and a rock-cut tomb containing three low trough-shaped graves. A hole to form a window had been cut in its wall, which we were told was part of its original form, enabling the disciples on the first Easter Day to see the interior without actually entering it. The doorstep was very worn, the result of visits of early pilgrims, our guide told us, and several rough crosses in red had been painted on the walls. There was a kind of ante-chamber which would permit the entrance of all the people mentioned as visiting the tomb of Jesus when His Resurrection became known. Before we left we were shown a strangely shaped piece of white plaster, which, we were informed, quite positively I regret to say, was a model of a shrine to Venus which Hadrian had built on this site.

It was natural that a good deal of bewilderment was caused amongst the men by this combination of an attractive garden with plausible arguments that here was the site of Calvary, and they demanded to know my views on the subject. They were not the only ones. Conversations I had with hundreds of men on leave in Jerusalem would inevitably lead to their question, 'What do you think about the Garden Tomb?' So I promised the men who looked to me as their guide around Jerusalem to investigate the whole subject to the best of my ability, and to tell them what I discovered. I incorporated my findings in a booklet which was published for the troops, entitled *Where did It Happen?* The material in that booklet is contained in the following pages.

I discovered that an ancient controversy was being renewed; not, however, on my part, but on the part of those who confused the troops by advertising an alternative site for Calvary and ridiculing the Holy Sepulchre. My attempt was to clarify the matter, and enable an intelligent man to make up his own mind on the subject by presenting the pros and cons of it. I may say that I particularly resented the fact that it was taken for granted on the part of some that, because I am a Methodist, I would accept as authentic a place which was owned chiefly by Nonconformists. I resolved to remain detached from the prejudices which have so long prevented clear and independent judgement upon matters such as these. But I found myself at variance with such a stalwart as Hugh Price Hughes. He paid a visit to Jerusalem in 1901, and he wrote in the *Methodist Times*, which he edited, on March 28th of that year:

'I was so convinced that this was indeed "the place where the Lord lay" that if an angel had suddenly appeared I should not have been at all surprised, but I should have turned to him with eager confidence and exclaimed, "That is where my Lord's body rested from Friday to the first day of the week, was it not?" I could not resist the desire to place my poor body on the very spot on which the Sacred Body once rested. For a space I lay there flat on my back.'

This quotation will serve to show how the Garden Tomb theory influenced even the most intelligent of the Victorian divines. It is not surprising that the same legends and decorations at the Holy Sepulchre which disgusted them should cause people even to-day, who have a superficial knowledge of these things, to turn hopefully to an attractive alternative for the Golgotha scene. Soon after he wrote the above, Hugh Price Hughes sent a letter to the *Westminster Gazette* to say that the only evidence of the traditional site was a foolish dream of the Empress Helena in A.D. 326. Did he not know that authentic history knows nothing of this dream, and did he never try to discover any historical facts in favour of the Holy Sepulchre? Such ideas as his have persisted, and in a recent book by a famous Methodist preacher who visited the Holy Land the view is expressed that the Garden Tomb is authentic. I do not think so, and I say why in the pages that follow. It should be remembered that this was originally written for men who were in Jerusalem and could visit the places mentioned, but the authorities I quote are, of course, accessible elsewhere.

Where did It Happen?

I do not think that it matters very much where Jesus died and was buried. What is of importance to us is that He is not dead any more, but is very much alive in the modern world, and is a living reality to people everywhere. After all, I would tell the men, if you had a friend who died you would be grieved, and would mark the grave in memory of him. But if you suddenly discovered that he was not dead at all, but alive and with you, it would be his companionship that would be a marvel to you, not the place where he happened to die and was buried. So it is with Jesus. It does not matter where He rose from the dead. What matters is that He is with us all the time. Not His empty tomb, but my full heart is all the evidence I need. Nor need we take the point of view that there is some virtue in the very rock of a holy place, some emanation that can be gained by kissing it, or that a prayer said there has more value than one said in London or New York.

I used to make it clear that although I would prefer to accept the Garden Tomb, because it has more pleasant surroundings than the Holy Sepulchre, yet I could not believe that it actually is the place where Jesus was buried; and although I did not care for the gloomy dilapidated church, with lamps and candles all over the place, I thought that the Holy Sepulchre was more likely to mark the true site of the Crucifixion and Resurrection of Jesus than anywhere else. Needless to say, if it is the truth we want, we will realize that the accumulation of both legends and decorations round a place has nothing to do with its authenticity, and that history is not a matter of taste, but of evidence. I am sure some people have come to believe that the Garden Tomb is genuine because they like the look of it! Had they seen it a hundred years ago, however, they would presumably have rejected it, because it was full of rubbish and there was no garden there. Such decisions are actually 'wish-fulfilments'.

It was necessary also for me to assure the men that there is no truth whatever in the statement sometimes made that 'Catholics accept the Holy Sepulchre and Protestants the Garden Tomb'. Protestants have the right of private judgement, and they can accept or reject whichever place they please. Sometimes the question of 'commercialization' was brought into the discussion, but that has nothing to do with it. Some visitors arrived in Jerusalem with the fixed idea that the holy places are 'commercialized', whatever they meant by that, and people usually manage to see what they are looking for. I think the idea originated from the books of travellers in the bad old days of the Turkish rule. Certainly there was never any charge for us to enter the Holy Sepulchre, and in the scores of times I took parties round Jerusalem, the only place where I was asked for money by a custodian of a Christian holy place was at the Garden Tomb! It was not for that reason, however, that I decided that the place is not genuine.

Jesus was Crucified Outside the City

A fact which has perplexed most people is that the traditional site of Calvary is inside the Old City, whereas it says plainly in Hebrews xiii. 12 that Jesus 'suffered without the gate', and in John xix. 20 that 'the place where Jesus was crucified was nigh to the city': therefore, obviously, not inside it. Mrs. Alexander's famous hymn:

> There is a green hill far away,
> Without a city wall,

naturally cannot be accepted as evidence, although men quoted that to me more than they quoted the Scriptures, possibly because they sang the hymn so often in childhood. They came to Jerusalem looking for that green hill, and were disappointed to be shown the Calvary Chapel in the Church of the Holy Sepulchre. They were very surprised, and slightly incredulous, when I pointed out to them that it nowhere says in the Bible that Calvary was a hill. All we can be sure of is that the Crucifixion was in a prominent place, as in Matthew xxvii. 55 we read that many women stood 'beholding from afar'. As Calvary was 'nigh to the city', it must have been to its north, for the other three walls were above precipitous slopes.

This difficulty is not a new one. Several pilgrims in past centuries recorded their doubts about the genuineness of the Holy Sepulchre because it was inside the city. An Englishman named Willibald, though, who visited Jerusalem in A.D. 754, decided that Queen Helena—who was supposed to have found the site of Calvary—

must have extended the city wall so as to include the Holy Sepulchre. He certainly did not mean, as some declare, that she transported the site of Calvary into the city for safety's sake. What Willibald wrote is in Vol. 3 of the Palestine Pilgrims' Texts. This does bring home to us, however, the obvious fact that the Emperor Constantine, Helena's son, who first built the Holy Sepulchre, could easily have extended the walls to include a Calvary outside it, had he so desired. As a matter of fact Byzantine churches were built outside the city, like St. Stephen's. Surely Constantine knew as well as we do that the Crucifixion took place outside Herod's city. As a matter of fact, I feel sure that he would never have located Calvary in such an unlikely place—under an abominable pagan temple, too—unless *he knew very well that at the time of the Crucifixion the city wall was in a different place.*

Where was the City Wall?

Now this idea, that the north wall of Jerusalem in the days of Jesus went through the middle of the present city, fits in with the facts we know. Excavations at Herod's Citadel show plainly enough the wall of New Testament days. It does not follow the line of the present wall, but it turns a corner at that point, and its wide curve points eastwards, towards David Street. Without any doubt it ran along the side of David Street, which was the moat outside it, and went straight across to the Temple Area. When we climbed up the steep lane which is the first on the right along David Street, and stood up there overlooking it, we were right on the line of the old wall. One can see from there, too, the dome covering the Holy Sepulchre and the Dome of the Rock where the Temple was. Calvary was apparently a little mound on a rise of ground just outside the wall here and plainly visible from the Temple, where the priests could see Jesus on the Cross, and mock Him, as we are told they did.

But in the days of Jesus there was a suburb to the north of this wall, and it had its own wall round it, some pieces of which have been found between the Antonia Palace (where Ecce Homo Convent is now) and the Holy Sepulchre. Other pieces of it show that it ran down towards the Citadel, which was Herod's Palace, somewhere near the present German Church of the Redeemer. This wall round the suburb is wall No. 2, and Calvary lay in a sort of L-shaped dent in it, rather like the dent you can see in the south wall, towards Zion, to-day. Look at the map for a moment. You can see the line of wall No. 2, which was the boundary of the city

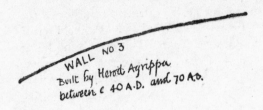

WALL No 3
Built by Herod Agrippa
between c 40 A.D. and 70 A.D.

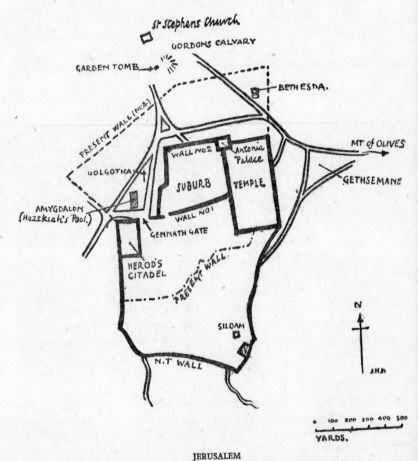

St Stephens Church

GORDONS CALVARY

GARDEN TOMB

BETHESDA.

PRESENT WALL (Nth.)

WALL No 2

Antonia Palace

MT of OLIVES

GOLGOTHA

SUBURB

TEMPLE

GETHSEMANE

AMYGDALON
(Hezekiah's Pool.)

WALL No 1

GENNATH GATE

HEROD'S
CITADEL

PRESENT WALL.

N

SILOAM

N.T WALL

JHD

0   100 200 300 400 500
YARDS.

JERUSALEM

——————— Line of Wall in New Testament times.
- - - - - - - - Line of Hadrian's Wall, A.D. 135.

when Jesus was crucified. The Holy Sepulchre stands to-day just outside where this wall was.

All this fits in very well with a description we have of Jerusalem written by Josephus in the year A.D. 70. He was a kind of war correspondent with Titus' army, which besieged Jerusalem in that year and destroyed it.

In the chapter describing Jerusalem (*Wars of the Jews*, p. 339 in Everyman's Edition) he says that in his day there were three walls to the north of Jerusalem, being three lines of defences. Wall No. 1 can be seen at the Citadel; wall No. 2, the one around the suburb, started from Gennath, a gate near the Citadel, and reached Antonia (top of p. 340); and wall No. 3 went right out to the 'caverns of the kings' and along to the Kedron Valley. Pieces of wall No. 3 were found in 1925 near the Tombs of the Kings, a quarter of a mile up the Nablus road, well outside the present wall. It was built by Agrippa after the time of Jesus. So it is the middle wall, No. 2, that interests us most, because it was the outer wall of Jerusalem in New Testament times. This, of course, cannot possibly be on the line of the wall we see to-day. Josephus says (p. 351) that there was a weak place in this middle wall somewhere to the north-west, which agrees with the idea that there was an L-shaped depression in it (Agrippa built wall No. 3 in order to remedy this); and (on p. 356) how Titus captured the outer wall, No. 3, and encamped inside it, being, however, out of range of the Jewish archers, which could hardly be true if those archers were on the line of the *present* north wall. And he tells (p. 376) how the Romans put up a bank at the Pool Amygdalon, which is now Hezekiah's Pool, to the north of David Street, and was thus outside the wall in New Testament times. So the wall to-day along the north of the city was built at a later time. It is wall No. 4, and has nothing to do with the situation of Calvary.

I ought to add that if one goes on reading Josephus' book one will find that on pp. 351 and 376, when he is describing the attack on the city, he changes his numbering of the walls, and calls the outside wall No. 1 and the inner one No. 3, and so on, as the defences were demolished.

Now, add to all this the following fact. There is nowhere along the *present north wall* any trace of masonry earlier than A.D. 135, when Hadrian built a Roman city at Jerusalem with a completely new boundary. As a matter of fact, the only part of it which does date from Hadrian is the Roman gateway we had seen half-buried beside the Damascus Gate. The foundations of the wall itself were put there in the fourth or fifth centuries A.D., so it is late Roman or Byzantine. The gateway looks like part of a triumphal arch of

Hadrian, and may not originally have been a gateway in the city wall. The Palestine Government Department of Antiquities made excavations at the present wall in 1938, and recorded their findings in the *Department of Antiquities Quarterly*, Vol. X, No. 1.

In a little book sold at the Garden Tomb, *Moriah, the Place of Sacrifice*, by L. T. Pearson, it says on p. 9 that 'through this gate Christ bore His cross to Calvary'. This is quite impossible. The gate was not built until long afterwards.

Constantine was not deluded by the appearance of the city. He knew that it was on quite a different plan from the Jerusalem of Herod's day, and the obvious place for the Crucifixion was 'nigh to the city'—much nearer the original wall, No. 2, than the green hill we can see, which is too far away.

Gennath, the gate mentioned by Josephus, outside which it is probable that Jesus died, means in Hebrew 'a garden', implying that a garden lay just outside that part of the city north of the Citadel, which would also be beside a public road and at a good place for an execution. We are told in John's Gospel that 'in the place where he was crucified there was a garden' and that the tomb was also in the garden. Two typical Jewish tombs, by the way, can be seen inside the Holy Sepulchre Church, in the Syrian Chapel off the rotunda behind the Tomb itself. They are called the tombs of Joseph of Arimathea and Nicodemus, but whether that be true or not, they certainly prove positively that once this place was outside the city, for people were buried there!

Also, eye-witnesses have described the remains of a rock-cut chamber beneath the marble Tomb of Christ in the Holy Sepulchre. Traces of quarrying there were seen in A.D. 670; pilgrims before the Crusades saw pieces of original rock in it; and when the place was rebuilt after a fire in 1808 evidences of a rock-cut tomb were seen. Pierotti, who wrote a book called *Jerusalem Explored*, describes in it his interviews with reliable witnesses who saw the actual sepulchre when it was being repaired. The foremost archaeologist of Palestine, L-H. Vincent, also gives evidence of the existence of a genuine tomb under the protecting marble in the Holy Sepulchre. His book, *Jerusalem Nouvelle*, is written in French. The tomb has been deliberately destroyed several times, so it is now reduced to a mere fragment of rock.

There is, therefore, no reason to reject the Holy Sepulchre because of its position within the present walls. On the contrary, it is in a very likely place.

The 'Invention of the Cross'

I do not propose to enlarge upon the legends and traditions that have gathered round the Holy Sepulchre, nor upon the circumstances which led up to its location, and the dedication of the church on September 14th, A.D. 335. Eusebius described how Constantine, after the Council of Nicea in 325, decided to 'make that most blessed spot, the place of the Resurrection, visible to all and given over to veneration', and found it 'against all hope', believing that Hadrian's temple to Aphrodite had destroyed all remains of it. E. T. Richmond's little booklet, *The Sites of the Crucifixion and Resurrection*, describes the excavations that were made at the time, how the hillside was pared away to leave a rock-cut monument round the tomb. The tradition that spanned the 300 years between Pilate and Constantine cannot be ignored. There were Christians in Jerusalem nearly all the time, and it is amazing that at the place they pointed to, under a long-established heathen temple, was found a tomb that agrees in every particular with the Gospel narrative.

There can be no possible doubt that the place located in A.D. 325 is the place now covered by the Holy Sepulchre, so the tradition is unbroken since that time. The approximate place of execution could be known, at any rate, just as we know to-day that the Turks executed people outside the Jaffa Gate, though nobody, I suppose, could point to the exact spot where one particular victim died. And on one point let us be quite clear. Eusebius, who described the building of the church at the time, says nothing whatever about St. Helena miraculously finding the True Cross at the site, and so locating it. That is a legend that arose later.

The story is that she discovered the wood of the Cross in a cavern under Calvary and by its miraculous powers proved conclusively that here was the right place. We need not believe all that, for those were credulous days, but the significant thing about it is that in the present Chapel of the Invention of the Cross is a cistern which could very well have been a reservoir for the garden. One pilgrim described holes in its roof for buckets. It was naïvely suggested to me that the word 'invention' means that Helena invented the whole thing! *Invention*, I would remind the men, is a Latin word which means 'discovery', a 'coming upon', in the same way as the word 'prevent' originally meant 'come before', as in the old prayer: 'Prevent us, O Lord, in all our doings.'

The Place of a Skull

All four Gospels relate how Jesus was taken to a place called 'The Skull', which in Latin is *Calvary* and in Hebrew *Golgotha*. It is clear, therefore, that the writers were referring to a definite location that had this particular name during the first century. It might be that 'Golgotha' is really *gal go'ata*, the 'hill of Goah', a place somewhere north of Jerusalem mentioned in Jeremiah xxxi. 39, or that the reference is to an eminence that resembled the top of a human head, much as we refer to the crown of a hill. It may even be that there was a legend, mentioned by Jerome in A.D. 400 and which has persisted until this day, that the skull of Adam was buried in a cave under the hill. It may be that the configuration of the cliff resembled a death's head or, less likely, that at the customary place of execution there were skulls displayed. The significant thing about this name is not that we can expect to get a clue to its appearance, but that the site possessed a name and could therefore be located. The early Christians certainly were interested in knowing where New Testament events took place. Long before Constantine built the Church of the Nativity at Bethlehem, for instance, Origen, who was in Palestine in A.D. 215, declared that he was shown the cave of the Birth of Christ at Bethlehem. They were interested in seeing where He was born, so we must not say that the Christians of that time were not concerned to know where He died. When afterwards they wanted to build a church over Golgotha, they pointed to the place where the Holy Sepulchre is to-day.

General Gordon had the extraordinary idea that the hilly range which runs north and south through Jerusalem parallel with the Kedron Valley resembled an enormous skeleton. He said that the feet were at Siloam, the pelvis at the Temple, and so on. He decided that the head was where the Moslem cemetery is, and was therefore the Place of a Skull. This was in 1883, although a German named Otto Thenius had suggested in 1842 that this hill might be Calvary.

Gordon had the most fantastic ideas about Biblical geography. One can find some strange suggestions of his about the Garden of Eden's situation, as well as of this skeleton lying across Jerusalem, in the *Palestine Exploration Fund Quarterly Statement*, in the volumes for 1885 (p. 79), for 1901 (p. 299), and for 1904 (p. 40). He was contemptuous about the idea of the hill possessing eyeholes like those of a skull, and insisted that the plan of the hill, looking at it from above, showed the outline of a human head. He lived before the invention of the aeroplane, or he would have been able to see his error, but he had seen a contour map of 1864 showing the line of 2,549 feet above sea-level in the shape of a skull! A line forming such a shape is purely accidental and temporary, because it passes over accumulated ground that could not possibly have been there at the time of the Crucifixion.

Besides, surely he did not mean to suggest that the Herodian residents called the place 'The Skull' because they had a contour map? There is no other way of seeing that shape. Gordon, I may add, also thought that a river would one day flow from this hill to sweeten the Dead Sea, and that Constantine built the Holy Sepulchre behind the Garden Tomb, where St. Stephen's Church is. No wonder that L-H. Vincent said that 'General Gordon deserves more fame for his heroic defence of Khartoum than for his theories about Eden and Calvary'.

If one stands in front of Gordon's Calvary, as it is called now, one can see, with a little imagination, two holes like eye-sockets. But we saw holes like eyes in several hills in Palestine, pitted as the limestone rock is everywhere with caves. Besides, it appears very likely that these particular holes were made by quarrying far more recently than 2,000 years ago. Anyway, the likeness to a skull is very superficial, and it is my experience that visitors never thought of such a likeness until I pointed it out to them. I am sure that the hill does not resemble a skull sufficiently clearly for it to earn the local name of Golgotha. Indeed, some people are simply unable to see any skull-like form in the cliff. Even in the book sold at the Garden Tomb, Rider Haggard, a novelist who is extensively quoted in it, but who can hardly be regarded as an authority either upon Biblical or archaeological subjects, tells how his nephew could not recognize any skull shape in the hill. So the resemblance to a death's head is not universally acknowledged. Such evidence as this that Golgotha is here is very flimsy indeed.

The Garden Tomb

Jerusalem is set in the midst of an immense cemetery. There are tombs along its southern border, notably at Akeldama; to the east, on both sides of the Kedron Valley; to the west, where the Herodian mausoleum is; and along the northern boundary. The tomb near Gordon's Calvary is not therefore an isolated one. Indeed, within a few yards of it there are many others very much like it. There is a series of rock-cut tombs behind the wall of the Garden Tomb, as we had seen beside the Church of St. Stephen, farther up the Nablus road. The lay-out of three graves round a little chamber cut in the rock is the customary fashion with most of them. They are considered to be tombs of the second century, used again in the fifth and sixth centuries as burial places for Christians, because St. Stephen's Monastery was there in Byzantine times. I do not think there can be much doubt that the Garden Tomb is part of this cemetery. In fact, E. T. Richmond, formerly Director of the Department of Antiquities in Palestine, declares that it offers no evidence of any work earlier than the Byzantine period, which was roughly A.D. 300 to A.D. 600 in Palestine.

It is as well to get the actual name of any authority who is quoted in these matters. I found that people were fond of saying airily, 'Archaeologists say . . .' when they had no proof of their statements. Scientists and R.E. officers who excavated in the city during last century were admittedly pioneers in digging round Jerusalem, and many of their claims have been modified by archaeologists of to-day. The Department of Antiquities keeps records of all modern discoveries, of course.

When we were at St. Stephen's, we saw the tomb inscriptions they have there. They are written in ancient Greek characters and date from Byzantine times. On one the men could make out for themselves, even though they did not know Greek, the letters NONNO and ONIC, which belong to the man's name: Nonnus Onesimus. Somebody inquired whether he was the Onesimus mentioned in the Bible! Actually, it says on the tombstone who he was. It reads:

'Special tomb of Deacon Nonnus Onesimus, of the Holy Resurrection of Christ and of this monastery.'

The Holy Sepulchre was called the Church of the Holy Resurrection (indeed, that is still the Arabs' name for it), and it is known that in those days some priests and deacons of that church were connected with St. Stephen's Monastery. Nonnus Onesimus was one of them, apparently, and was buried in this cemetery.

What has this to do with the Garden Tomb? In the little book called *The Garden Tomb*, by A. W. Crawley-Bovey, which is sold there, on p. 38, two inscriptions are quoted, said to be in St. Stephen's graveyard. One is:

'To Nonnus and Onesimus, Deacons of the Church of the Witness of the Resurrection of Christ.'

The other is:

'Buried near his Lord.'

It can be seen how inaccurate the first one is. There is nothing on the tombstone about two deacons, but of only one with two names, and there is nothing about 'witness'. Yet the writer of that little book says that here is a proof that a church existed nearby, presumably where the Garden Tomb is, as a witness to the Resurrection! We really ought to be accurate when quoting things like this.

When did such a church exist? In Byzantine times? No, because we know that the Holy Sepulchre was built then. Before Constantine? Certainly not; it is a Byzantine inscription. And what of 'Buried near his Lord', which we are told means that the deacon was laid to rest close to the tomb of Jesus? Such an inscription does not exist, and there is no evidence that it has ever existed. I have looked at all the fragments of tombstones at St. Stephen's; and nowhere there, nor in their museum, nor in the report issued when excavations there were finished in 1894, is there the slightest trace or reference to such an inscription. Where is it? What is the name of the man who saw it? When did he see it? According to L-H. Vincent, who wrote a little book in French on the *Garden Tomb*, the phrase 'Buried near his Lord' originated in an American newspaper, the *North Christian Advocate*, in 1889!

The Tomb Itself

The Garden Tomb was accidentally discovered in 1867 by a Greek, and at that time it was full of rubbish and bones. It changed hands several times, and in 1892 it came under the control of a number of trustees, with the aid of a public subscription, who were charged with the duty of keeping the garden and tomb 'sacred as a quiet spot'. It aroused wide interest in Evangelical circles at the time, as in those Victorian days there was less archaeological knowledge than to-day about Jerusalem, and there was a great deal of disgust at the excesses and abuses of the holy places. It was a welcome change from the ornate Holy Sepulchre to see this bare rocky tomb in a carefully laid out garden with a skull-like formation on a green hill nearby. The tomb is, however, cut in a quarry face, not in the scarped face of the limestone hill itself, and it is doubtful if the quarry was there in New Testament times.

The famous D. L. Moody preached to a congregation on Gordon's Calvary, and so did Dr. Talmadge. The most that can be said for the place to-day is that it is a pleasant spot outside the city, and it is interesting to see what a tomb in a garden looked like. Many of the trustees are British Israelites, and their book is produced by the Covenant Publishing Co., Ltd., which does publishing for the British Israel World Federation.

There is, nearby, a wine-press of uncertain date, which it is suggested shows that a garden used to be there. These are very common round Jerusalem. Presses were found all the way up the valley of Gethsemane. There are also the marks, with a channel, of what appears to have been a pool. It is claimed that it was a font, but it is not at all like one. Probably it was part of the stables which are known to have been there in Crusader times. Stones of a wall outside the tomb suggest that the stables extended from the face of the cliff, and a wide feeding trough still lies at its entrance. If for many years this narrow tomb was used as part of a stable, it is not surprising that the step is worn. We need not conclude that it was worn by pilgrims venerating the tomb! If any one imagines that this trough —admitted as of Crusader origin in the *Garden Tomb* booklet on p. 42—is a groove for a rolling-stone, let him go to the Tombs of the Kings, near St. George's Cathedral, to see a genuine rolling-stone, and let him notice the difference.

There were crosses on the wall, of course, as in other tombs used later for Christian burial, and it was not unusual to alter graves (if indeed this one has been altered) to fit tenants other than those by whom the tombs were originally used. In any case, surely it is not seriously suggested that masons worked on the grave to make it fit the body of Jesus on the night of the Crucifixion? One of the St. Stephen's tombs has been quite changed from its original form. It cannot truly be said that two of the graves in the Garden Tomb are not completed. They have been used many times for different purposes. The place was full of bones when it was found. Nor is there any evidence that the remains of a stone wall outside it were once part of a church. There is a hole in the wall of the Garden Tomb, but such an aperture to illumine the tomb and allow the women to see its interior on Easter morning is not demanded by the Gospel records. Indeed, they imply the opposite, as we get the impression of a sepulchre that was completely sealed when the stone was placed before its entrance. The Garden Tomb could fit the details of the Easter story as we know them just as many other tombs do, notably the Tomb in the Holy Sepulchre.

Besides, the Garden Tomb is not particularly a rich man's tomb. As I described in the last chapter, I had the good fortune to be present in June, 1942, at the excavation of a first-century Jewish tomb on the Mount of Olives, which had the usual three benches round its interior and was full of bones. It was of the style of grave for burying people of ordinary social standing, and such tombs are quite common round Jerusalem. We do not know how rich Joseph of Arimathaea was, but emphasis is placed upon his wealth in the Gospel record, so we could expect a special sort of tomb. We can see in the Kedron Valley one or two tombs made by rich men just before the time of Jesus. They are cut out of the solid rock of the hillside, making distinct and permanent monuments, so that men later believed them to be the tombs of Absalom and Zechariah. It is not impossible that this was the sort of sepulchre that Joseph made for himself, if not so large and without an elaborate roof, into which the body of Jesus was placed. That also may account for the 'monument', as they called it, round which the rotunda of Constantine's church was built. At any rate, if Joseph's masons did not cut such a monument out of the hill, those of Constantine did around the original grave. It may even be that the artistic rock-cutters of Petra were employed upon this tomb. The semi-barbaric kiosk of marble we see in the Holy Sepulchre to-day is its nineteenth-century successor. But there is nothing in the Garden Tomb to suggest a rich man's grave. Professor R. A. S. Macalister wrote in the *Palestine Exploration Fund Quarterly Statement*, 1907, p. 232: 'Nothing whatever can be said in favour of the tomb.'

The Relic of Venus-worship

When one visits the Garden Tomb one is shown a queer-shaped piece of white plaster which is said to be a copy of a carved stone found in some debris near the tomb in 1923 by a Miss Hussey, who was looking for some relics of the Venus-worship by which Hadrian is known to have desecrated the tomb of Jesus. Hadrian's temple to Venus could not have been here, however, because it seems certain from the records that the Holy Sepulchre church was built on its site, within the present city walls.

Now I am not saying that this lady was determined to find some such object as this, and that her search was rewarded much as Queen Helena's was, who looked for the True Cross and found timber that answered its description, but I do think that excess of zeal hindered calm judgement in this matter. E. T. Richmond, the archaeologist mentioned earlier, says that this object has been proved to be *a model carved by a Danish sculptor only fifteen years before it was found!* This man used to live there as caretaker, and he carved little models like this, which he sold to visitors.

A certain professor, who is quoted as saying that this object is a genuine relic of a pagan cult, wrote to *The Times* on September 16th, 1924, to deny it. He said that the stone is not a copy of the temple of Aphrodite (another name for Venus), and it is wrong to connect this stone in any way with an altar belonging to the goddess and still more with any question concerning the situation of the Holy Sepulchre, with which it has nothing whatever to do. Now that is plain and definite. There is no evidence that a shrine of any kind was ever at the place. This carved piece of stone is not authentic. And there is no reason to believe that one or two holes in the cliff face at the tomb are the niches of a Venus *columbarium*, which it does not resemble.

Mount Moriah

The last point I want to deal with is that contained in a pamphlet called *Moriah, the Place of Sacrifice*, by L. T. Pearson, who used to live at the Garden Tomb. In it he propounds a new form of an old theory: that Gordon's Calvary, the hill long known as Bezetha, is in reality the peak of Mount Moriah, the hill upon which Abraham tried to offer up Isaac, and where later Solomon built the Temple, and it is, therefore, God's chosen place of sacrifice. The writer says that Moriah is a long backbone of rock running from where the Temple used to be up to this eminence outside the city, that Solomon built the Temple on the *southern* portion of Moriah, and (p. 6) that 'God had to preserve this northern summit of Moriah for the last sacrifice ever to be acceptably offered'.

This is all part of a complicated argument about the death of Jesus being 'a burnt offering and a peace offering' on Mount Moriah, the traditional Jewish place of sacrifice, and at the same time a sin offering, which was made outside the city. Furthermore, he says that God ordained that the Jewish Temple should be built on a lower part of Moriah, and the city wall should go across the hill, so that Jesus could be sacrificed on the northern height outside the city. All this is reminiscent of General Gordon's notions. Now, everybody is entitled to his own opinion about a matter like this, but when it comes to using such a phrase as 'This northern end of Moriah is Golgotha', the answer must be made: that statement goes against the facts.

Bezetha is not Moriah. Mount Moriah for thousands of years has been the name of the hill on which stood the Temple and on which now stands the Dome of the Rock. It is completely unwarrantable to declare that a ridge of hills is all one hill. A contour map shows how the land drops into a natural declivity between Moriah and Bezetha. One might as well say that Mount Scopus is the Mount of Olives. Besides that, 2 Chronicles vii does not say that the mount, but the house, i.e. the Temple, was hallowed, that God's name should be there for ever. There is nothing in the Bible that says either that the Temple was built on a lower part of the holy Mount Moriah, or that the sacrifice of Jesus would take place on that Mount; nor is it required by any orthodox doctrine of the Atonement.

He shared our pain. He died our death. That is the tremendous truth about Calvary. Where it happened is purely a matter of speculative interest. Why it happened is overwhelmingly important. The Cross is the climax of fellowship between God and man. It is the eternal emblem of love, that He has identified Himself not only with human birth, and human life with its joys and tears and temptations, but that He is at one with us in sorrow and in death.

What is the truth about Calvary and the Tomb? Not that it happened here or there, but that Jesus is alive, and leads us with a pierced hand.

CHAPTER IX

EASTER

In the year of our Lord 192, before Constantine the Great and Helena, before the Invention of the Holy Cross, Narcissus was Bishop of Jerusalem, and he, when he was going to hold service on Easter Even, was told by his servants that there was no oil either in the jar or in the lamps. When the holy and believing man heard this, being full of faith, he ordered the servants to draw water and bring it to him. When the water was brought to him, he prayed, blessed the water, and bade them pour it into the lamps. Then of a sudden, by a wondrous power unheard of in any other age, the water took upon itself the fatness of oil, and being lighted from heaven, made the light of the lamps shine more brightly than it was wont to do.

FELIX FABRI, A.D. 1480.

LIKE Christmas at Bethlehem, Easter in Jerusalem is an unforgettable experience, and we who were stationed in the Holy City, and those who could contrive to get leave there at that time took advantage of every opportunity, not only to see the age-old ceremonies of the Eastern Churches, but to visit the scenes of the sufferings and Resurrection of Christ and to worship there in our own way. This chapter consists of extracts from my diary. They recount some of the things I saw and did during Easter, 1942. Much the same happened the following Easter, except that then I was able to preach on Good Friday morning on Mount Calvary, at an open-air service on the roof of the Holy Sepulchre.

Saturday, March 28

The day before Palm Sunday is called 'Lazarus Saturday' by the Eastern Churches, and the Holy Week services begin with the ceremonial entry of the individual patriarchs into the Holy Sepulchre during the afternoon. This year the Orthodox Easter occurs at the same time as the Western. This happens every three or four years, for the Eastern Churches use the obsolete Julian's Calendar. In consequence, this year the ancient rules made for this eventuality will apply, and each Church will be enabled to hold its own ceremonies without interfering with the others. It so happened that the published plan of services (it looks like a Methodist circuit plan!) took no account of summer-time, and I reached the Holy Sepulchre Church an hour too soon—at 2.30 p.m. This was a fortunate thing, because the crowd that gathered later had not yet arrived, and after watching the preparations being made, altar-cloths being spread in the Coptic chapel behind the Tomb, the kindling of wicks in a multitude of glass vessels of oil, and men climbing ladders to light the immense candles before the Tomb and round the Stone of Unction, I mounted the steps leading to the Calvary Chapel and took a vantage-point by the balustrade overlooking the Stone. I had a clear view, too, of the great door of the church, and I spent the time watching the strange medley of people as they came in and stood beneath me.

There were representatives of many branches of the Christian faith, distinguishable either by their features or their garb. There were priests of the Eastern Churches in black flowing robes and tall hats, all with long beards of black or grey; Franciscan monks in brown habits; Copts in turbans; Christian Arabs, often poorly dressed; Armenians who appeared to be rather more prosperous; Greeks in Army uniform, officers and men; as well as many members of the Empire forces in the variety of dress of the different units: khaki and blue varying the grey of nursing sisters and the darker blue of Australian V.A.Ds. Priests and monks as well as laymen and women and little children were constantly kneeling and bowing forward to kiss the Stone of Unction that lay under a dozen immense alabaster lamps, all now shining between the flanking candles whose big flames flickered quite 20 feet above the ground. The Moslem doorkeeper, of hereditary honour, sat in his great cubby-hole lined with carpets, and the District Commissioner, with a cross of palm in his button-hole, stood awaiting the first patriarch, the Latin, to arrive.

As the time drew nearer, more people began to congregate round the Stone of Unction, and two files of choir-boys wearing crimson cloaks lined the way from the Stone to the Rotunda, in which lies the Sepulchre itself. I looked above me. The bricks in the vaulted roof lacked mortar between them, and appeared to be about to fall on us. The walls, where they could be seen between the criss-crossing timbers that held them up, were dank and peeling. And yet there was an awesomeness about it all. The massive wooden doors were closed for a minute, only the candles giving us light, and then they swung open to admit a short procession of priests followed by the Latin Patriarch. Preceding them walked three dragomans, or *kuwasses* as they are called, in scarlet and gold and fierce black moustaches, loudly banging their staffs before them to clear the way. The D.C. went forward and bowed a greeting. In front of the Stone the Patriarch stood a moment while a crimson robe with a hole for his head was dropped over his shoulders. He was an old man with a white imperial beard. Italian by race, he carries a Vatican passport, and thus he is a neutral and can go and come as he chooses in these days of war. After some crossing and censing of himself, he knelt upon the cushion placed with a piece of carpet in readiness for him against the Stone, and bowed himself over it with the sign of the Cross. I noticed that he did not actually kiss the Stone. Then, forming into procession, the boys and the priests and the Patriarch moved slowly into the Rotunda, chanting as they went. Each held a candle; one bore a cross; another, a banner. As the Patriarch pushed between the thick wooden planks that obstruct a free entry into the Rotunda, I wondered if he was thinking of the spacious grandeur of St. Peter's in Rome, and comparing it with the dinginess of this, the heart of Christendom.

Next to me, leaning upon the balustrade in the crowd that had now gathered on the top of Calvary, was a young Greek monk in flowing black with a rimless black hat and a good-sized dark beard in spite of his youth. In an atrocious mixture of English, Greek, and Arabic, he commented to me upon the scene, pointing out representatives of various Churches and nations. He seemed to regard it all with a good deal of humour, and his smile became broader when I said 'No' to his inquiry whether I was a Catholic and 'Yes' when he asked if I was a Protestant. He told me his name was Christopheros.

At intervals of half an hour arrived in similar manner the Orthodox, Coptic, and Armenian Patriarchs, in that order, the Syrian bishop passing into the church meanwhile with very little ceremony. Each had representatives of his own community to welcome him, and each was greeted by the D.C. A different carpet and cushion was placed in readiness for each to kiss the Stone, after he had stood first to be arrayed in scarlet. Each ceremony exceeded the last in brightness of colour and richness of ceremonial. As was quite common, the Orthodox Patriarch had sent a bishop to deputize for him, so Christopheros informed me. One by one, the bishop took great books bound in silver and ornamented with enamel pictures, and some ikons and the like, and, kissing them, returned them to their bright-robed bearers, who in their turn kissed his hand that held them. He kindled censers with incense from elaborate silver boxes some of them carried, and three times swung the censer over the Stone and over the priests and the people. A sickly cloud came up to me as I leaned over, high above their heads. Then he took a cross of flashing blood-red rubies and carried it through the crowd, blessing the people as he walked slowly round the 6-foot slab of limestone which is the Stone of Unction. The procession in its turn entered the Rotunda.

The Armenians had the largest crowd of all, and their ceremony was even more elaborate. Their Patriarch stood to be robed just inside the door, and was dressed in a gorgeous garment of blue and gold and white. Beside him I saw my friend, Father Cyril, in a bright purple robe, directing the ritual. These are truly Oriental Christians, and beside them the Roman Catholics look like Nonconformists. It was a wonderful scene from where I stood, and worth waiting to see. When at last the Patriarch had kissed the Stone and blessed the people, he moved into the Rotunda and the throng followed him.

I went quickly down, and along the ambulatory that encircles the Orthodox Cathedral, in order to enter the Rotunda from the other side. I paused to see the Latin procession as it returned from the Franciscan chapel, with the red-robed Patriarch following it. At one place they all knelt and chanted prayers, each boy and priest and bishop holding a candle and a book, lighting up the gloom with a medieval beauty. There was a crowd milling about the Sepulchre when at last I found myself under the great dome, and through it pushed priests and monks of many kinds, in bright robes and drab habits. The Coptic bishop made his way past me, flicking holy water right and left upon the people, and I was unlucky enough to get a great splash of sweet-smelling liquid on my face and the front of my uniform.

A bearded Syrian priest stood by me, and in excellent English courteously inquired whether I was a priest, as he noticed my black tie. I replied that I was a Methodist minister. He expressed a little puzzlement, and at his request I explained to him what Methodists are, regretting in a way that I was adding to the number of the divisions of Christianity represented in the Holy Sepulchre that Easter, but at the same time realizing that here was the focus-point of Christendom, and the more of us who were there the better. Since he imagined that Methodism was an insignificant little sect, I told him of the 40 million Methodists all over the world. He then informed me that, like the Armenians and Copts, his Church was Monophysite in doctrine. I remarked that only the previous week Father Cyril of the Armenians had told me that his own Church anathematizes the Monophysite heresy, and that they are wrongly described as such by the Latins and Orthodox because they use an old formula saying that Christ had but one nature, although they believe this means that His two natures, human and divine, were mysteriously fused into one. My companion agreed with this interpretation of the doctrine. He invited me to attend the Syrian Ceremony of the Bridegroom's Coming next day at St. Mark's Church, and I promised to be there.

I pushed through the crowd inside the church, and stepped out into the bright sunshine. In a shop nearby I bought for one piastre a cross made of long, thin palm-leaves, to send home to my small son in London.

Palm Sunday, March 29

I rose at 5 a.m. and walked under the clear stars to the Central Y.M.C.A. building to join a party of some forty people, some of them my men, and the rest Jerusalem officers, residents and visitors. We went by bus to Bethany, about three miles out of the city past Gethsemane on the main road to Jericho, and we climbed to the ruins of a Crusader castle above the village. We stood in the early light and looked at the square stone houses, the hills towards the Dead Sea stretching away like waves, and the purple curtain hung across the skyline which is the mountain range of Moab in Transjordan. The sun peeped over the Moab hills, and as it rose above them we sang 'Christ, whose glory fills the skies', and, after a prayer and a reading from the first chapter of John's Gospel, 'When morning gilds the skies'.

Then we started the climb over the Mount of Olives. It was a lovely scene, fresh and peaceful. The spring flowers and grass were under our feet, and the air was fragrant with the smell of the country in early morning. As we mounted higher, the view expanded, and we saw the silver of the Dead Sea in the distance and the Judean hills about us, with the Frank Mountain to the south. This path is one of the most authentic of the holy sites, for Jesus could scarcely have crossed the Mount of Olives by any other route. We came to the height, with Olivet higher beyond it, which is the traditional site of Bethphage. Behind a wall was a Russian church. On that turn of the path we halted for another little service. We sang 'Ride on, ride on in majesty', and 'Rejoice, the Lord is King'; and the reading was from Matthew xxi.

The path then led us to the top of the Mount of Olives, with a beautiful terraced valley to our left, and we went on past a few Arab houses with dirty children on the doorsteps, and women gossiping while a man wiped mud from a patient cow, whose tiny calf stood beside them. An Arab on a donkey passed us with a morning greeting, and we went between the high walls of some Russian compounds. We passed the Church of the Paternoster, leaving the Chapel of the Ascension on our right, and began the descent towards Jerusalem, down an old path widely stepped. A little way down in the wall on our left was a tablet marking the place of the Weeping over the City, and opposite this the ruins of an old mosque. This stood on the site of a church mentioned in Crusader itineraries. We entered the field beyond the ruins, and stood about or sat on the rocks and looked over Jerusalem. This is a vantage point for one of the loveliest sights in Palestine, especially at that hour, with the morning sun behind us shining on the domes and towers of the city. The Dome of the Rock, on the site of the Temple, stood behind the old wall as it has done for 1,300 years, and in that light every detail was plain to us, even at that distance. We could imagine how it had appeared to Jesus, with the gold shining on the front of the white House of the Lord in the centre of the Sanctuary, and the slope to the skyline within the city wall covered with flat-topped houses huddled together, and on the horizon the square bulk of Herod's Citadel.

The scene for us was indescribably lovely, and one felt like weeping to look at it. Here Jesus yearned to gather her people together under His wing, here He wept because they did not know the things that belong unto peace. Our voices rose in the still morning air with 'Glorious things of thee are spoken, Zion, city of our God', and 'Hail to the Lord's Anointed'. As one read from Matthew xxiii, and a Scottish Army chaplain spoke for a few minutes on the Entry into the City, the bells began to peal from the Russian church below us in Gethsemane. Its peaked domes shone between the cypresses and olives, and a jolly tinkling peal rang out across the Valley of the Kedron.

I want to record here the prayer we said together as we stood on that hilltop. It was written by Arthur Rugh, a former Jerusalem Y.M.C.A. secretary:

'Our Father, Father of all men, on this holy hill we lift our hearts to Thee. We thank Thee for fellowship with those in every land who wake to worship Thee. We thank Thee most of all for Him who loved this city though it crucified Him. We thank Thee that He chose to leave home and beauty to risk His life here that all men everywhere might live abundantly. Come into our hearts this morning and help us to follow Him. Bless this troubled city, over which He wept, and bring peace to Jerusalem. Bless with us this morning all who in this city or anywhere woke with anxious hearts. Pardon all our selfishness. May Christ come triumphantly into our lives this morning. And as we follow Him down into the city accept anew the dedication of our lives, that all men may soon love Him who offered here His life for a weary world. We offer our prayer in His name. Amen.'

Down by the entrance to the Latin Garden of Gethsemane, into which we looked for a moment at the flower beds with their sweet-scented stock and profusion of colour, and old, old olive trees, we regained the buses which then took us round the Old City wall to our starting place. After breakfast I went to the Central Y.M.C.A. Auditorium and took part in a National Day of Prayer church parade. There were hundreds of troops present, and it was a large and very smart assembly. The Assistant Chaplain-General read the prayers, and Major-General McConnel the lesson, and I preached the sermon. There was a march-past afterwards, and then the General talked for a while with the chaplains.

In the afternoon I saw about thirty of the members of the Wednesday Fellowship off to Bethany from the Damascus Gate, but I did not go on the Olivet pilgrimage a second time. They joined about a hundred people led by the Anglican Bishop, and afterwards they told me that it was all very impressive. The Roman Catholics in their procession carried palms and banners and made a very colourful picture. I was glad, however, that I had elected to go with the little group in the morning, before the crowds congregated on the hill. It was very hot, and I walked back through the Old City and out of the Jaffa Gate. Just outside I saw a little grey-bearded Orthodox priest furiously fighting with a big Mohammedan donkey-driver. They wrestled and pushed one another, to the amusement of the crowd. I pushed myself between them, to receive a loud stream of Arabic from them both. I put my arm about the little priest and led him away. He was trembling with anger, but I calmed him down, pointed to my clerical collar and then at him, and told him to remember that he was a *qassis* (priest). He smiled and nodded at that, and apologized, and we parted with '*Ma's-salameh*' and '*Allah yusallimak*' ('Go in peace' and 'May God preserve you'). Strange that when a priest of the Orthodox Church and a Methodist minister wish to exchange greetings, they should use as their word for God the name of an early tribal deity in Arabia.

Soon after five o'clock, I went with two or three young local preachers in khaki to the Armenian Cathedral of St. James, the historic seat of the first Bishop of Jerusalem and the burying place of the head of St. James the Less. The great and beautiful church was bright with the light from its hundreds of hanging lamps of olive-oil, and every sacred picture was veiled by a curtain, including a huge curtain across the screen which encloses the apse, on a raised dais. This 'stage effect' is due to the dramatic form which many Armenian services take, and no doubt was the forerunner of modern secular drama. High in the gallery behind were women and children; and men, crowding it, stood in the pewless body of the church. Before the altar curtain were boys and girls, and some adults, clad in the brightest of robes of many beautiful colours and designs, some stiff with brocade and elaborate embroidery in gold and silver. Each held a long candle which was lighted from a big one carried by a boy in the centre. The Patriarch was dressed in a robe of blue and red, and the higher clergy in purple, while the others and a choir of youths lining the sanctuary were in black robes. It was the famous Armenian Ceremony of the Coming of Christ, symbolizing Judgement Day. The ikons were veiled as a sign of waiting, and beside each, all round the church, stood a child whose task it would be to pull aside the curtain when the time came. The singing and chanting of the priests was singularly beautiful. They had some movement and processing, of course; and at intervals for the reading of the lessons or of a long list of donors of gifts, priests and choir and people squatted on the floor; or whenever they felt like it.

It was all very happy and informal, in a way, and yet it was an impressive ceremony, especially when the Bishop went up on to the dais before the curtain and, flanked by two youths in bright robes, besought entrance into Paradise on behalf of the people. Between his petitions he knocked loudly. A voice behind the curtain, representing God the Creator, answered him, and there followed a seemingly interminable dialogue, with the Bishop beseeching admission. It was chanted in Armenian, but I had Canon Bridgeman's little handbook with me, *Jerusalem at Worship*, and was able to follow some of the dialogue, as follows:

Patriarch: 'Open unto us, O Lord, open unto us the door of pity; to us who call upon Thee with weeping.'

Voice within: 'Who are these that I should open? For this is the door of the Lord, and the righteous enter therein.'

Patriarch: 'Not alone the righteous enter, but also sinners justified through confession and repentance.'

Voice within: 'For this is the gate of Heaven and the vale of sadness, which the Lord promised to Jacob; a rest for the righteous, a purgatory for sinners, the kingdom of Christ, the dwelling-place of the angels, the assembly of the saints, a safe haven, the house of God.'

Patriarch: 'Open unto us'. (This was repeated very many times, with hymns between, and many variants.)

Voice within: 'Come, ye blessed of my Father, inherit the Kingdom prepared for you from the foundation of the world.'

Patriarch: 'Open unto me the gates of righteousness that I may enter into them and give thanks unto the Lord.'

Then came the climax of the ceremony. All the curtains were drawn and the veils removed from the pictures, and the altar was revealed in a blaze of lights. The singing rose to a joyful crescendo, to symbolize the entry into heaven. I thought how much we missed in our own worship at home when we eschewed the dramatic element. It was more than a show to the people there. It had a symbolic and religious value. I know I wished I could have a bright-coloured robe and a candle and sit on the floor before that great curtain, to rise and share in its joyful revealing of the glories of heaven. The Armenians have had a long and sad history of persecution, and it seemed to me that their patient endurance for the joy set before them was symbolized by that Oriental display of childlike faith.

We hurried through some narrow cobbled streets to be in time for a similar, but in many ways different, ceremony, that of 'The Bridegroom's Coming' at St. Mark's Church. This tiny Crusader church stands on the site of an earlier one, a tablet from which is preserved in the wall and relates in Old Syriac (the nearest language to the Aramaic of New Testament days) that the early Christians believed here was the house of John Mark, to which Peter went after his escape from prison. Incidentally, the church is a possible site of the Last Supper and Pentecost. The Syrian Christians here are few and poor, but they maintain ceremonies dating from very primitive times. We stood by a picture of the Mother and Child—believed to be painted by St. Luke—over a silver font. The women stood at the back of the church and the men at the front, and the altar was curtained. Before it a deacon stood and recited prayers, and there was a procession outside and inside the church of boys in white, clasping candles and singing lustily, a few robed priests, and the Bishop with a big flat hat shaped like a pointed onion bulb. An immense silver cross was carried by a lad, and it rested by me. I saw that it was worked in a myriad designs in filigree, with many little bells around it. A ragged, unshaven Syrian lifted his little boy of two to see it, and the child, who was grasping a long, thin, lighted candle, gaped at the scene open-mouthed.

I and the three Methodist local preachers who were with me felt completely out of place in this ancient church, with its people in native robes, its strange ceremonies by candlelight, and the smell of incense and the weird ululations of the priest's voice. It was as though we were intruders from a modern world looking into a page from the remote past. Nothing had changed for centuries. This was the scene here when the Christian faith was still young. Maybe we were standing on the place where the first disciples met together in the days of the Acts of the Apostles.

But all I could think of was the unreality of it all. At one juncture in the service all the candles were doused, and the children had to sit in darkness. One little boy would not blow out his candle, and resisted with indignation every effort of others to do so, until somebody succeeded in extinguishing it, and he sat angrily complaining in the darkness. I sympathized with that little boy. Children are the same the world over, whatever language they speak or religion with which they are labelled. It was his own little light and he wanted to keep it. He hated the darkness, and so did I.

We crept quietly out of the church, and left that fantastic scene behind us—the quaint rites and half-forgotten symbols of a vanished age. One of my companions doubted whether that church ever saw any conversions. They had ceased to expect such things, of course. In their maintenance of traditional ceremonies they had lost their primitive evangelism. And where the Fire of Pentecost fell upon the Apostles, to set their hearts aflame with zeal and love for souls, a poor, struggling remnant wail and chant liturgies from dusty books, and a child cries because his candle is put out.

We hurried to the Y.M.C.A. canteen for a gospel service with the troops, led by a sturdy staff-sergeant and addressed by a young lance-corporal. The men sang the choruses together and heard a simple message from the text, 'What think ye of Christ?' No greater difference could be imagined between the two scenes, that in the old Syrian church and that in this cheerful soldiers' canteen. It was a day of contrasts for me.

Monday, March 30

At ten in the morning I went to meet Farik Guindi Tekla, a Coptic Christian who wants to be a priest in his own Church in Egypt, since, he told me, his mother had consecrated him from his birth to that end, and he is studying Greek and Hebrew here on his own account, and other subjects unfamiliar to his priests in Egypt. Farik is his own name, Guindi his father's, and Tekla his grandfather's. He learns Hebrew from a Liberal Jewish Rabbi, to whom he took me this morning. He is Dr. W., and lives in a modern flat, and was most cordial. I asked if I might attend his Passover service, and he was very willing to invite me. He is a German Jew, speaking excellent English, and told me of his views on Christianity and on Zionism.

He does not regard Jesus as a prophet, but as one of the great moral teachers of Judaism, perhaps the greatest. He believes in co-operation with Arabs in Palestine, and says that peace in the world must come from Jerusalem, the holy city of the three great religions, Judaism, Islam and Christianity There is room for all to co-operate, and peace here will bring peace everywhere. He said that the apparently irreligious youths in the Jewish communal settlements were religious without knowing it, for they kept the command-ment, 'Thou shalt love thy neighbour', and are beginning to form their faith after first excesses. There are many young people there who are very rich, yet have not a penny in their pockets. The Jewish nation is unique, and has a unique part to play in the world. Simply as bankers and merchants and dance-band leaders scattered about the world, Judaism cannot function properly. It needs a national consciousness to enable it to function as it should, although very differently from modern forms of nationalism. Jews can function for the peace of the world, but they can only do that when they have learned to work on the soil and cease as much as possible to be so abnormal. Only in Palestine, he thought, could such a national consciousness be fostered. Brazil or some such place would only produce another Diaspora and national rivalries. Arabs have rights here. Their nationalism and that of the Jews here is possible—indeed, an example for the world. It seemed to me that, although more tolerant than most Zionists, he scarcely did justice to the Arabs.

He was kind enough to take me to see his synagogue, a basement of a block of flats in the newest part of the city, and equipped as an air raid shelter. It followed a conventional model, with the rolls of the Law in a wooden ark in a corner behind the pulpit. Some old synagogue curtains brought from Germany hung on the walls, and some fringed prayer-shawls. I was interested to see the sign of the priest represented: two hands with fingers spread to make the Hebrew letter *shin*, for a blessing. This sign is made by Cohens (priests) after their hands have been washed by Levys (Levites), at the close of the services. At the Wailing Wall it is common for members of the priestly families to make this sign at certain prayers, but they do so under their prayer-shawls. Orthodox Jews avert their gaze from this holy sign as Aaron did from Moses, for *shin* stands for Shaddai, Almighty, one of the sacred names for God.

Dr. W. also took me into the Jewish Bezalel Museum, and I saw relics of Jewish life from many parts of the world, particularly a table laid for the Passover, with a silver case for the *matzoth* and bitter herbs, goblets, books, etc. We went through the art gallery, with many paintings by Jews, including a genuine Rubens. We looked through the School of Art, too, and altogether it was an interesting and profitable morning.

At four, I visited Sir Flinders and Lady Petrie, and stayed about half an hour. Sir Flinders, nearly ninety years old, was in bed at the British Hospital. He was very active in mind, and talked to me a good deal about his work, and reminiscences of his childhood in Woolwich. In the evening I went to one of the barracks and conducted a Holy Week service in the church room. I began a series on the personalities of Holy Week, and spoke on 'Annas'.

Tuesday, March 31

I had a busy day of conferences and duty, with the second Holy Week service in the evening.

Wednesday, April 1

The third Holy Week service was conducted in conjunction with the Wednesday Fellowship, and after an address by a visiting chaplain, I led a Communion Service for over thirty men who gathered for it in our upper room at St. Andrew's House.

Although it was late when I was free to go, I made my way in the light of the full moon to the home of the rabbi I met on Monday. It was nearly eleven o'clock when I ascended the stairs, and I was prepared to leave if it seemed too late to enter. But his door was wide open, and I saw the people within seated round the table. The door had just been opened, I learned, as part of the ritual after the third drink of wine, to allow guests to depart. They had just finished singing the Hallel psalms (cxv-cxviii), and they made me welcome. A chair was given to me at the table. They had been holding their ceremony—the *Seder*—since about 7.30 that evening. There were several children present, a Jewish South African soldier, and four or five guests, including a Professor of History at the Hebrew University. It was the first day of the Passover, and they allowed me to eat of their *matzoth* (unleavened bread), bitter herbs (horseradish sauce—very nice), and *charoseth* (clay), a pleasant mixture of apples, nuts, raisins, and cinnamon, and to sip some wine. On the table also were: salt water, to symbolize their tears; a piece of cooked shankbone of lamb, representing the Passover sacrifice; and an egg, which meant the Temple. The 'clay' is reminiscent of the making of bricks in Egypt, the bitter herbs of suffering, and the unleavened bread of their haste in leaving the land of bondage, when there was no time to wait for the yeast to work.

The head of the house, Dr. W., continued reading the *haggadah*, or 'telling forth', being the traditional account of what was meant by this feast. He did so in a sort of monotonous chant. Then one of the guests began to chant the weird song like a nursery rhyme

about the Holy One who slaughtered the angel of death who killed
the butcher who slaughtered the ox, and so on through water, fire,
stick, dog and cat, to the refrain *chad gat yo!* ('only one kid!').
It may be that the 'only kid, which my father bought for two
suzim', stands for Israel, and the other ones in the song for its
persecutors.

It was a memorable experience for me, and strange to join in a
Passover, to eat the *matzoth* and sip the wine, in an upper room in
Jerusalem, directly after partaking of the Lord's Supper. Afterwards
I talked with the company about the ceremony's significance, and
of various Jewish sects in Jerusalem, and some local legends. It was
half-past one when finally I got to bed at the officers' mess.

Maundy Thursday, April 2

'Maundy' is, of course, a corruption of the 'mandate' that the
disciples received at the institution of the Lord's Supper, the 'new
commandment' to love one another. The Germans call it 'Green'
and the Greeks 'Great' Thursday.

I had secured a ticket from the District Commissioner for the
Orthodox feet-washing ceremony, and went with several other
chaplains to the Convent of Abraham in the Holy Sepulchre at
9 a.m. It was in strong sunlight, and a large and happy crowd had
gathered. The courtyard is an elevated space surrounded by still
higher buildings, and we had forms to sit on in a good raised
position. The atmosphere was like that of a Bank Holiday crowd at
home, and the people pressed around a platform rigged up in the
centre, below us, surrounded by iron railings and containing twelve
cushions on two forms, with two thrones at one end. On a roof-top
facing it was a holy picture hanging, surmounted by the branch of
an olive-tree, to symbolize the Mount of Olives. This kept falling
sideways during the ceremony, and several times a man climbed on
to the roof to secure it. Beside it a hatless man in a yellow robe
stood in a sort of pulpit. He was the Gospeller, and intoned the
relevant passages from the Scriptures throughout the service, in a
sort of nasal wail. The distinguished guests, this year mostly Greek
officials, were accommodated nearby on a low rooftop.

A procession emerged from a little doorway. There were choir-
boys in black, who took up a position in the corner of another
adjacent rooftop and sang several hymns later in the service; priests
in black tall hats; priests in pale blue, with golden criss-cross scarves,
who carried lighted candles, some three candles tied with ribbon
and large blue rosettes, signifying the Trinity, and others two
candles, similarly tied, signifying the two natures of Christ (this last

[Photo by J. Melhuish.

THE MOUNT OF OLIVES.

Bottom left is the Latin Gethsemane, and the Russian compound is in the centre, with the Place of Weeping and the Ascension Chapel immediately above.

THE TOMB OF JESUS.

[*Photo by W. Portsmouth.*

to emphasize their difference from the other Eastern Churches).
Twelve bishops followed, with black veils hanging over their
shoulders; and behind them came the Orthodox Patriarch, long-
white-bearded like Santa Claus, and immensely dignified, wearing
white and gold vestments. He is considered to be a king, so he wore
a large golden crown shaped like a teapot cover. The King of
Greece walked with him, in Army uniform.

First they stood in a group away from the platform, and a bunch
of flowers in a large jar was carried towards the Patriarch, and then
preceding two of them, representing Peter and John, it was placed
in the centre of the platform, where stood a great silver ewer and a
bowl. The Gospeller was chanting meantime, and the carrying of
the flowers represented the man bearing a pitcher of water in the
Gospel story. The procession then made its way to the platform, and
His Beatitude seated himself with His Majesty next to him, and the
bishops sat six on either side before them. Several priests and
deacons went up on to the platform as well, and it all looked rather
a squash. Several had lighted candles, incongruous in the bright
sunshine.

Then followed the service, which was long, the chant of the
Gospeller being interspersed with readings by the Patriarch and
others, in a monotonous sing-song, and with hymns by the choir.
A youth up in the choir received a sharp poke from the black-
bearded leader for not singing up well enough. There was one
priest on the platform whom I termed the R.S.M. He seemed to
be telling everybody what to do, including the Patriarch. Then the
long-awaited moment came. His Beatitude was solemnly divested
of his outer regalia, and wrapped with a large bath-towel round his
portly middle and left shoulder. He proceeded to wash the right
foot of each bishop, beginning with John on his left and ending with
Peter on his right. I did not notice any colloquy with Peter, but it
might have taken place. There was a loud hubbub from the crowd
the whole time, children were crying in the heat, and the whole
atmosphere far removed from that of worship. The bishops had
easily-removed footgear, and apparently no socks. The Patriarch
walked round and bent down to the foot of each one, assistants
carrying the water for him.

He was robed again, and proceeded to have a discussion with
them, representing Christ talking with the disciples, several of them
making remarks—all in Greek, of course, and quite inaudible—
about the meaning of the feet-washing, the giving of the New
Commandment, and Christ's approaching departure, so I learned
afterwards. I thought the next part of the drama very sweet. The

M

Patriarch went down a little way into the crowd, and three bishops, representing Peter, James, and John, seated themselves on the steps of the platform and composed themselves for slumber. It was delightful to see those old men pretending to be asleep, while the old man acted the part of Jesus in Gethsemane, turning and questioning them, and receiving no answer from their recumbent forms. The Gospeller chanted the narrative of the Agony meanwhile.

There were some prayers, and then the procession left the platform, moving slowly through the crowd while the great bells of the church began to peal. The king wore dark sun-glasses. The Patriarch took the bunch of flowers, dipped them in the water with which he had washed the feet, and flicked it over the people as he walked. Some women dipped handkerchiefs in the water, and others appeared anxious to get it on their faces.

I pushed my way out of the crowd and found with difficulty a passage along the labyrinth of the convent which adjoins the Holy Sepulchre. Round in the courtyard before the main entrance to the church I mounted a narrow, dirty staircase in the right-hand corner. It led to the roof of St. Helena's Chapel, where the Abyssinians live, and then a wider set of stairs took me to the Coptic chapel in the Convent of St. Anthony. This large, gaudy place, yellow with gilt and covered with crude, sacred pictures, was crowded with Egyptians, sitting quietly on a few wall pews and on the floor, while the Coptic Bishop intoned a sermon in Arabic from a pulpit at the back. I was courteously led in and given a chair beside the Anglican Bishop and a canon of St. George's Cathedral, in the very centre of the people, and we sat facing the altar with our backs to the preacher. Before us were twelve men in white and yellow robes, squatting on the ground. They had just had their feet washed. They sat patiently waiting for the sermon to finish. I noticed that many of them had at least one bad eye—typical Egyptians! I am told that the feet-washing in the Coptic ceremony is not confined to the twelve appointed, but anybody in the congregation may be washed. I was too late, however, to see that.

I dozed during the sermon, and was aroused to discover that the Bishop had descended from the pulpit and was shaking hands with us, while everybody looked on in silence. He used halting English, and said he was 'veree glad' to see us. He wore a black-and-gold turban and a yellow robe. Somebody whispered that the service would last for two more hours, so we shook hands with the Bishop and departed. I accompanied Dr. Graham-Brown, the Anglican Bishop, to the pavilion the Abyssinians had erected in a corner of their rooftop, where he had his hand kissed and a lot of dumb show went on between him and the black priests. He then gave me a lift in his car out to St. George's Cathedral, where I visited the book-shop.

At 3.15 I was at the Armenian Cathedral again, where last Sunday I saw the Ceremony of the Coming of Christ. I had a ticket for their feet-washing ceremony, and I was led through the crowd, mostly of men standing under the hanging lamps, to a seat within the wide sanctuary. There were many visitors, especially distinguished members of the British community, as this is the most popular of the feet-washing services. It is a ceremony conducted with great beauty and reverence. I looked up and saw that the gallery high under the roof was full of women and children. A highly decorated blue curtain hung across the dais. A choir of boys clad in gaily em-broidered robes were below it in the centre, and on either side of the curtain stood deacons carrying candles, censers, and silver boxes of incense.

The drawing of the curtain gave a theatrical effect to the whole affair, and revealed the Patriarch seated to the left of the 'stage', and twelve priests on chairs facing us, six on either side of the altar. The Patriarch wore a very tall gold-and-white mitre. The priests had blue cloaks clasped across their shoulders. Each had a lighted candle and a cross, and with the latter made the sacred sign at appropriate moments during the service. Like all the Eastern Churches, the Armenians cross themselves from right to left, unlike the Latins, who go from left to right. All the priests wore the tall pointed black cap of the Vartabeds (monastic priests), except an Anglican canon who had been invited to take part. His bare head and clean-shaven face looked incongruous in that hooded, bearded company. There were hymns and prayers and Scripture readings, and, finally, divested of his mitre and scarf, the Patriarch received each priest, who crossed the stage to where he was kneeling, to have his right shoe removed and the foot lightly washed and dried with a towel. The Patriarch put the chrism, the sign of the Cross, on each foot, with his finger dipped in a great white mould of fat on a plate nearby. During this ceremony the choir sang, in clear, sweet voices, the story of the scene in the Upper Room. H. C. Luke gives a translation of one of their songs. Here is part of it:

A new mystery has He now revealed. On His knees He sank, and with a towel
    Himself He girded;
And washed, in order, their feet in a basin, to set us an example.
Thereby men of lowly rank He lifted up and received into heaven;
While he who was proud came to ruin, and nevermore stood up. . . .
My heart is terrified. Horror has possessed me for Judas;
That the Lord of all, on His knees before him, should fall.

The whole service was beautifully and devoutly conducted. It was closed—a fine gesture of Christian fellowship—by Dr. Graham-Brown, wearing an Armenian bishop's mitre, who in English read the Gospel for the day, and pronounced the Benediction.

I had hoped to be able to go on to the Church of St. Mark to see the Syrian feet-washing service, which I was told is the most primitive form of this old custom, with interesting features. But there was no time. I had to be at the Central Y.M.C.A. at 5.30, so after tea I went there. I had been asked to conduct a Communion service there, and then a service after a pilgrimage to Gethsemane.

The Last Supper Room, in the Jesus Tower of the Y.M.C.A., is a beautiful chamber with a cushioned divan which runs round the walls, and a low, broad octagonal table in the centre. Pictures are on the walls and the atmosphere is quiet. It was a most memorable service. I spread my Communion cloth on the table before me, and the bread and wine. Many people were there, but only a few soldiers, as it was not a suitable hour for them to be off duty, but the only convenient time for the service and pilgrimage to be held. There were some Arab Christians present. We sang 'When I survey the wondrous Cross', and I followed the order of the Methodist Church, all of us partaking of the elements as we sat round the table. The Eastern furnishing, the high window overlooking the Old City, and the simplicities of the service, together with the realization of the hour and the day, made it the most impressive Communion service I have attended.

Afterwards we walked across to the city wall, and round it over Zion, past the Ceonaculum, the traditional Last Supper Room, and down by the Temple wall, some of the lower courses of which may be the very stones whose size the disciples commented upon; then we went over the Kedron Valley and up to that part of the Garden of Gethsemane which is within the wall of the Russian compound round their church. It was a lovely evening, clear and sunny, with fragrant air from the pines and a gentle wind in the treetops. We found a quiet place where a grassy patch lies under some cypress trees, and we stood or sat on rocks, and sang 'My faith looks up to Thee', and later, 'Jesus, the very thought of Thee'. After prayer and a reading, I gave a brief address, but we all felt that we would rather be quiet there in the Garden on Good Friday Eve, and we each said our own prayers where Jesus prayed that night. That hour in the secluded corner of Gethsemane is one I shall always remember.

Some of us looked into the Russian Church of St. Mary Magdalene, which lifts its domes above the compound. Priests and nuns were around a group of lighted candles at a crucifix in the centre of

the church, and were chanting prayers in Old Slavonic. It was their
Four-hour Ceremony of the Holy Passion. They have fine voices.
It was getting dark, and the others of my party departed, but before
I returned I went into the Latin Church of the Agony, the newly-
built mass of mosaic, covering the traditional Rock of the Agony.

The crowd which had attended the service of the Holy Hour
there had just left, and I went in through the main doors, opened
for this occasion. The flood-lighting of the ceiling made it look far
less ornate than it does in daylight, and I sat on a chair and looked
at the really fine painting of the Agony which is over the high altar.
It was most impressive to me in that light, and at that hour.

I went back through the Old City, along the dark and deserted
Via Dolorosa, very tired. After dinner, I attended our fourth Holy
Week service for troops in Christ Church, and then very wearily
I found my bed.

Good Friday, April 3

It rained in Jerusalem on Good Friday. I was far too tired after
my busy day yesterday to rise in time to attend the Anglican procession along the Via Dolorosa at 6 a.m., as I had intended to do. I
conducted a service at one of the barracks, with a good attendance,
at 9.30, and then drove to the Damascus Gate, where I dismissed
the car, and walked along the narrow streets to the police barracks
on the site of Antonia Palace. I went up on the roof and sat on the
parapet. It was an interval between showers, and I sat looking for a
while at the Temple Area, where many Moslems wandered about,
not yet finished with their feast of Nebi Musa, which is always held
at the same time as the Orthodox Easter, to make sure that there are
plenty of Moslems in the city when the Christians congregate there.
The Mount of Olives lay to my left and the domes and towers of
Old Jerusalem to my right. Below where I was sitting Pilate had
his judgement court on the first Good Friday.

When other people began to climb on to the roof where I was,
I moved away, and descending to the street of the Via Dolorosa, I
knocked and gained admission to the Ecce Homo Convent. I was
a frequent visitor, and the sister at the door told me in French that I
could go down into the crypt, where they preserve the 'Pavement'
of John xix. 13. There I walked on the worn old stones which Jesus
trod when He began the journey to Calvary. In a corner a large
group of negro soldiers were kneeling, crossing themselves devoutly. A young man wearing the badge of the Friends' Ambulance
Unit stood by me. A Sister of Zion, in black habit, crossed the
Pavement slowly with downcast eyes.

After a while I quietly left that holy place, and walked along the Via Dolorosa, with its scattered groups of people. The Roman Catholic services would not begin for an hour yet. I met two of my Methodist lads, and we went together to the Church of the Holy Sepulchre. On Calvary there were many people, and a blaze of candles came from the Orthodox altar. In one part a little group of soldiers were kneeling while a chaplain read prayers from a book. A number of Greek priests chanted before their altar. Palestinian Christians and Greek visitors were everywhere. I fear that for me in that crush the top of Calvary on Good Friday morning was no place for prayer, in the way that I wished to pray.

I met two Y.M.C.A. workers from New Zealand, and the five of us walked round the Tomb and adjacent chapels, but the crowd was very great, and we were glad to get out into the fresh air. It was inevitable that there should arise a little friction amongst these excitable people at this season of the Christian year, when so many services were taking place in the same church. That morning, a policeman told me, there had been a difference between some Orthodox and Roman Catholic priests, and last Sunday morning the Copts and Syrians had a little scrimmage about a chair being carried in a procession. But in view of the number of services held and the excitability of the people involved, order was kept very well, on the whole. While I was walking towards the Roman Catholic Chapel of the Apparition, I received a violent shove in the back. I turned in surprise, and found it was one of the American Franciscan monks going through the crowd into his chapel, presumably to pray. I preferred to go the other way.

But what evidence is here of the catholicity of the Christian faith, if not of its charity! There can be heard a babel of tongues as various branches of the Church begin their services. But it is not the Tower of Babel again, for they have an underlying unity. One can distinguish Syriac, almost the Aramaic in which Jesus preached the gospel; Greek, in which Paul wrote; Coptic, the language of the ancient Pharaohs; Indo-European Armenian from the Caucasus; Arabic, the speech of Islam and 'tongue of the angels'; and Latin, the language in which the Western world was evangelized. And all were mourning the death of Christ, at the place where He was crucified.

The Orthodox Church would hold a service at which they adore a piece of the True Cross, and the Latins would be having their ceremony of the 'Taking Down from the Cross' later that evening. They take a jointed figure from a crucifix on the altar, place it on the Stone of Unction, and then lay it in the Tomb until Easter Day.

The Eastern Churches would also be having their services of the Imperial Hours, of the Entombment, and of the Winding Sheet.

After tea with the men at an Army canteen I took a party of twenty for a walk along the narrow top of the Old City wall, led by Rev. Eric Bishop, of the Newman School of Missions. It was 5.15, and still rather showery. We went first to St. Stephen's Gate, which faces eastwards, and he told us of the two brothers who started to build the wall from there, each working in opposite directions. They met ten years later at the Jaffa Gate, on the other side of the city. It was finished in 1542, exactly 400 years ago.

We mounted the wall, and got a fine view of Olivet. B. said that he thought the summer residence of the Greek Patriarch on an adjoining height was most likely the place where Jesus descended to Jerusalem on Palm Sunday, as that would allow the 'great multitude' to go out to welcome Him. Beneath the wall on which we walked he pointed out a fig tree thick with early fruit, showing that it could be expected as early as the Passover in a sheltered spot. Strangely enough, a hundred yards farther on we saw the bare branches of a withered fig tree! We had a grand view of the city and of the Temple Area as we walked.

We turned the corner by the fine, low lines of the Rockefeller Museum outside the wall. A large herd of sheep and goats were being driven across the road as we reached the top of Herod's Gate, often called the Sheep Gate. We had an unusual view of the Crusader Church of St. Anne, by the Pool of Bethesda, from this narrow ledge, no more than a yard wide, on which we stood. Right along the northern wall we went in single file, and saw Gordon's Calvary on the one hand and the Bezetha section of the Old City on the other. B. was pointing out all the time the various landmarks to us, and telling us their stories. It was fascinating to make this unusual tour of Jerusalem on Good Friday evening. We came to earth at the Damascus Gate.

Saturday, April 4

To-day I saw the most amazing spectacle of my life. It was the unbelievably pagan saturnalia of the Holy Fire in the Church of the Holy Sepulchre. I was told by the District Commissioner to be in my place by 11.40 a.m., although the actual entry of the Orthodox Patriarch into the Tomb would not be until 1 o'clock. I decided to go at 10.30, however, because of the crowds. In spite of the fact that, in wartime, there are very many less pilgrims in Jerusalem, there was a great throng trying to enter the church, with many Greek troops among them. The mass of people along Christian Street appeared to be impenetrable, but a donkey with wide burdens across his back was beaten on by his driver who wished to reach some place along that way, and the laughing crowd opened to let him through. I followed in his wake, and got to within six or seven people of the line of police ahead of the crowd. My 13 stone of weight and 6 feet of height enabled me then to get to the front, and my ticket allowed me to step within the circle of police. A police-officer led me down the steps to the group waiting before the closed doors of the church. 'They call this Christianity,' he said, à propos of the milling mob.

I waited about an hour in the bright sunlight. An Arab youth told me he had been there since 7 a.m. A Russian woman with a boy of ten asked if she could stay by me all the time, as she feared the crush. I regretted that it was not possible for me to look after her, as I should have to go to the place in the church to which I was allotted. I suggested that it was not wise for her to take a child into that crowd, but she said she wished to do so. I had attired myself in an old battledress uniform, with no stick nor camera to lose, and it was as well that I did so. When the great doors opened, and the crowd was allowed to press in, I was caught in a furious stampede. The police—unwisely, I think—charged the crowd to fling it back, and women and children were screaming as they were crushed. It was completely impossible for me to remain by the Russian woman and the child, who were quickly whirled away from me in the mêlée. I have never before entered a church in such a fashion. I was carried in with the flood of people and deposited breathless before the Stone of Unction.

Beneath the Rotunda were a number of chairs facing the Edicule, or chapel covering the Tomb. These were reserved for the King of Greece and other distinguished visitors. My ticket allowed me to stand beside the entrance to the Tomb, and thus I had a very fine, close view of everything that took place. I took up my post, felt myself to see that I was still whole, examined my sandwiches and found them squashed but edible, and began to make a few notes on the scene. There was an immense noise of people talking and shouting. They were everywhere. Right up to the high ceiling were people, men and boys climbing on every foothold of the timbers that filled the spaces between the pillars. The dismal cupola, its paintwork peeling, echoed with the noise from those in the topmost balconies. Police were everywhere. The great candlesticks which usually stand before the Edicule had been removed for safety, but lamps hung there still, and round the walls. And still the crowds entered. The Rotunda is not very large, but 5,000 people were massed within it. It was nothing like a church service. Add to the picture of an English football crowd the excitability of Orientals filled with religious fanaticism, and one can imagine the scene.

The District Commissioner and some high officials and ecclesiastics stood by the Tomb entrance, and when the King of Greece, George II, entered with some of his staff officers and Princess Irene, Prince Peter's wife, there was great clapping and cheering from the people. An old water-carrier, following an ancient custom, brought in an old rusty petrol-tin filled with water, and gave the D.C. a drink. He sipped it, and handed the man a 50-piastre note. Suddenly through one entrance appeared a crowd of men—Syrians, I believe—carrying others on their shoulders, who waved their arms and screamed, their cries being taken up by the people. This happened several times. Some bearded Greek priests doing duty by the Tomb entrance beside me were wrangling about a pair of scissors. A lady by my side who spoke Greek told me that they were arguing as to who should cut the broad white tape which sealed the door. The one who claimed the scissors assured the others that he would give them a piece to keep. The District Commissioner's *kuwass*, in blue, baggy trousers and with a golden coat of arms on his tarbush, sealed the door with wax and white ribbon, and it was duly inspected by the D.C. It was to be opened when the Orthodox Patriach arrived.

A Franciscan monk stood by. He lowered a lamp hanging over the door and extinguished the light. He was there in the capacity of an observer. Otherwise the Latins have nothing to do with the ceremony. The Greek-speaking lady talked with one of the priests. He told her he was thirty-two. Younger than I, and with his great beard he looked sixty, at least! He informed her that this was the first time for 1,300 years a king had been present in the Holy Sepulchre at Easter. I have no means of verifying his statement. Certainly Crusader kings were here. Doubtless he was referring to Heraclius, and meant kings only of the Orthodox faith.

Everybody had a candle, ready for the Holy Fire. Father Cyril of the Armenians came across to me and gave me a lovely long white candle with a twisted line of gold and a sacred picture on it. I had no wish to use it, however, so I handed it to a Greek standing behind me who seemed anxious to have one. The crush was worse by this time, and I scarcely had room for my feet on the ground. There was a great din, not only from the cries of the throng, but especially from the throats of some frenzied natives, who uttered a peculiar piercing ululation, rather like the supposed cry of the Red

Indians. This cry is often used in the East at funerals to scare away evil spirits. The noise became louder when a procession with thirteen great tattered banners appeared, bearing almost unrecognizable sacred pictures, and by some mysterious means forced a passage three times round the Tomb, with priests and boys singing, and followed by the Orthodox Patriarch. The front of the procession caught up with its rear, and thus they encircled us, representing all the Eastern Churches. Singing seraphically, with a candle in his hand and wearing a bright blue robe, I recognized the pugnacious little priest whose fight I had interrupted last Sunday.

When the banners came opposite the entrance to the Tomb the third time, they were carried away into the Greek Catholicon, and a hush fell upon the assembly as the Patriarch prepared to enter the Edicule. He was divested of some of his robes and his golden crown as he stood only 2 yards from where I was. He looked a tired old man, with an untidy mop of white hair and a great white beard. He moved slowly, and with immense dignity. An Armenian bishop accompanied him into the Tomb.

A few minutes later the whole place was in a tumult. A torch appeared through a porthole on either side of the Edicule, from the Chapel of the Angels, and was snatched by a waiting runner. Hands with candles were raised, and with astonishing rapidity the whole place was ablaze with candlelight. The light passed from one to another, right up the clambering figures on the walls. The Armenian, clad in white, who rushed away with his torch, took it with surprising speed up to the Armenian Patriarch, who sat at a high balcony, and he waved it over the crowd. The noise was deafening. The great bell of the church began to peal. Men and women holding bundles of lighted candles waved them in the air. Why that jostling, fighting, yelling mob waving flaming candles did not burn themselves, I do not know.

The superstitious believe that the appearance of this fire is a yearly miracle from heaven. There was a miracle. It was that no conflagration was caused. I stood in my sheltered corner and gazed fearfully at the scene, expecting catastrophe at any moment. Many tragedies have occurred in the past, but as far as I know, there were no accidents on this occasion. The D.C.'s secretary and some police officers yelled to those on the wooden girders to extinguish their lights, and with some demur they did so. I saw one man dangling over an arch, ready to drop down, but the heat from candles beneath him made him rapidly pull himself up again. Another man was solemnly putting his hands through the flames from somebody's torch, and passing them over his face. The Holy Fire had fallen again from Heaven. God had not failed them. Everybody was happy.

The ceremony symbolizes the victorious light of the Resurrection, and it is first mentioned by Bernard the Wise in the ninth century. Of what strange pagan rite is it a survival? Up till the last war, runners would carry specially prepared torches all the way to Jaffa, where a ship was waiting to convey the fire to Odessa, whence it spread to the village churches throughout Holy Russia. To-day it is carried to the Orthodox churches in Palestine. It was a most incredible sight to see in these modern times at the Tomb of Christ.

The Patriarch emerged, and handed a bunch of lighted candles to the D.C. There were thirty-three of them, representing the years of our Lord's life. He then made a dignified exit into the Catholicon. The Franciscan monk lowered the largest lamp that hung before the Tomb, and kindled it again from the candle of the man standing next to me. People began to disperse. I found it necessary to go right round the ambulatory in order to gain the main door. It was half-past two, and I felt very tired. My sandwiches were welcome.

At five o'clock I took my camera and mounted the roof of St. Helena's Chapel, where the Abyssinians were preparing to hold their annual ceremony of Searching for the Body of Christ. Several men were with me, and we were fortunate enough to be able to climb a ladder on to the roof of one of their little houses. I sat there facing the opening of the great tent they had constructed, and could see the area below, with the chapel dome rising in the centre of the courtyard. It was a sunny afternoon, and the whole atmosphere had the pleasant formality of a vicarage garden party. Were it not for its gorgeous trappings, I might have imagined the pavilion to be a marquee on some village green in England. The ceremony is usually held at night, which is said to add an atmosphere of mystery to the whole affair. Blackout regulations, however, caused it to be held in the afternoon, when one was better able to appreciate the splendour and at the same time the normality of it.

Below us, preparing for their preliminary prayers, were dark-faced Abyssinians arrayed in robes of every imaginable colour. One man wore an apple-green jacket with wide yellow stripes on his baggy trousers: two *kuwasses* were in pale blue and gold, with great curved swords at their sides and mighty staves in their hands; a black waiter wore his boiled shirt and black tie, but with a cloak of crimson over his shoulder; there were robes of gold and white, of deep blues and reds and purples, and of a barbaric motley defying description. Children wore immense crowns of gilt or silver, backed with crimson or blue and descending to the ears. The Abbot wore a magnificent crown, and his black, bearded face was solemn beneath it as he began the ceremony.

It was a corner of Africa there on the roof of the Holy Sepulchre. I had been told that the ceremony was a mixture of native *voodoo* and Christianity. It appeared to me to be nothing of the kind. It was far more dignified and reverent than most of the religious ceremonies I have seen this Easter. Doubtless the customary darkness gives it an air of magic. But in broad daylight it could be seen for what it was: a slow procession of simple native Christians commemorating the burial and Resurrection of Christ in a way that was natural to them. There were none of the excesses or frenzy of more excitable Orientals.

Led by the two *kuwasses* in blue, who smote their staves upon the ground, the procession passed beneath us with infinite slowness. There were many large umbrellas of blue and red, and others of fine golden filigree work. There were banners, and two drums upon which the bearers beat their hands with monotonous rhythm. Two priests held silver *sistra*, or rattles, which they solemnly shook. Four bells hanging behind us under the ruined Crusader canons' arches began to jangle. Nearly every one carried a lighted candle. A solemn chant rose from the people, and their abbot followed them with dignity. Quite half of the procession consisted of visitors: British officials, Army chaplains, nursing sisters, and sightseers of all kinds, most of them carrying candles and pacing slowly behind the black priests. They were enjoying themselves, and entered into the spirit of the thing. Black primitive Abyssinians are not the only ones who like colour and drums and processing. Standing in the crowd below me, I saw the Moslem doorkeeper of the Holy Sepulchre; and three monks were talking together, one in the white of a Dominican, another in the brown of a Franciscan, and the third wearing the black of a Benedictine. A child with black eyes, frizzy hair and a face of shining chocolate smiled up at me. Women sat on the ground with their backs to the walls of their crude native huts and nursed their babies.

A turbaned Coptic bishop joined the procession. The drums throbbed, the bells jangled, the candles shone, the voices chanted, the robes and crowns glittered. They all were children at play: the Abbot, priests and people of Abyssinia, and the District Commissioner, the High Commissioner's Chief Secretary, a Princess of the Hellenes, the American Consul-General, Anglican clergymen, and colonels and majors of the British Army!

The procession passed into the pavilion again after rounding the courtyard three times, and the spectators dispersed. With difficulty,

I persuaded Hailé Selassie's grandson, who was playing on the pavement beneath me, to fetch a rickety ladder to enable me to descend.

Easter Day, April 5th

I had hoped to be able to go to the celebrations this morning at the Russian Cathedral, for I had heard that the singing there is very beautiful, and the scene memorable at the close of the ceremony, when the old Russian priest joyously salutes his people with the kiss of peace on Easter morning. But their service started immediately after midnight, lasting till dawn, and I was far too exhausted after yesterday's adventures to spend the night, as one can profitably do, I am told, in the Holy Sepulchre, to see the diversities of ceremonial; and to go into the Russian Cathedral in the early hours of the morning. As a matter of fact, by their curious custom of anticipating services, the Easterns begin to celebrate Easter on the evening before, perhaps after the fashion of the Jews, whose day always begins at sunset; and since, of course, they cannot have Communion in the evening, Easter Mass is said early on Saturday morning!

I had my duties to attend to, and I conducted an Easter Day service in one of the barracks. There was a good attendance, and we greeted our Risen Lord with traditional 'Alleluias'. The usually bare chapel was fragrant with Easter lilies the Colonel's wife had provided. Twenty Methodist lads remained for a Communion service. Some of them had attended the early morning service at the Garden Tomb, which, if it is not the authentic sepulchre, at any rate provided a happier setting for worship on Easter morning than the tawdry Tomb itself.

In the afternoon I took some twenty-five men, in the heat of the day, to see the Russian Cathedral, which lies near the Jaffa Road. Its domes have not the customary onion shape of the earlier Church of St. Mary Magdalene in Gethsemane. It is more modern and more tastefully appointed, although lined, of course, with holy pictures of questionable merit. Children were greeting each other with kisses on the cheek, and they joined together in a service. We did not linger long. We went on to find the Abyssinian Cathedral behind the Street of the Prophets. Before we left the grounds of the Russian Cathedral, we were interested to see a huge half-quarried column of stone lying nearby. It is Herodian in date, similar to some that Josephus describes, still to be seen in the Temple Area. Either its quarrying was abandoned, because of the big crack across it or for some other reason, or it was deliberately left in that position to mark the boundary between Judah and Benjamin, which ran somewhere here and then passed across the area of the Temple, leaving the House of the Lord in Judah and the Altar in Benjamin.

The Abyssinians have a large rotunda for their cathedral, set amid shady trees and with a profusion of broad beans growing within its precincts. They had presumably been 'digging for victory'. A black priest, with dumb show, exhibited to us a large illustrated book all about some saint who worked miracles, of which he seemed very proud. Some crude pictures hung upon the walls, especially one of three old men with long beards, which a black boy who spoke English informed us was the Holy Trinity. The altar, rather like the Edicule in the Holy Sepulchre, was in the centre under the dome, and the congregation presumably gathered round it in the ambulatory where we walked. The services are sung in classical Amharic, the boy told us, which nobody but the priests understand.

We thanked our host and departed, going to the Newman School of Missions, which many of the men had not visited. B. showed us his treasures: the Ptolemaic inscription from Gaza, the Samaritan inscription, and some ancient manuscripts in his library, where we saw on the wall a little engraving of John Wesley. I stayed with Mr. and Mrs. Bishop to tea, with six of the men who were newcomers from England. Afterwards I walked with my party to the Holy Sepulchre, and we quietly went into the Tomb for a moment. Few people were about, and for that reason the hour of dusk on Easter Day was the best time to enter the Tomb. The whole place, the decorations and the priests, looked tired, as though glad that all the celebrations were over at last. Crowds had been there that day, some of them a great while before dawn, to worship their Risen Lord in their own way at the very place where He conquered death, the last enemy of man.

I conducted a service for troops at Christ Church at 7.30, and afterwards we had a social hour for them until ten o'clock, and I was glad to make my way to my bed. Easter in Jerusalem has been for me a mixture of excitement and solemnity. I have been amazed and bewildered and at the same time inspired. When Jesus entered Jerusalem for the last time, it must have presented an appearance very different from the city of to-day, but in some ways probably very similar to it, both in the scenes it presents and the nature of the people, who are nowadays at once as arrogant and as lovable as those He knew.

CHAPTER X

SAMARITANS

Our fathers worshipped in this mountain.
THE WOMAN OF SAMARIA.

THE Samaritan calendar is a relic of Byzantine influence in Palestine, and is not easy to understand. It is dependent upon the Greek calendar, and the Passover is held on the evening before the full moon of the Greek Nisan and is therefore always after April 12. In 1942 the Samaritan Feast of the Passover was celebrated at sunset on April 29, more than three weeks later than the Jewish Passover, yet the previous year it was a day earlier than the Jewish feast. I have compared the dates for some years back, and their 14th Nisan occurs at varying intervals. Certainly when I attended their celebrations on the summit of Mount Gerizim it was on the eve of the second full moon after the spring equinox.

April 29 fell upon a Wednesday, and to travel north to Samaria and see the sacrifices at sunset would mean that I could not be present at the Wednesday Fellowship, and I was very reluctant to be absent from it even for once. The week before, however, I mentioned it to the members, and they urged me to go to Samaria and tell them all about it when I returned, while they arranged to hold a debate in my absence. The subject which one of them suggested, by the way, and which they decided to discuss, was something to do with the primary need of Christianity either for evangelism or for better co-operation between the Churches. Unfortunately, it was not possible for me to take any of the men with me. On the rare occasions when they could get forty-eight hours' leave, they preferred, not unnaturally, to spend it in more congenial ways than exploring the obscurities of some ancient cult. So I went by myself, securing a lift in a friend's car northwards early on that Wednesday morning.

That road, now a well-metalled thoroughfare, is loaded with the traffic of history. Those surrounding hills were familiar to Israel under the Judges, to the kings of the two kingdoms, to priests and prophets, rulers and rebels, through the Old Testament and the New. Jesus trod this road as He went back to Galilee through Samaria, and Saul *en route* to Damascus and the bright and shining light awaiting him. Crusaders and Saracens, Turks and Allenby's Army knew it too, and during the 'Troubles', as residents refer to the

Palestinian clashes with the Government in 1936, there were many popular hiding-places for snipers among the giant boulders fringing this road, especially in the chasmic 'Robber's Valley'. But everything was peaceful as I sped smoothly along those forty miles between Jerusalem and Nablus. There was no suggestion of local 'troubles' nor, indeed, anything to remind one of the fact that these quiet hills stood in the centre of a mighty whirlpool of war, like the stillness of the heart of a tropical typhoon: 'a core of sweetness in much bitter', as Mary Webb says.

Away to the left I could see the minaret of Nebi Samwil against the sky. Until very recently this was pointed to as the location of Mizpah, but the excavations of Professor Badè, in 1932, have revolutionized those time-honoured but erroneous theories. At the hill I passed shortly afterwards to my left, Tell en Nasbeh, he found the site of Mizpah, with the wall and its gate destroyed by Sennacherib in 701 B.C. Most interesting of all, Badè found amongst some ancient ornaments a beautiful agate seal with an inscription in ancient Hebrew: 'Belonging to Jaazaniah, servant of the king', and with a device of a cock with long spurs on its legs. It is in the Rockefeller Museum in Jerusalem. Now, if you turn to 2 Kings xxv. 23, you can read about this very man, Jaazaniah, who was amongst the captains of the forces who left Jerusalem when it was destroyed by Nebuchadnezzar, and joined the new Governor, Gedaliah, at Mizpah, with all their men. This extraordinary discovery locates Mizpah, and at the same time gives confirmation to an Old Testament story. Jaazaniah is also mentioned by Jeremiah in xl. 8, and he describes in the next chapter how seventy men were slain by Ishmael, the son of Nethaniah, and their bodies thrown into a pit at Mizpah. Just such a pit full of bones has been unearthed by Professor Badè. So it was from this eminence, and not at yonder Nebi Samwil, that Samuel judged the people, and all the events associated with Mizpah took place. The stone Ebenezer, I imagine, was erected somewhere between here and Ain Karim. And it would be, of course, on this eminence that Judas Maccabaeus formed his headquarters before his successful attack on Antiochus Epiphanes at Jerusalem. The latest archaeological finds at Tell en Nasbeh date from the Maccabaean period.

This location is at Ramallah, beside the Old Testament Beeroth, and just before I reached it I saw the remains of an ancient Roman road continuing its desolate course through the fields to the left. This, possibly, was the route that St. Paul followed when he was taken to Caesarea on the first stage of his long journey to Rome. I had pleasant memories of Ramallah itself, where American

[Photo by L. Duenner

THE SAMARITAN HIGH PRIEST AT PRAYER DURING PASSOVER, 1942.

[See page 191

SISTER JOHANNA WITH SOME OF HER PATIENTS

missionaries of the Society of Friends often entertained the members of the Wednesday Fellowship.

Farther north, and away to my right, lay the village of Bethel on its hilltop. I recalled a visit I made there a few weeks earlier to see it and the site of Ai, the modern name of which is Et-Tell, about two miles to the north-east of Bethel, with the Valley of Achor between them. A French archaeologist, the late Madame Krausse-Marquet, made excavations at Ai at about the same time as Dr. Albright was digging at Bethel, just before the war. They discovered that whereas the site of Ai had been unoccupied from about 2000 B.C. to 1000 B.C., there was evidence that Bethel was thoroughly burned at the time of the Hebrew invasion, about 1200 B.C., and shortly after-wards re-occupied. In Joshua viii there is an elaborate account of the destruction of Ai, however, and the present theory is that, since archaeologists have found ruins of the time of Joshua at Bethel instead of at Ai, the later author of the seventh and eighth chapters of the Book of Joshua confused Ai with the nearby Bethel. He might have seen a flourishing city at Bethel, whilst Ai was desolate, and decided that its desolation was caused by Joshua, whereas the truth is that it was a ruin for 800 years before Joshua appeared. The very name Ha-Ai means 'the ruin'.

Apart from some pathetic crops among the rocks and a few 'neighbour's landmarks' of piled stones, Ai is 'a heap for ever, even a desolation, unto this day'. Bethel is now a little Arab village with a few fig orchards, and a marvellous view. I thought of the dream-ing Jacob of long ago, and of Amos of Tekoa, who thundered his denunciations here, unless the capital of Israel then was farther north. They still 'build houses of hewn stone' as they did in his day.

The story of Achan has a parallel, by the way, in some facts unearthed at Gaza. Lady Petrie described to me the discovery that she and Sir Flinders made of what appeared to be the complete and deliberate destruction of all the possessions of a family, probably for some such act of treachery as that of Achan. She showed me a photograph of a basalt table that had been wantonly smashed in the same vengeful manner. Apparently, therefore, the practice of 'liquidating' such undesirables as Achan who had offended against the solidarity of the tribe, by utterly destroying them, their families and their goods, was a Semitic practice going back well over 1,000 years before Joshua assaulted Bethel. As I surveyed that desolate valley I wondered which of the many heaps of stones covered the remains of the unfortunate Achan. I remembered, too, the promise of Hosea, a greater than Joshua, that the Valley of Achor,

N

or Troubling, should be a door of hope. We needed such a promise in these dark days of trouble.

Shiloh, away to our right further on, held a reminiscence of Achan, for his crime and his fate were quoted there where the Israelites viewed with misgiving the erection by the tribes of Reuben and Gad of an altar of their own to the Lord. It appeared to them to be a similar case of disloyalty, but they were convinced otherwise by the Reubenites. This historic spot, the scene of Joshua's division by lot of the Promised Land among the Hebrew tribes and of Samuel's childhood in the house of Eli, Shiloh in the land of Canaan, later to be destroyed, as Jeremiah announced, is now marked by a series of ruined churches dating from the Byzantine period. I remembered a rainy day when a party of us in a couple of cars ventured to Shiloh for a picnic among its deserted green hills, only to get stuck in the muddy track until we could be rescued. But a memory of an olive orchard with its trees rising from a blue mist of bird's-eye, and of red anemones and yellow buttercups and white Stars of Bethlehem spangling the verdant meadows, will long remain with me. As we sped past it, I thought of the beautiful mosaics which the Danish scholar, Dr. Schmidt, had unearthed in those lush fields, and covered carefully with low walls and roof. In one place we had found the remains of an early Christian *agape*-room, which reminded one member of our expedition of the *pain-bénie* in churches in France, and me of what was perhaps the last Methodist love-feast in London, when we passed round some old mugs made for that purpose which somebody had found, and we rather self-consciously sipped water and ate biscuits and gave our testimony. What a memory to have of a London Mission church in far-away Shiloh!

It was a delightful hour's journey to Nablus. The hills, now yellow, now green, now brown, rolled away on either side, and in their clefts were wild roses and clustered honeysuckle, with towering hollyhocks and the lesser though equally noble blue spikes of cat-mint. Scattered along the sheltered valleys were irregular olive trees, their leaves silver in the sunlight. As we mounted the rise before the steep and winding descent to the Vale of Lubban I marvelled at

> The smooth enamelled green
> Where no print of step hath been,

a brilliant smudge of jade that lay below me to the left, and I coveted the eye and hand of an artist to capture its beauty and keep it all my days. This hilltop marked the boundary of Samaria and

Judea in the days of Jesus, and there would have been an inn somewhere here, just within Judea, perhaps where a decrepit *khan* now
stands, to enable Jews travelling through Samaria to pass straight
through that country without stopping for the night. Before me I
could discern not only the majestic outline of Mount Gerizim, but
on one occasion through a gap I had a glimpse of the snow-topped
peak of Hermon on the far horizon.

The road wound uphill again when the valley was crossed and we
rounded the hulk of Gerizim which towered above us to the left,
to stop for a while at the entrance to the long valley between
Gerizim and Ebal, in which lies the town of Nablus. Down a gentle
slope to my right I saw a wall enclosing some trees and church ruins
and I followed a footpath which brought me to its gate. I was at
Jacob's Well, not merely the location of a story of Old Testament
patriarchs, but the scene of one of the most beautiful stories in the
Gospels, the meeting of Jesus with the woman of Samaria. It is
almost certainly the identical place. An unbroken tradition locates
this well—in a country where wells are not plentiful—as the one
regarded in the time of Christ as the well of Jacob. Jerome describes
a church that was standing here in A.D. 404. This was destroyed by
the mad Khalif Hakim, and the Crusaders built another, with the
high altar above the crypt containing the well. Destroyed again by
the Moslems, it lay deserted for centuries, except for the visits of
pilgrims and occasional services by Orthodox priests, who finally
bought the land at the beginning of this century and started to build
a fine new church. Work was discontinued during the 1914–18
War for lack of funds, and it was never completed. Now half-built
walls and a few pillars stand about the site in an air of desolation.

I found the way down to the Crusader crypt, and the thin sound
of chanting came to me as I descended the old stone steps. I saw the
head of the well in the centre of the crypt. An altar was behind it
and a lectern by the wall before it, at which stood a little bearded
priest and a woman of middle age. He was reciting prayers in a
monotonous drone and she was making the responses. There were
a few candles and ikons about the place, and light from high windows. They took no notice of me as I walked across to the well and
sat on its stone edge to peer into the depths. Far below I thought I
caught a glimmer of reflection on the surface of the water, but it was
very dark. How strange it was in that gloomy cavern, so different
from when the well-head had been in the open air and Jesus had sat
where I was sitting, under the shade that covered the well, while
flies circled in the shimmering noon heat and a woman slowly
paced, head erect under her earthen waterpot, towards the Man

who held the key of her life in His hands. How little did she know that she would date her life from that moment, that the greatest sermon in the world would be spoken to her, a congregation of one, in conversation with this tired traveller. How gently He talked with her; how delicately He spoke first of this water and then of the water of life which He could give to her so that she thirsted no more; how subtly He roused her curiosity as to who He was, and then revealed the truth. 'I that speak unto thee am He.' Did He really say that, here where I was sitting? I had that hushed feeling we have within us at rare and sacred moments. I was on holy ground.

The prayers ended and the priest walked across to a peg on the wall, on which he hung his scarf, while the woman lit candles stuck on a sort of tin plate and lowered it into the well for me to see the ancient stones that lined it. Then she lowered a bucket into the far depths and brought it up spilling over with clear, cold water which she poured out for me in a little metal mug. I sipped it as I would the sacrament, and the words of the Lord Jesus came to me as though I heard them myself: 'Whosoever drinketh of this water shall thirst again, but whosoever drinketh of the water that I shall give him shall never thirst.'

Outside again and across a few fields I found the tomb of Joseph under a white Moslem dome with some fig trees nearby. It was a dirty and stained plaster cenotaph with rotting orange peel and stubs of candles on flanking stumps of stone, and pieces of rag tied on its railings, as Moslems are fond of putting at the tombs of their prophets. The place had been built in its present form in 1868, and except for a few paving stones which might have held Crusader markings, it contained nothing of historic interest. Probably, however, this is the place which always had been associated with the record in Joshua xxiv. 32: 'And the bones of Joseph, which the children of Israel brought up out of Egypt, buried they in Shechem, in the parcel of ground which Jacob bought.'

I walked across Jacob's Field to see the excavations of the Tower of Shechem, which stood in the days of the Judges in this command-ing position at the entrance to the valley. Diggings have revealed the huge uneven stones that encompassed the fortress, and in one place a great double entrance, apparently a fortified gateway. Those rough stones, hidden for centuries beneath the soil and grass by Jacob's Field, the existence of which was unsuspected doubtless when Jesus passed that way, were probably the ones that confronted Abimelech and his men when they piled boughs around the tower and burnt it with the thousand men and women it contained. The story is to be found in the ninth chapter of the Book of Judges.

There was history, sacred and profane, in every yard of the ground that I was treading.

Over by the roadside again, I passed through the filthy streets of the Arab village of Balata, built around a flowing stream, and under some shady mulberry trees were broken columns of what, incredibly, looked like Assuan granite. A little Arab boy, proud of his school English, told me that one house was the 'house of a prophet'. An old man was lying fast asleep on the ground in the shade of a tree, but I could not be sure whether he was the prophet! The village is named after the word *badanos* (oak), and is believed to be the site of the plain of Moreh of Genesis xii. 6 because of the more exact location given in Deuteronomy xi, as well as of the oak under which Jacob buried the strange gods and ear-rings of his household, according to Genesis xxxv. 4. The strong Samaritan belief to this present day is that the slope above Balata, the hill of Moreh, part of Gerizim, is the Mount Moriah of Abraham's sacrifice on which the Temple should have been built.

Away to the north, on the slopes of Ebal, I could see the square stone houses of Askar, which may be the site of the city of Sychar mentioned in John iv. When I went along the road to Nablus, I realized why from time immemorial a city has been in this valley. It is the sheltered and fertile watershed of Gerizim and Ebal, which rise in noble rounded contours on either side. To-day, as in the past, it is an important centre of local government. Shechem used to be nearby, where at Solomon's death Rehoboam foolishly threatened the northern tribes with severer penalties than those of his father, which resulted in the split into two kingdoms. It was the capital of Samaria, and destroyed by the Romans, to be rebuilt after A.D. 70 to the honour of Flavius Vespasian, and named Flavia Neapolis, the New City, from which 'Nablus' is a corruption.

I wandered through its long, crooked streets, with vaulted bazaars and many minarets of mosques, several of which are former Crusader churches, until I found the hospital of the Church Missionary Society, where I was given generous hospitality for that day and night. The hospital is a series of fine old buildings lying on the southern slope of the valley, with a grand aspect of Mount Ebal from its garden, which greeted me with a profusion of scent and colour. Other guests were there to see the Samaritan Passover that evening, and so it came about that I mounted the steep ascent of Gerizim accompanied by three young C.M.S. missionaries. We carried sandwiches and a flask of tea to fortify ourselves during the lengthy proceedings, and toiled up the hillside well before the hour of sunset, which was about half-past seven.

Gerizim, holy mountain of the Samaritans, is 2,800 feet above sea level and 1,254 feet above the level of the valley from which we climbed. Groups of people, most of them Jews from surrounding settlements who desired to see the only surviving reminder available of what the ancient Jewish Passover must have been like, were climbing the hill between trees and clumped hollyhocks on the lower slopes and then over open grass and white rocks amid brown soil.

As we came towards the Samaritans' camp, pitched in a hollow under the very peak of the hill, we were met by several lads in robes of thin blue and silver stripes and wearing red tarbushes on their heads, like Egyptians. I have before me now as I write the piece of paper one of them pinned to my shirt in return for a contribution for, as it says on the paper under a line of Arabic characters, the 'helping of the Samaritan's school'. The idea of a 'flag day' had apparently spread even to this obscure corner of the world! Those boys amongst them who belonged to the priestly families—about a third of the male population—were unshaven, and embryo beards of red hair clustered about their cheeks. Centuries of inter-marriage has guaranteed the continuance of the characteristic Biblical physiognomy of broad features and long noses. One of them was a deaf mute, but another spoke good English, and I inquired of him what was the language they used between them-selves, as I wondered whether they still spoke Samaritan. But he told me that they speak Arabic, the ancient Samaritan tongue being the formal language of ritual.

In a wide plateau some 200 or 300 yards from the actual summit of Gerizim lay the white tents of this little community. Every Samaritan, including invalids and a few who lived in Tel-Aviv and Tulkarm, had come to the holy mountain where they would remain for the next seven days. There were about twenty tents, in two orderly rows except for one or two separate ones, one of which, I understood, was to accommodate any Samaritan who fell ill and was liable to die during the Passover. In that case, he would be carried to the tent by Moslems, plenty of whom were about among the curious sightseers. The 'Good' Samaritan, who, unlike the priest and Levite, was not afraid to touch a possibly dead body by the side of the Jerusalem–Jericho road, was presumably an exceptional man. A point about that parable is that the Samaritan had as many rules about the ceremonial uncleanness of touching a corpse as had the Jews, but was willing to risk contamination in order to discover whether the man was alive and needed help.

I remembered a band of godly women in England who arranged

outings for old-age pensioners. They called themselves 'The Samaritan Society', and I wondered what they would say if they could see some genuine Samaritans to whom they had likened themselves.

Oranges, black-coloured drinks, and sweetmeats were on sale from some stalls, and the whole atmosphere was reminiscent of a Sunday-school treat at home. A few Palestinian policemen stood about the place and directed us towards the centre of interest beyond the camp, where we could see a crowd around an open space. I was interested to notice that the tents were not ornate Eastern pavilions nor picturesque Bedouin bivouacs, but prosaic bell-tents of regulation design. Their rule is that all tents must be white, and the English standard pattern must have appeared to the Samaritans as being specially made for use at their Passover! A similar incongruity lay in the fact that the smaller boys, who wore white at the service like all the other male Samaritans, had baggy trousers made from coarse calico flour bags. I could see the blue stencilling of the maker's name on the seat! The tarbush, which is not the common male headgear in Palestine, was worn by practically every man and boy. I remembered the account of a visit to the Samaritans which was paid by Sir John Mandeville, a pilgrim to the Holy Land in the middle of the fourteenth century, who described the red head-dress they were required to wear. Is the red tarbush a survival of that old law?

In the open space formed by visitors sitting and standing round a wide rectangle, we saw the furnace and the altar being prepared for the approaching sacrifices. The furnace was a wide, deep pit lined with stones and containing a fire which was constantly fed with bushes of dry wood. In the little ill-printed book a Samaritan priest sold to me for 1s. there is a circle drawn to illustrate the fire, and within it the words: 'This is the furnace tacken [sic] from the time of Abraham.' The altar, to my surprise, was not a raised table or cairn of any kind, but a trench lined with stones, and with a circle at either end, so that its shape was that of a dumb-bell. A fire was burning in a part of the trench, and over it on a grid stood two great blackened drums of water gently simmering. Some rather Victorian-looking armchairs awaited distinguished visitors within the arena, and seven fat lambs contentedly munched the grass in a corner.

These were the lambs that were to be slain at sunset. Carefully tended so that they would be perfectly healthy and unblemished, they were born in the month Tishri of the previous year. This ensured that they were of the age and condition stipulated by Moses. The number of lambs for the Korban, as the sacrifice is called, depends upon the number of people taking part in the ceremony, but they prefer to slay in multiples of seven, as they believe that this ensures the prevention of any blemish on the animal or any error in the act of slaying. The slayers of the *Korban* must kill the lamb with only one sweep of the knife, and the victim must make no sound. If it is wounded or cries out it invalidates the sacrifice, and the body must be burned.

We went into a little enclosed part of the camp containing a wooden hut and one or two tents, which was the dwelling-place of the Samaritan High Priest, Mazliach Ben Pinchas, and found him sitting at the door of the hut smoking a cigarette. If it were not for the modern touch of the cigarette, he would have presented a picture of a typical Old Testament patriarch. He had a silver turban on his head, a long dove-grey robe and a beautiful big white beard. He stood and shook hands with us and obligingly stepped out into the sunshine to allow us to photograph him. He spoke no English, but a young British police sergeant nearby kindly acted as interpreter. We asked him how many Samaritans there were.

'About two hundred and forty,' he said.

'Your numbers are increasing, then?' I asked. I understood that only a few years ago the Samaritan population had been 145. He assented to this, and said that improved conditions under British administration had resulted in a lower rate of mortality. At least, that is what he meant to convey by long explanations duly translated by our worthy interpreter, who added that about half a dozen Jewish girls had married Samaritans during recent years, which enabled them to avoid excessive intermarriage. Their numbers have been scanty since the Middle Ages, and it is remarkable that this ancient people should have persisted as they have. Apparently there are no signs of them dwindling and becoming extinct.

When I inquired whether Mazliach Ben Pinchas considered himself to be a descendant of Aaron, I received a very involved and confused answer by which I understood the High Priest to say that his ancestry was connected with the Levites. But I could not be sure of his meaning, especially as the police sergeant showed signs of not being very interested in the conversation and probably did not translate very carefully. It may be that there is some truth in the theory that the priestly line fell back upon the Levitical family to maintain it in the seventeenth century. There is a letter of that time in the British Museum which was written by the Samaritans to an imaginary Samaritan community in England, asking for a member of the family of Aaron to be sent to them in order to maintain the high-priesthood. They long had the curious idea that communities of their people flourished in Europe, probably a memory of prisoners taken by the Crusaders. Another pathetic appeal to France was made last century.

We asked to see the famous Roll of the Pentateuch, and were admitted into the hut where High Priest No. 2, who spoke English, duly exhibited it to us. There have been stories about various copies of this manuscript, of varying ages, being shown to visitors, but apparently it is their oldest and most treasured copy that is produced on Mount Gerizim at the Feast of the Passover. The case was a most interesting object of what appeared to be silver, cylindrical in shape and hinged to enclose the two rolls of the ancient parchment. It was covered with carefully engraved pictures of the altar and temple furnishings which Joshua was believed to have placed on Gerizim. Besides birds and bushes, there was a seven-branched candlestick, the Holy Ark, lamps, shew-bread, vestments, priests' staffs, pitchers, a chalice, and a number of other indistinguishable objects. Whilst the Roll itself, with its archaic characters plainly discernible, is not, as they say it is, written by Abishua, the great-grandson of Aaron, it probably dates from the early Christian era and is the oldest of its kind in the world. The parchment is made from the skins of sacrificed lambs.

Who are the Samaritans? This is a subject upon which many volumes have been written and it is the cause of much controversy. It is not possible for me to do more than mention a few facts and suggestions about the origin of this interesting people. The Jews have always declared that they are the descendants of Assyrian colonists who intermarried with the remnants of the ten tribes of Israel after the invasion and captivity of Shalmaneser, as related in 2 Kings xvii. This mixed race, it was said, learned but a garbled version of the religion of 'the god of the land', and have persisted in their delusions ever since, recognizing only the Pentateuch, the first five books of the Old Testament. But in 2 Chronicles xxx there is an account of Hezekiah inviting Israelites, men of Ephraim and Mannasseh, to the Passover at Jerusalem, most of whom refused to come. This suggests that it was recognized in those days that there were Israelites in the land, as distinct from foreigners, who would be welcomed to join in the ceremonies at Jerusalem, and who for their part refused to be tempted to share in the glories of Solomon's Temple. Later, also, in the time of Josiah, there is a reference to Israel as well as Judah. The Samaritans claim to be descended directly from these Israelites. Their name might have its origin in the Hebrew word for 'guardian'. They say it means that they, and not the erring Jews, are guardians of the Law.

When the Jews were rebuilding Jerusalem the Samaritans offered assistance, which Ezra refused. The Jews declare that this was justified, as the Samaritans are a mixed race. They themselves however, deny this, and insist that they are of true Israelitish stock, that they alone have preserved the ancient traditions, and that the Jews are schismatics. They claim pure descent from the families of Ephraim, Manasseh, and Levi who escaped and remained completely separate from the Assyrian invaders. What is more, they declare that Moreh, on Gerizim, is the true Moriah where Abraham tried to offer up Isaac, and is thus the true site of the Temple; and that Eli was not in the true priestly line, but that the Jews wrongly accepted him. David, they insist, knew all this, and that is why he did not build the Temple in Jerusalem; but Solomon, influenced by his foreign wives, erected his Temple on a false Moriah. Competent scholars find it difficult to decide the amount of truth in these conflicting ideas, so it remains for me to say, as one of our college tutors used to put it: 'There is much to be said on both sides.'

There were many Samaritans in New Testament times, and we are all familiar with the encounters Jesus had with them. It is interesting to notice that He told the ten lepers that He met on the border between Samaria and Galilee to go to the priests. One of them, the one who returned to thank Him, was a Samaritan. Did he go to a priest in Samaria, whilst the others went to a Jewish priest, if they were Jews?

Samaritans were plentiful and powerful in the early Christian era, and although there is evidence that many of them became Christians, in Byzantine times they massacred many monks, including the Bishop of Neapolis, and went burning churches as far as Bethlehem. Justinian waged war against them and destroyed their army in Transjordan. He sold 20,000 of them into slavery in Persia and India. There are records of many Samaritans in Damascus in the thirteenth and fourteenth centuries, but now all that remains of the ten tribes of Israel is this tiny community living under canvas on this hilltop during Passover, and at other times clustered into a huddle of mean houses around a little dark synagogue in the back streets of Nablus.

Theirs has been a history of troubles and risings, and they have not always been able to come up on to this plateau. They were excluded from Gerizim for about forty years by the Turks, but about 100 years ago the British Consul intervened and the Samaritans purchased the land. As the little book I bought from them naïvely says: 'Since the Five Books of Moses say that anyone who fails to do his duty with regard to Passover commits a great sin and is to be killed, therefore we find that all Israelites do their best to fulfil their obligations.'

The time drew on for the ceremony to begin, so we took our places in the crowd, and watched the proceedings. Some notable visitors were seated on the armchairs, including the acting High Commissioner, the District Commissioner, and a high Moslem official. The Samaritan men, all clad in white except for the High Priest and two other priests in green, divided into two parties, some to pray and some to stand by the altar-trench to be the 'workers'. The 'prayers' all faced towards the east, it may be because the traditional site of their temple was a few hundred yards from them in that direction. Each had a rug, on which he occasionally knelt and bowed his forehead to the ground. The prayers were chanted in a wailing sort of sing-song. The crowd was very close to the worshippers, but the latter appeared unconcerned, as were the lambs frisking in a corner. I was struck by the resemblance to the Moslem mode of prayer, both in prior ablutions and prostrations on rugs. I later learned that Gaster believes that the Moslems owe a great deal to Samaritans, and the similarity runs to the liturgy itself, some counterparts of which are in the Koran. At one juncture the people cry, 'There is no God but one', reminiscent of the Moslems' *La illaha illa 'llah*.

As the sun began to dip down to the western skyline, the High Priest stood on a block of stone and, facing the people, recited the Exodus account of the institution of the Passover, while the workers made ready to kill the lambs. Then he cried, '*Shatu attu!*' ('Slay!') and one by one the lambs, with no apparent struggle and without a sound, had their throats slit in one sweeping movement of a great knife. As each one was killed successfully, the onlookers clapped and cheered, and the participants worked themselves into a sort of frenzy, chanting and singing all the time. They poured blood into bowls and, dabbling their fingers into it, they spread wide red fingermarks on the foreheads of the firstborn boy of each family. I saw a little boy of about six years of age delightedly dripping with gore. The carcases were then plunged into the boiling water in the drums to soften them and facilitate fleecing them. Then they were hoisted on to crosspieces of wood and the entrails were expertly removed. These were laid on sticks across the fire at one end of the altar trench, and duly burnt until not a trace or odour of them remained. Salt was rubbed into the remainder of the carcase of each lamb, and the right foreleg cut off for the priest's portion. Care is always taken to break no bones and to account for every fragment of the animal. A search is made next morning and every remnant is burnt. Also, the law is that nobody but a Samaritan is allowed to touch the *Korban*, and police were at hand to keep the crowd back and prevent any deliberate or accidental violation of this law.

It was getting darker, of course, and the furnace in the pit was flaring as workers stoked it up. Oil lamps were produced and everything became a little confused as groups were formed here and there, where a priest was chanting prayers, or a girl reading the Scriptures—in very good Hebrew, one of my missionary companions told me—and others attended to the carcases. The moon was rising and many of the visitors departed. We were determined to see the whole of the ceremony, so we spent this interim period before the resumption of the main ceremonies by walking about the broad expanse of the hilltop. Before it got properly dark we were able to see the wonderful view from the topmost peak, where stands the dome of the Moslem tomb of Sheikh Ghanem. Here maybe, in the dim long-ago, was a Canaanite and later an Israelite high place. We could see, far below, the outline of the ruins over Jacob's Well. How obvious it was that the woman had pointed to this great mass on which we were now standing, and said: 'Our fathers worshipped in this mountain.' Far to the left lay the bulk of Ebal, some 300 feet higher than Gerizim. It is called the Mount of Curses, since Joshua assembled the people round the Ark to hear the law of Moses, and the curses were uttered on the slopes of Ebal, and the blessings on the opposite slopes of Gerizim. Far away up the valley to the northwest was Sebastieh, the old Samaria itself, now excavated and revealing remains of Israelitish glory.

There were some ruins nearby, and we inspected them as well as we could in the waning light. They seemed to consist of a great octagon whose walls held the outline of side chapels. This is all that remains of the Byzantine church to the Virgin built by the Emperor Zeno in A.D. 474. It is probably on the site of Sanballat's temple, which was destroyed by John Hyrcanus in 120 B.C. The words of Jesus to the Samaritan woman suggest that worship was carried on there at that time, so it is possible that Herod rebuilt their temple for them. The Samaritans say that Hadrian destroyed it in A.D. 135 to build there his temple to Jupiter.

We sat on the great stones and watched the activities below us round the leaping flames of the fire in the pit. Immediately beneath us lay the enclosure formed by a wall of rough stones, within which the Samaritans declare is the site of Abraham's altar on Mount Moriah and the true Holy of Holies. There is a platform of rock with a depression in it which may once have been a Canaanite place of sacrifice, especially as a pit full of human bones has been found nearby. There is also a cairn, supposed to be Joshua's Twelve Stones. Formerly this site was the scene of some of the prayers and the reading of the Torah in the Passover service. Dr. Thomson relates how he saw the Samaritans praying there in 1898, and a man to whom I spoke on Gerizim, an Arab, told me, that he had seen the same thing more recently. But now the whole of the service is conducted on the lower plateau.

We could hear the sound of chanting as the priests read the first fifteen psalms and continued the preparations for the consignment of the victims into the pit. As they chanted and wailed, their hands were raised before them palms upwards, and occasionally they wiped their hands over their faces, a habit I am told they have when they pray in their synagogue. When all was ready, they ran a long sharp pole through each carcase and lowered it into the pit, where embers were glowing, and covered the whole with criss-cross timbers and clods of earth, till nothing could be discerned of what lay below except the ends of the poles emerging from it. This common oven suggests the rustic simplicity of a small village, with its own high place and communal oven because of scarcity of fuel. We were looking back through the dim centuries at age-old customs persisting into the modern world; but we moderns were the intruders, not the Samaritans. They were at home here. This is where they had worshipped for centuries, and in this manner. Maybe in generations to come they will still be observing these weird old rites and ceremonies. It did seem to us, however, to lack any spirituality whatever. There appeared to be no meaning in it all, except the maintenance of tradition. All was well so long as the correct words were said at the correct time and particular actions were made at the appropriate moment. The whole thing was a living museum-piece, a show to goggle at by many and apparently with no vestige remaining of a spiritual content. It was as dead as a Tibetan prayer-wheel.

Sitting up there above that strange assembly, that piece of Old Testament in the flesh, the four of us, young ministers of the gospel, had a prayer meeting. My eye had been on my watch, because I meant to observe the Fellowship of Silence of the Wednesday Fellowship, when the members would stand in silence and remember and pray for the folk at home and all absent friends. I knew they would be thinking of me at ten o'clock, too, so I told the others about the Silence, and we observed it together. There we were, on that moonlit hilltop where so many prayers through dark centuries had been raised to the god of the Canaanites and to the Yahveh of the Israelites, to Jupiter of the Romans, and to Mary, Mother of

God, of the Byzantine Christians. We joined ourselves, not only with loved ones far away and friends in Jerusalem, but with the people of the stations where the missionaries worked. And we prayed for the people before us, vainly slaughtering animals when Christ our Passover had been slain for us, and would, if they followed Him, lead them out from a greater captivity than that of Egypt: the bondage of dead ceremonies. The words came back to us: 'Neither in this mountain nor in Jerusalem . . . but in spirit and in truth.'

After some sandwiches and hot tea from a flask, we descended to the plateau and watched the groups of men at prayer. I searched in vain for any sign of blood upon the lintels of the tents, although I had read of observers seeing hyssop dipped in the blood and sprinkled over the doors, and the fact that it was part of the ceremony was plain in their own booklet. I asked the High Priest why this had not been done. He was resting by his hut. It was a pity to disturb the old gentleman. His answer was a very vague one. He muttered something about a feud that was going on between two of the families, but turned off the conversation by informing the police sergeant that he thought the sugar ration was too small! Our interpreter added that the Samaritans in Nablus were notorious possessors of illicit stills, in which they made the potent *arak* that the Arabs loved to obtain and which intoxicated them so easily. There really was a feud, I understood, as one more progressive family was demanding a school for the Samaritan children and an improvement in the synagogue, which the conservative High Priest refused. He waved his hand towards one tent, and said in Arabic: 'They are the people causing all the trouble,' and would tell us no more about the lack of blood on the tents.

The Samaritans observe the Sabbath with a greater strictness than that of the Jews, who have any number of legal loopholes to make the rules easier for them. But amongst these people there are no evasions, and they keep the feasts of Pentecost and Tabernacles and other ceremonies in due season. In this respect, at any rate, they are Israelites indeed in whom is no guile.

At about half-past twelve, when the lambs had been in the pit for more than three hours, with due ritual they were removed. I stood by the pit edge and watched the young men as they feverishly pulled away the earth, grass and sticks that covered it. When the space was clear, a strong aroma of roast lamb came up to us. The poles were raised and the steaming carcases pulled off and placed on seven large platters that were held ready. Away to the tents sped the boys with the meat, where women and children sat waiting with *mazoth* (unleavened bread) and leaves of bitter lettuce ready to share out.

I walked across to where the High Priest and his family sat in a circle, girded about and with sandals on their feet, and I watched them eating. The enactment demanded that they should eat in haste, and cheerfully. This they did all the more readily because they had been fasting all day, but I must say that the sight of a hungry, bearded priest reaching over the shoulders of others for a great smoking piece of meat, grinning and gorging himself as he stuffed it into his mouth with greasy fingers, was no pleasant sight. When the men had finished, the women began to eat, and we left them at that late hour, enjoying the dramatic climax of an exhausting ceremony. They were eating the Passover as their fathers had done for generations on their holy mountain.

We stumbled downhill in the moonlight and our footsteps echoed along the narrow, empty streets of the sleeping city of Nablus, under the weird outlines of domes and arches, to find our resting beds. Above us on the hilltop slumbered the weary guardians of an ancient tradition which once again they had faithfully fulfilled. Except, maybe, in one particular. I still do not know why they sprinkled no blood on their doors.

CHAPTER XI

LEPERS

> When I lived in sin, it was very painful to me to see lepers, but God led
> me into their midst, and I remained there for a little while. When I left
> them, that which had seemed to me bitter had become sweet and easy.
>
> St. Francis.

For several weeks I tried without success to arrange for the members
of the Wednesday Fellowship to visit the Leper Hospital in Jerusalem. The cold, changeable weather we experienced in the early
weeks of 1942 caused a mild epidemic of influenza, and it affected
the nursing staff of the hospital. The sisters who had not fallen
sick were far too busy with their extra work to attend to a party of
visiting soldiers. So we postponed our visit until the finer spring
weather came, when Sister Johanna, the Matron, not only invited
us to see the patients and the work of the hospital, but asked us to
stay to tea. I warned her that at least twenty of us would be coming
—actually there were twenty-seven—but she was undismayed, and
we duly gathered at our customary Sunday rallying point at St.
Andrew's Hostel in the centre of the town.

I led the men, in khaki and R.A.F. blue, past the Moslem burial
ground of Mamillah with its old pool once thought to be Hezekiah's
Upper Pool of Gihon, over the hilltop which in the last few years
has been covered with the stone houses of modern design that
constitute the Jewish suburb of Rehavia, and downhill again towards Katamon in the valley, a remote section of new Jerusalem
where many British residents live. On those slopes, above the
many quiet homes hidden amid trees and gardens, lie the grounds
of the Moravian Leper Hospital, obscure behind old stone walls,
and unknown even to many of the oldest inhabitants of the city.

An Arab girl, in a Sunday dress of black silk embroidered with
red, was awaiting our party at the gate, and led us along a garden
walk to a peaceful courtyard in the midst of surrounding buildings,
where Sister Johanna came to welcome us. I had met her several
times before, and had called at the hospital at Christmas-time, when
the patients had received gifts in a candle-lit hall greenly decorated
after the style of an old-fashioned Christmas. For twenty years
Sister Johanna has laboured amongst the lepers, dealing gently with
a multitude of trials and difficulties, and displaying that infinite
patience which has produced so sweetly placid a mien. She was clad

in a simple black habit and apron and old-time nurse's cap. These good sisters—four of them to attend to the needs and treatment of thirty lepers—are missionaries who are devoted to the selfless calling of caring for the pitiable creatures in this hospital.

We looked about us. The flagged quadrangle was surrounded by two-storied buildings with a balcony round them, fringed with the green beds of ferns and shrubs. Under the raised brick centre, the sister told us, was a great water cistern after the Arab style, fed by pipes from the roofs. Our heavy boots rang on the stone floor of the corridor as we followed her black figure as quietly as we could from ward to ward of the hospital. Only two, or at the most three, beds were in each great airy room, with the stone floor scrubbed clean and never a rug or mat to harbour dust.

We saw the women's quarters first. Most of the patients were out in the garden, but a few were abed, or sitting in easy chairs in the quiet of the room. Most of the women were Jewesses, one of very great age and another no more than seventeen. As we peeped into the wards, at the sister's invitation, some greeted us with the universal Jewish greeting, 'Shalom', Hebrew for 'peace'. Others, however, turned their disfigured faces away from us and we did not embarrass them by remaining long. The girl of seventeen had first shown signs of the disease some three years earlier, and already the thickening countenance and harsh voice were noticeable. She looked twenty years older than she was. The old woman in another room, who sat at a table and ignored us completely as we passed, was a recent admission and she had not been proved to be a leper until after her eightieth birthday. It is possible, however, that she had had the disease within her for a very long time. The leprosy bacillus has an incubation period of anything from one to twenty years.

Before we went into the garden, the sister took us, filing as quietly as we could, through the men's wards. Most of them were Arabs. In the first room we entered, two young men were sitting talking together, their faces marked with the dreadful nodules.

'One is a Moslem,' Sister Johanna told us, 'and the other is the only Christian patient we have. He is a Jew who was baptized a few months ago. The patients have liberty always to observe their own religions, but we never make a secret of the fact that we minister to them in the name of Jesus.'

We grouped ourselves in his room, where he sat up in bed under a number of brightly-coloured religious pictures. His name was Jeshua, and I greeted him with 'Kef halak?' ('How are you?')

'El hamd'lillah,' he replied, 'quais katir' ('Thank God, very well').

'Thank God, very well!' Is that what I would say if half my face

o

were eaten away by a devilish pestilence that every one seemed powerless to control, and my body ached with a pain I knew would never leave me whilst I lived?

The sister told us his story.

Jeshua, whose name was that of his Lord, formerly shared this room with a young Armenian who suffered a great deal of pain, but who endured it patiently with the faith and hope of a Christian. When finally he died, his courage and peace had so impressed Jeshua that he was constrained to find for himself in Christ the secret of inner strength and serenity possessed by this young Armenian Christian. The result was that he came to know Jesus as his Saviour, and was baptized. The difference in his life had been amazing. There he was in the bed his friend had occupied, under the pictures his friend had owned, waiting for an end that was not far away, an end that he knew would be but a beginning. His one desire was to be able to pass through every pain and endure death with the calmness he had seen in the friend who had gone before him. Was it not Origen who said that the finest apology for the Christian faith is the way Christians live their lives?

Some ignorant Jews believe that leprosy, 'the first-born of death', is the only disease which persists in the hereafter. Dreadful thought, that one must be unclean for all eternity! And that fearful superstition was not the least of the depths from which this young Jew had been delivered. It was not easy for him to maintain his faith among other patients who were unbelievers. But he had found the answer to his need both of body and soul in the simple piety of the Moravian sisters.

At one time lepers were legally judged to be 'dead', and in Europe it was the custom to hold the service for the dead when a person was discovered to have the disease. The contrary was the case in this man's experience. He had found, not death, but life.

We had a little service in that room, the troops standing vigorous and full of health, and the frail leper lying in his bed. We sang 'Jesu, Lover of my soul' and 'Lead, kindly Light', and we prayed together. He did not understand our words, but we were at one with him in the fellowship of faith and prayer.

'Ma's-salameh,' he said ('Go in peace').

'Allah yusallimak,' we replied as we filed out ('May God preserve you').

We went to the bedside of a bearded old Jew with a little black smoking cap on his head. He was from Lithuania, and the sister said that it was very difficult for her to understand the queer Yiddish that he spoke. But he had lived in the United States for a while, and when it dawned upon him that we were British he managed to croak some English words to us, and pointed to a large photograph that hung upon the wall. It was of a group of large and prosperous-looking Jews, his six sons and two daughters, who he told us lived in Chicago. He was extraordinarily proud of them, but we could not help feeling how pathetic it was that this old man, who had brought up a large family to prosper in a distant land, should end his life so sadly, gripped at the end by the age-old dread of leprosy. His form of the disease was the worst of all. It had affected both his nerves and his limbs instead of the one or the other, as is more common. He slept nearly all day, but at night he would rise and wander about his room, eating bananas, playing with a few tiny objects in his cupboard, and looking at the photograph on the wall. In the morning the sisters would find his room in disorder and the old man fast asleep on the bed.

Another and another patient we saw, each affected differently by the disease, some indetectably except to the eye of the expert, and others obvious to us all, with fingers dropped off, limbs withered to stumps, and faces cracked and hideous. The face of one man was covered with bandages, and we did not pause to worry him. We passed on and left the sister to lean over and comfort him with gentle words.

We were shown the bandaging-room. The sores and broken skin must be dressed every day. Sometimes two hours are spent in binding up the separate open sores of the patient. Often the patient has had the same open place on his body dressed daily for years. What fortitude he needs, and what infinite patience on the part both of those who minister and those who are ministered unto. There is no man more philosophic, who has learned more by the things he has suffered, than the leper. And no man more hopeful. The scourge of the centuries is laid upon him, but he still clings to the hope that somehow, some time, the skill and knowledge of men will deliver him. An outcast, a prisoner, unclean of body and pitied by every one, harbouring within him secrets that have never yet been fully revealed, he persists in the blind hope that one day he will be cleansed of his plague. He has a stoic calm: he has learned to wait.

The nerves which carry the impulses of the body are the trophic nerves, and it is these that the disease usually attacks. Like an intricate, mysterious signalling system, the trophic nerves inform the body of cuts and burns and bruises, carrying not only a warning pain, but the message that destroyed cells and tissues need to be restored; and so the process of healing comes about. But no impulses are sent along the system when this disease attacks it. A leper burns his hand or cuts his finger, and the body receives no warning to repair the damage. The wound remains open, pus accumulates and foul ulcers form. Damage cannot be taken care of, for the delicate lines of communication are cut, and the body remains ignorant of its wounds. There is no pain when the trophic nerves are gone. The flesh wears away, fingers and toes fall off joint by joint, the body is defenceless against the attack of germs of all kinds, and lepers succumb to influenza and tuberculosis, neuritis, rheumatic fever, and a score of other besieging ills. They rarely die of leprosy. The body rots and they remain alive, living corpses. The last two patients in this hospital to die were aged ninety and a hundred and eight respectively.

It is difficult to give these poor souls other things to think about beside the prolonged act of rotting and dying. They are often very fond of music, though their fingers can seldom wield an instrument and their voices are usually harsh and croaking, owing to the effect of the disease upon their vocal chords. There was a radio-room in this hospital, however, in which they could sit and listen to music from the Jerusalem station and from farther afield. As in countless other places, the wireless linked up these innocent captives with the outer world from which they were barred.

We went into the garden. It was a wide series of plots along the hillside, with a coppice of fir trees under which the grass was splashed with the crimson of anemones and the white and blue of daisies and bird's-eye. Occasional almond trees gay with blossom were scattered across the grounds, but for the most part the garden plots were full of vegetables: onions, peas, and cauliflowers flourishing in the rich red soil, albeit stony, of course, like all the fields of Palestine. Both men and women were occupying themselves with hoe and rake, often in a desultory manner, pleasing themselves how they worked. The result was not the orderly garden the Matron might desire, but the principal object was to give the patients some occupation.

We grouped together under some fir trees and watched a poor, wretched creature in an enclosure of her own busy with a copper ewer of water. Leprosy had attacked her brain, and she had been hopelessly mad for twenty years. She had no hands, but thrust the stumps of her arms through the handle and lifted the pitcher to her scarred and distorted face. She had the delusion that it was the Moslem prayer-time, and for hours she would mutter her petitions to Allah, cleansing herself with water after the Moslem fashion. Since 1923 she had dwelt in that little house in the hospital grounds, after being rescued from a life of beggary at a gate of the Old City, where she had found the exhibition of her withered limbs to be a source of profit. I thought of all that had passed in my own life since 1923. I reviewed the years of schooldays and of commercial life in the City of London, of study and of local preaching, of happy cycling days in summer through leafy Essex lanes, of making great decisions, and dreaming great dreams, and making the great discoveries of youth and life and love; I remembered college days, and the glad early years of ministry in the drab streets by a London terminus; and marriage, and a glorious tour of Italy, and strenuous mission work in Old Kent Road; the delight of our little boy in tiny wonders; the coming of war and the sundering of family life; adventures with the Army in East Anglia and Aldershot, in Cape Town and Khartoum, in Abyssinia and Syria; and now my life in the Holy City. And all that time, which was such a kaleidoscopic pattern of experience and life to me, had been but the monotonous passing of years for that poor soul, a leper, unclean and deranged of mind, hidden from life; of the world, but not in it.

The lepers cultivate their garden plots on rough terraces which stretch along that hill slope, and they have a fine southern view of the hills around Bethlehem and away over to Hebron. We wandered amongst them, and whilst some were shy, most allowed the visitors to take photographs of them while they worked. They greeted Sister Johanna with obvious pleasure, and she talked volubly to them in Arabic. I was interested to notice a Jewish lad wielding a spade alongside some Arabs, and found that they are the greatest of friends, and Arabic has become his usual speech since he has lived here. Here is the Brotherhood of Leprosy. The disease takes no account of rank or race or wealth or creed, but binds all together in a fellowship of suffering. The insidious, invisible bacilli conspire to destroy the age-old human barriers of race and religion.

Before the house there is a quiet garden edged by trees and girded by a high stone wall. Later, in June, I saw that garden rich with masses of purple bougainvillea, with oleander trees weighed with bright pink blooms, and, hanging from the wall, the mystic passion-flower, with its three nails and five wounds and crown of thorns in each intricate blossom, blue and white amid the dark green leaves. We walked slowly across the garden, and looked up at the words JESUS HILFE cut in stone across the front of the house. It means 'Jesus, help', and I remembered one of the other workers in the hospital, Sister Katherina, telling me how she saw it when first she arrived here as a stranger, and the sister who met her told her, 'You will need that.'

'I have needed it many, many times since then,' she had told me; 'and always His grace is sufficient for me.'

We could not help noticing a patient talking to two visitors in a corner of the garden. She was a Jewess, and they were her husband and little boy about seven years old. She was not permitted to touch them, and they stood about 2 yards from her, talking in low tones. It seemed overwhelmingly pathetic to us, who had been separated for so long from our wives and children, to see a mother who was compelled to keep her distance from her child; who could see him occasionally, but knew that she never could make him a garment, never cook a meal for him, never embrace him again.

Sister Johanna's dark form preceded us, and we mounted the stone steps into what the men immediately termed 'the M.I. room', not, I may say for the benefit of the uninitiated, a room designed for Military Intelligence, but for Medical Inspection. There were bottles of medicines and drugs covering the shelves on the wall, and the sister gave us a little lecture on the treatment of leprosy. Her English was excellent, but occasionally she made us laugh by a smiling misuse of English idiom. Hers was such an informal and friendly air that we did not attempt to conceal the amusement she caused when she said some authorities 'swear at' a certain drug, when she meant that they 'swear by' it. We explained the difference to her, and she was delighted at her error. The sisters who come to work here have the burden, not only of equipping themselves for the specialist task of leprosy nursing, but can seldom use their native language except to one another. They must learn Arabic and Hebrew in order to speak to their patients, and English in order to enjoy the wider fellowship outside the bounds of their compound.

Both Arab and Jewish dermatologists and specialists in leprosy visit the hospital to attend to the patients, and we learned something of the treatment that is given. The sister showed us a bottle of a chaulmoogric oil preparation known as E.C.C.O., Dr. Muir's formula, which is made from a herb found in India. The patients receive a regular, usually weekly, intramuscular injection of this, and a mixture of chaulmoogric acids is also injected into the separate nodules on the skin. We saw some tiny dermal needles that are used for this purpose. It is also possible to take a form of this preparation internally, and little capsules of hydrocanus Wightiana oil were made up in that room and some of the patients took them before meals. Other drugs, strychnine and camphor and so on, were there for particular needs, and we heard, what we had already known about insulin for diabetics, that the supply of the necessary drugs was a difficult and expensive matter in time of war.

Instances of the arrest of cases of leprosy in Palestine are common, but so far a complete cure has not been known. Some patients have been discharged with the progress of the disease retarded, but there have not been up to the present any of the dramatic cures from the disease known in other more extensive centres of research and treatment in the leper colonies of India, Africa and China. There are about 200 lepers altogether in Palestine, many of them living rent free in some cottages provided for them in the village of Silwan, the old Siloam across the valley south-east of Jerusalem. The worst cases, of course, are cared for by the Moravians in this hospital.

The disease is not very contagious, at least in temperate climates. It is far easier to catch a cold than to catch leprosy. Cleanliness is the secret of preventing contagion, and there is no cleaner place in Jerusalem than the Leper Hospital, where dwell the abhorred and the 'unclean' of society. The disease is conveyed by touch or by dirt, but with proper precautions it is not impossible to prevent its spread. The difficulty is to find a cure for leprosy, and that is a romantic and fascinating task which engages scientists in colonies and research laboratories all over the world, and some dramatic stories are told both of their successes and their failures.

One in every 600 or 700 people is a leper. There are 3,000,000 lepers in the world altogether, 1,000,000 of them in India and another 1,000,000 in China. Forty thousand are in Burma, which at the time I am writing this is being invested by Japanese aggressors. What will happen to them, and to the multitudes of others who have hitherto had what attention and treatment the science of the Western world has been able to give them? There are hundreds of lepers in the United States at the present time, dozens of them in New York. There are some in Europe, even as far north as Iceland, and a few in Great Britain. Palestine has known them from time immemorial, and in the Old and the New Testaments we find mention of them. So when we visit the Holy Land we behold, not only the hills and valleys and cities that Jesus saw, but pathetic, disfigured faces and withered limbs, like those He knew.

What had been accepted as a scourge of God He saw as a sad result of man's ignorance and uncleanness, and he fought against it. The spirit of rebellion against dirt and disease and the painful maladies amongst men that shut them from their fellows and cause them to despise themselves is a spirit that His followers have inherited. It was wonderful to us to see His work of healing still being done. 'These, and greater things than these, shall ye do.' Where Jesus cleansed the leper, these Moravians were doing the same, in His name and for His sake. The meaning and implication of all this was put into a phrase by one of the men, who whispered to me:

'I reckon this place is more holy than the Holy Sepulchre.'

He was right. The beauty of holiness is in character and personal love and service rather than in sanctuaries full of baubles. 'Let your light so shine', not from a crowd of altar lamps, but from 'good works'. 'If your son ask bread, will ye give him a stone?' Yes, too, too often the stone of Byzantine architecture for the bread of life. As we wandered round the holy sites in and around Jerusalem men often inquired whether such and such a place was 'authentic'. Very few of them are. But one 'authentic' holy place we have seen: it is the Leper Hospital of the Moravians. The building was erected in the eighteen-eighties, but in spirit it dates from the New Testament.

We sat on chairs ranged round a larger room with a window looking upon the hills of Judea. Sister Johanna presided at a tea-pot and we passed round plates of cakes. There was a homely, godly atmosphere about that room; and none of us will soon forget the picture of the saintly sister serving us as willingly as she had satisfied our curiosity and interest all the afternoon, and as ceaselessly active as in her devotion to the poor creatures under her care.

One of the men had found a Moravian English Hymn-book and seated himself at the piano. Pictures of Count Zinzendorf and Martin Luther stared at us from the walls, but unabashed we sang some of Charles Wesley's hymns, all the more readily when I had explained the connection between the Moravians and the Methodists. Without the Moravian Church very probably there would have been no Methodist Church. John Wesley was greatly affected by their piety and calmness when he travelled to Georgia in the days before his conversion, which took place in a Moravian meeting in London. I wished that we could have sung one or two of John Wesley's translations of the hymns of Zinzendorf, his Moravian contemporary, but the tunes were not familiar to us. We looked, however, at the words:

> Eternal depth of love divine,
>   In Jesus, God with us, displayed;
> How bright Thy beaming glories shine!
>   How wide Thy healing streams are spread!

> Still, Lord, Thy saving health display,
>   And arm our souls with heavenly zeal;
> So fearless shall we urge our way
>   Through all the powers of earth and hell.

This spirit of unyielding zeal in attacking the evils that beset mankind was a characteristic of Wesley that he gained from the Moravians, and it is exemplified in this branch of the Moravian missionary work. The 'healing stream' had spread as far as this. The term 'Moravian', like 'Bohemian', was once used to connote a nation in Czechoslovakia, but now describes people of any race who think and live in a certain way. There are many Moravians in England, and they are responsible for a great missionary work; and all, on the Continent, in England or America, are characterized and animated by the same simple piety and love for others that first attracted Wesley and influenced him so profoundly. Like St. Francis, whose first gesture at his break from convention to a life of poverty was to kiss a leper, those Moravian sisters have inherited the spirit of Jesus, who Himself touched lepers and made them whole. It is perfect love that casts out fear. It was something like the testimony of St. Francis that Sister Johanna gave us when we had sung our hymns. She told us in her low, quiet voice about the power of prayer that alone enabled the sisters to do their work, giving them courage and endurance in every difficulty, and affection for the poor souls committed to their charge.

The Knights of St. Lazarus, who founded lazar-houses for lepers all over Europe in the Middle Ages, have their successors to-day in these Moravian sisters, bless them.

A soldier's income is not great, and piastres, of the value of $2\frac{1}{2}d$. each, were precious, but when one of our number went round with the hat, the contributions of twenty-seven men amounted to 300 piastres for the Leper Hospital. I shall always remember the plaque on the wall which held in German the words of St. Paul:

SEID ALLEZEIT FRÖHLICH

which, being interpreted, means 'Be always happy'.

CHAPTER XII

NEW JERUSALEM

Jerusalem is a small town of big things.

G. K. CHESTERTON.

EIGHTY years ago there were barely a dozen houses outside the walls of the Old City. To-day Jerusalem spreads over valleys and hills to the north and west, so that now but a fifth of the population resides within the old walls, and there are broad streets flanked by modern office buildings, banks, department stores, cinemas and blocks of flats designed in square piles of white stone. Pleasant suburbs, such as the Greek Colony with new villas in gardens, or the former German Colony with its shady avenues of pines, lie on the fringe of the modern city; while in the new Jewish quarters, built in very recent years, crowds of mansion flats rise often eight stories above the streets in monotonous white, straight lines. The luxury hotel, the King David, stands in proud modernity in contrast with the ancient stones a few hundred yards away. Cinemas have such names as 'Zion' and 'Eden', while restaurants in the modern thoroughfares of Ben Yehuda Street and Princess Mary Avenue are known by names more reminiscent of the central Europe from which proprietors and customers have recently come.

The finest building in New Jerusalem, dominating the city with the highest tower in it, is the famous Jerusalem home of the Young Men's Christian Association, the 'Central Y.M.C.A.', as we called it. I have often mentioned it in this book. All that was best in the social life of the Holy City, not only for men in uniform, but amongst young Arabs and Jews, centred in that pinnacle of white stone with adjacent buildings clustering at its foot. It seemed to possess everything a young man could want: a library with thousands of volumes, many of them in Arabic and Hebrew, as well organized as any borough library in England, with a huge section devoted to devotional and theological subjects; the only swimming-pool for hundreds of miles; a gymnasium with rooms for boxing, wrestling, squash courts, all under an immense dome; a large concert auditorium; hostel bedrooms and public restaurant; an Army canteen and billiard rooms; a soda fountain; tennis courts; a football ground; and a multitude of other amenities of that kind. It stands on a hilltop outside the west wall of the Old City, the fences of its sports grounds blue with profuse convolutions of Morning

Glory and with a garden containing most of the trees and flowers mentioned in the Bible. A broad terrace lies before it from which the tower rises over 150 feet. All the material for its building was quarried from the ground on which it stands. Once a Georgian monastery was on this site, and excavations revealed remains of ancient tombs.

It was built with American money, and cost $1,300,000, a million of which was given by the American coffee-king, James Newbiggin Jarvie. He wished none but the Divine Name to be carved on it, so the foundation stone that Lord Plumer laid on July 23rd, 1928, reads simply: 'These buildings are given to the glory of God and in remembrance of His only begotten Son.' But since the millionaire's death his portrait hangs in the reading-room and a tablet at the entrance declares that the building is the fulfilment of his inspired vision. But his was only the money for it. The inspired vision was Dr. Harte's, whom I met when I went to Galilee. When he was in charge of the Y.M.C.A. work in Jerusalem after the 1914–18 War, he took Mr. Jarvie, who was visiting the Holy City, up to the Mount of Olives and told him of a dream he had for many years, to build a worthy youth centre in Jerusalem. He had laboured in the East and in central Europe and had kept always in his mind that desire. His friend later gave him the money that made his vision a reality.

So the man responsible for this great Y.M.C.A. building was Dr. A. C. Harte, a Methodist minister of the United States. I had not found Methodism very prominent in the Holy Land. Indeed, my presence in Jerusalem was a completely unworthy representation of my Church, inadequate in view of the important part Methodism plays in the One, Holy, Catholic and Apostolic Church. I felt that particularly on the occasion when I dressed myself in official robes and sat beside the Moderator of the Church of Scotland and the heads of the Eastern Churches in the capacity of representative of my Church at the service in Christ Church commemorating the centenary of the Anglican bishopric in Jerusalem. But here was a characteristic contribution Methodism had made to the life of New Jerusalem. There is another of which I shall tell before the close of this chapter.

The 'Y.M.', as all the troops naturally called it, is an overpowering place. Accustomed as we were to canteen huts in Army camps, few of us could believe for a while that this was the Y.M.C.A. when first we saw it. It functions splendidly under executive officers who come from the U.S.A. and work every detail of organization with typical transatlantic efficiency, so it is not for me to criticize it.

But it was difficult to feel at home in it. It was like being in a cathedral, or in a museum, or a rich man's club. It was a show-place, I felt, and I was never properly at ease in it. However, to say even these mild truths is perhaps an ungrateful return for so much kindness I found there, and many privileges. The kindly General Secretary, Mr. Miller, came several times to the Wednesday Fellowship to tell us of his work and of the building's origin and growth, and one Sunday afternoon he invited a crowd of us to tea there to meet Dr. Harte, who was visiting him from Galilee, and to explore its halls and tower while he explained its symbolism to us.

It is full of symbolism. Every corner has some meaning. The threefold nature of the structure itself represents the Trinity. Twelve cypresses lining the path to its door stand for the Twelve Apostles. The crown-shaped ceiling at the entrance, with its cruciform plan, means that there is no cross without its crown. The oratory below the great Jesus Tower is a tiny, hushed sanctuary below ground, lit through a star-shaped aperture by a bulb that lights a world-globe at the same time as it lights the 'Star of Bethlehem'. It contains an altar of twelve unhewn stones from Bethel, reminiscent of Joshua's altar; and tablets in the wall depict quarrelling brothers becoming reconciled before offering their gifts. This place marks the first stage in man's quest for God. The second stage is symbolized by the Upper Room, on the first floor of the tower, the chapel with an octagonal 'Last Supper' table and surrounding Eastern divans where I celebrated Holy Communion on the night before Good Friday, 1942. The final stage is represented by a beautiful little sanctuary within the dome right at the top of the tower. Its ceiling is a star-lit heaven and around its rim are the words: 'They that wait upon the Lord shall renew their strength.' A frame without a picture in it behind the oaken door is inscribed: 'Whom having not seen, ye love.' There is always silence here, and solitary prayer.

I cannot tell of all the symbols in the building; the carvings on its cornices, the inscriptions on its portals, the emblems in shapes and forms in this picture and that pillar. It is a deliberate and elaborate sermon in stone, with every allusion imaginable appropriate to its situation and its function. Mr. Miller led us round the building on that Sunday, and explained everything. But we could not take it all in at one visit. We were often in and out of the place to visit the library or recreation-room, and it was only by custom and familiarity that the full impression of the place affected us as it should. The capitals of the many columns along the grand terrace are carved to represent beasts or flowers mentioned in the Scriptures. The entrance is flanked by red columns crowned with two fine sculptures: of the Woman of Samaria with a water-pot on her head, and of the Lamb of God. A giant bas-relief 16 feet high of Isaiah's six-winged angel is set half-way up the face of the great tower. We saw to the left in Arabic the words: 'There is no God but God;' to the right in Hebrew: 'The Lord our God is One;' and between them in Aramaic the very syllables that Jesus uttered: 'I am the Way.'

Underfoot at the door is a mosaic reproduction of the Madeba map of Jerusalem. Just inside the vestibule we looked up at an elaborate and highly coloured wooden ceiling which dates from the seventeenth century, and had been brought from Damascus, with a conical-shaped fireplace in the wall that came from the same house.

We ascended by lift to the observation gallery above the carillon high in the tower. There are thirty-five bells in the carillon, the largest weighing $1\frac{1}{2}$ tons. Often on Sunday evenings we listened to the hymn-tunes, many of them Evangelical favourites of England and America, ringing across Old Jerusalem and New. Especially do I remember the evening of Easter Day, when pink mares'-tails were traced across an azure sky and the bells clashed out 'Alleluias' as I walked homewards after a service. The men of my party were very interested in them, and in the complicated connections with the console below, from which they were played. The observation gallery has bronze bas-reliefs at each of the four sides to mark the view and to identify the landmarks in every direction. Several times in this book I describe the wonderful views from high places in Palestine: the Mar Elyâs Monastery on the Bethlehem road, the minaret at Nebi Samwil, Mount Gerizim, Mount Carmel, the Mount of Olives; and each I have thought better than the last. So I will refrain from saying that this is the finest view in the Holy Land, lest I contradict other things I have said elsewhere. But this I will say: it is only from this, the highest point within Jerusalem, that one can appreciate to the full the varied character of the Holy City, for the ancient narrow streets around the domes at the Temple site and the Holy Sepulchre can be seen immediately below, and over the grey-stone walls the rising tiers of ultra-modern blocks of flats in straight lines. Here at a glance one can see the Old World and the New, the Orient and the West, rubbing shoulders, jostling each other; and to the distant horizon those eternal hills to which the ancients lifted up their eyes.

The auditorium—the Golden Hall of Friendship—has an elaborate stage and orchestra pit and a four-manual organ with nearly 3,000 pipes. A man can pass through the largest pipe; the smallest is the size of a lead pencil. I have addressed a big church parade from its stage on a National Day of Prayer, and heard my voice booming through the hall as though I was in a cathedral. Under it are situated the Army canteen and billiard-rooms, and it was there that the Wednesday Fellowship held its informal Sunday evening canteen services. On its outer walls are carved the words: 'In Essentials, Unity; in Non-essentials, Liberty; in All Things, Charity.'

At least one other room was of special interest to us. It was the George Williams Room, situated above the board-room containing an exhibition of the work of 1914–18 prisoners of war. Sir George Williams began the Young Men's Christian Association in London on June 6th, 1844, in a business house, and here was an exact reproduction of his little room. It is panelled in oak, with solid early-Victorian furniture and wide London windows, a replica in every detail of the birthplace of the Y.M.C.A. It was used for Bible classes, and to perpetuate the memory of the founder. It was while we were in Jerusalem the news was received that the original building had been destroyed during a London air raid. . . .

It is impossible for me to describe all the modern buildings in Jerusalem: the Hadassah Jewish Hospital on Mount Scopus; the Hebrew University and Library; the Jewish Agency; the modern Yeshurun Synagogue; the fine new hospices of various religious orders; St. George's Anglican Cathedral; the Ophthalmic Hospital of St. John of Jerusalem. I can attempt, however, to give an impression of New Jerusalem as it affected us who perforce dwelt there, or visited it during the course of leave or duty whilst in the Middle East. It was always a surprise to men to discover how European is Jerusalem to-day, with its grand avenues, tree-lined between clean white buildings, its up-to-date hotels, its Y.M.C.A., when they expected dirty, smelly, narrow streets. They do not find the Old City quarter until they search for it beyond its enclosure of sixteenth-century wall. But dirty houses and mean streets are not confined to the Old City. Like other modern cities, Jerusalem has its slums, and high rents have caused many of those new Jewish flats to become overcrowded. Beggars sprawl across the pavements of the modern streets crying out in Arabic and Hebrew their time-honoured supplications and their invocation of the Deity as beggars did in Solomon's city and in Herod's, in Byzantine and Crusader Jerusalem, under Mameluke or Turkish rule. Clothes may change and streets may change, but 'the poor ye have always with you', and the New Jerusalem will remain very much like the Old until there is a new spirit: justice and righteousness in human life, an equitable distribution of wealth, a divine value placed upon human nature. The New Jerusalem appears 'out of heaven from God' when the true seat of holiness is known: that there is no temple but the temple of the human heart.

The Scots' Memorial Church of St. Andrew is part of modern Jerusalem. It stands on high ground by the railway station across the valley from the south-west corner of the traditional Mount Zion, and its square, white tower beside a domed church and hospice is a bold landmark on that side of the city. It was built in 1927 to commemorate the part played by Scots in the Last Crusade, and to be a worthy centre for the work which the Church of Scotland has done in the Holy Land for nearly 100 years. To-day there are Scottish missionaries in various parts of the country, with their own hospitals in Jaffa, Nazareth, Tiberias; many schools, many centres of evangelism. Theirs is a Presbytery with its own Moderator, and throughout the Middle East we found the influence of the Church of Scotland to be far-reaching. There are hundreds of Arabs in Palestine and beyond it who are, strange as it may sound, members of the Church of Scotland.

In some ways I think St. Andrew's is the loveliest church in the Holy City. Its modern lines are soothing to the eye. Inside, its white walls curve overhead, and a marble Communion table is in a rounded apse, with oak pews and stone side pulpit. Every pew is marked with the name of a town in Scotland, whose gift it was, and the names of Highland regiments are upon the wall. Set in the floor in the centre of the east end is a metal tablet 'in remembrance of the pious wish of King Robert Bruce that his heart should be buried in Jerusalem'. But why bring a piece of Scottish stone for the minister to stand on, when there is all the Holy Land to use?

I was several times invited to preach there, and each time the experience was a memorable one: in slow dignity behind an Arab beadle to enter the crowded church, full mostly in these days with men in khaki, though in peacetime with pilgrims and students from Scotland, and to sing the 'paraphrases' beloved north of the Tweed. This beautiful Presbyterian church was the nearest we Free Churchmen could find to our own atmosphere of worship until Wesley House was opened, and we loved to attend its services. I well remember the Watchnight Service I conducted there one New Year's Eve after a party the Wednesday Fellowship gave in St. Andrew's Army Hostel, where we met every week. As we came out of that service each one of us tolled the bell, and afterwards there were reels and Highland flings in the lounge of the hospice.

St. Andrew's Hospice, next to the church, is a home straight from Scotland. It is yet another of the national hospices for modern pilgrims to Jerusalem. It had a function to perform in wartime, as ever, for there was always need for a home in the Holy City for members of the Forces on leave. I myself gained much kindly hospitality there; and it served as a centre for social work for troops in that part of the Middle East. Many of us Sassenachs first tasted haggis on Burns' Night in Jerusalem, brought in by a 'varlet' in khaki to the accompaniment of the pipes, and greeted by a recitation of the national bard's 'Ode to a Haggis'.

Not so imposing as the Y.M.C.A., and hidden at the distant north-east corner of the Old City, is the Archaeological Museum. It is a wonderful piece of architecture, however, designed in low, white outline with a blue-tiled pool in its centre courtyard, and sculptures by Eric Gill, who describes in his autobiography how he worked happily amongst the native labourers, dressed as an Arab. John D. Rockefeller sent $2,000,000 for such an establishment in Egypt after the First World War, but for some reason it was not used, and he gave it to Palestine. It is said that when later he saw the building he inquired of his secretary whether it was one million or two that he had given! It is the headquarters of the administration of the Department of Antiquities of the Government of Palestine, which only in recent years has been able to organize and co-ordinate archaeological investigation in the Holy Land.

The Museum was more than once an object of our excursions, when we would rove through the centuries from Stone Age Palestine to Bronze Age and Iron Age, through Herod's Jerusalem and Hadrian's Aelia Capitolina, Byzantine Christendom and the Moslem invasion, the Crusader rule and the Saracenic restoration. We saw the conquerors from Egypt and Assyria and Babylon, Greece and Rome and Persia, Arab and Frank, by means of the relics of their rule, the implements, the inscriptions, the statues, the homely household articles, the tombs and bones they had left behind them, mute evidence of the pageantry of history and of the transitory nature of imperialism. The library, too, I found to be a wonderful place, equipped with the newest system of indexing, where sometimes I spent hours gleaning many things to tell the members of my parties when I led them around Jerusalem.

The pleasantest, most peaceful spot in the Holy City, more attractive even than the Latin Gethsemane, which is disturbed by so many visitors, is the quiet court which lies between two wings of the Museum. A long artificial pool in its centre is fringed with blue clumps of lavender, and goldfish swim under waterlilies of white and yellow, while around it descend broad pavements of white stone. Few hours could be more placid than those spent on a seat in the tiled recess under the tower at one end of the court, between the sculptures of ancient Rome and the modern figures cut by Eric Gill.

There is a tall tree in the midst of the buildings of the Museum, rising high above its roofs. It is said that the former Moslem owner of the land would say his prayers under that tree within view of the Dome of the Rock, when he was too old to visit it, and in his will recorded the wish that if the ground was sold it would be under the condition that nothing obscured the view of the Dome from that tree. Fortunately the tree is tall enough to look across the rooftops to the sanctuary on Mount Moriah.

The Street of the Prophets is long and winding, and where it begins near the Damascus Gate it passes through the oldest part of 'New Jerusalem', among gloomy tenements and dirty alleys. But for the most part it is fringed by stone walls overhung with shady pine and pepper-trees. The Palace of the Abyssinian Emperor is in this street, and the Swedish School, and the erstwhile German and Italian hospitals. But most significant of all, and the place in it best known to my friends and to me, was the Newman School of Missions. It deserves a place in this chapter on New Jerusalem because although the house, 'Thabor', was one of the first dozen houses to be built outside the Old City and is thus over eighty years old, its function is up-to-date and its spirit as fresh and new as anything in the Holy City.

Dr. Schick, the famous Jerusalem architect and archaeologist, built 'Thabor' for his home in the middle of last century, and housed there the models of the Temple which were later accommodated at the German Lutheran Church of the Redeemer. Bishop Newman, of the Methodist Episcopal Church of America, acquired the house in 1888, but died before he could make it his home upon retirement. He was chaplain to the Methodist President of the United States, Garfield, who was assassinated in 1897; and he travelled extensively in Bible lands in the eighties and nineties of last century. His widow dwelt in the house for several years, and in 1910 she bequeathed it to American Methodism, and for a year it was a Methodist Biblical Institute. During the First World War the Turks used 'Thabor' as an officers' mess, and from 1920–6 it was the home of Dr. Harte while he was planning the building of the Central Y.M.C.A. At Easter, 1928, was held the great conference of the

P

International Missionary Council on the Mount of Olives, and two days afterwards the 'Newman School of Missions' was opened as a training-centre for missionaries of any denomination, as well as a language school open to Government officials, nurses, and doctors from various local hospitals, and to other students of Arabic, Hebrew, Syriac, Biblical and theological subjects, and the comparative study of religion. The loan of the premises and a substantial grant for the maintenance of the work is the contribution of Methodism towards missionary endeavour in the Middle East. The School works under the auspices of the United Missionary Council of Syria and Palestine, and members of the staff are from various societies. Over 600 students, of many nationalities and from more than thirty different Churches or societies, passed through the School in its first fourteen years of life, besides a great many more who regarded it, as chaplains and many members of the services did, as a spiritual home and dynamic centre of Christian thought and activity.

The rambling structure of old stone, added to in the course of years as necessity required, with library and classrooms round the walls of its compound, gives the whole house an informal effect that is delightful. The little guarded door in the wall, with a lookout window above and a heavy bar in a socket to secure it, is a reminder not only of recent political 'troubles', but of turbulent times in far-off days when it was a dangerous matter to dwell outside the city walls. Behind the main house is a flagged courtyard whose old wall in early summer was a blaze of glory from climbing geraniums which hung it with a curtain of scarlet, while around were lilies in enormous pots, and masses of blue passion-flower, shady pepper-trees, a glorious lilac and, flourishing like the wicked, a green bay tree.

I have pleasant memories of a little group sitting round the Greek New Testament on Friday afternoons in 'Thabor' library, of the summer school some chaplains were able to attend, and of the visits the Wednesday Fellowship sometimes made to that old courtyard for moonlit gatherings, when we would have a service in the open air and afterwards take Holy Communion in the tiny chapel with its bay window protruding into the street, when we used the Methodist Service Book that Dr. Mott and other leaders used at the united Easter Day Communion of the World Missionary Council on the Mount of Olives, and felt at one with a great multitude who had known and loved this place. Best of all, one of the rooms in a corner of this rambling house was set aside for the use of the men as a reading-room, and welcome it was for us to get away from barracks and Army life, and rest in that book-lined room, with easy chairs and rugs underfoot and an old engraving of John Wesley on the wall. And none of us will forget teatime on Sundays at 'Thabor' and the overflowing hospitality of our hosts, the Rev. and Mrs. Eric Bishop, at Christmas and Easter.

Methodism in Jerusalem does not vie with other historic Churches for the possession of 'holy places', but has made its own unique contribution to the life of New Jerusalem. In the Y.M.C.A., built by a Methodist minister, it contributed the kind of social work which Wesley inspired; and in the Newman School of Missions, the only Methodist property in the Middle East, it maintains that emphasis upon learning, and intellectual equipment for God's service, which Wesley ordained. The catholic spirit of Wesley is maintained here, for the principal of the School is a minister of the Church of England, and its students represent almost every shade of religious thought and life.

Among a few old stone inscriptions preserved at 'Thabor' are two that are specially interesting. One is from a Samaritan synagogue at Gaza, dating from early Byzantine times, revealing how far Samaritan influence reached in those days. The words on it are from Deuteronomy iv. 29–31, and are in archaic script. The tablet, about 20 inches by 8 inches, is set in a classroom wall. Nobody knows how it got there. Probably Dr. Schick acquired it. But it is unique, and is the oldest and largest Samaritan inscription that is known. Dr. Schick also acquired by some unknown means one of the four known boundary marks of the ancient Levitical city of Gezer, dating from the second century B.C. It has both Greek and Hebrew characters, and marks the limit of 2,000 cubits from the city (see Numbers xxxv. 2–5) to show the boundary within which a fleeing homicide could claim sanctuary, and beyond which no Jew could travel from his home on a Sabbath. The stone is a broad one, and is set upside down in the outer wall of the library. Only recently has its significance been realized. Doubtless the astute old archaeologist wished to disguise his possession of this treasure from the knowledge of the Turkish authorities. In addition to these two inscriptions, we saw, set in the wall of the soldiers' quiet room, a plaster copy of the Greek tablets which were set at intervals in the wall of the Inner Sanctuary of the Temple in Herodian days, warning 'strangers' to keep out upon pain of death. Trophimus the Ephesian would have seen such an inscription as this when he entered the Court of the Gentiles with Paul. In the library of the School are preserved many book treasures which the present principal has accumulated.

The Newman School of Missions epitomizes the New Jerusalem. It does not do so by means of a modern building, but by its spirit. The Holy City as John the Seer saw it, with no temple therein, was a spiritual reality, 'coming down out of heaven from God'. That is the spirit we found at 'Thabor'.

CHAPTER XIII

RUSSIANS

The House of Zacharias ... is situated at the foot of a mountain west of Jerusalem. In this house of Zacharias the Holy Virgin came to greet Elizabeth.

THE RUSSIAN ABBOT DANIEL, A.D. 1106.

THE Arab village of Ain Karim, buried in a valley among smooth and rolling hills about three miles west of Jerusalem, is one of the pleasantest spots in Palestine. There is something very satisfying about a journey to it. With very little trouble, it is possible to 'keep right on to the end of the road', albeit the road is a bumpy one and the Arab bus decrepit. The road leads nowhere else, as though its builders decided, with good reason, that once at Ain Karim visitors would be content to remain there. The village is not one that is discovered by a traveller in his wanderings, for it lies on no other route that he may be taking. One hears about Ain Karim and makes a special journey to see it. And it is worth seeing, with its cypresses punctuating the scenery like so many exclamation marks. Its name is a true one, 'gracious spring', and within the hollow of the wide horseshoe curve round which meanders its single street lie watered gardens in descending terraces rich with vines and figs, with marrows, cucumbers, and the black-fruited egg-plant, while all around are the guardian hills towering over the village; and more hills, brown and studded with olive trees, roll away where the valley opens towards the distant sea.

Nobody knows exactly why, but Ain Karim has since the sixth century been associated with John the Baptist, and it is identified with the city of Judah in the 'hill country' mentioned in Luke i. 39, where dwelt Zacharias and Elizabeth. A church was built above the inevitable 'grotto' where it was said that John was born, and another at the other end of the very long village to mark where Mary lived with her kinswoman Elizabeth for three months. The Crusaders elaborated the theme, and since their day a number of legends have accumulated round 'St. John-in-the-Mountains', as they called it. To-day there is a native Moslem community with a mosque by the picturesque stream in the centre of the village, and monasteries and convents of Franciscan monks and nuns, Sisters of the Rosary, Orthodox priests and Russian nuns; and their various establishments within the village and on the hillslopes around provide one or two church towers that contrive to add, fortunately, to the beauty of the scene. Ain Karim is, incidentally, the Bethcar where, according to the seventh chapter of 1 Samuel, the battle occurred in which the Philistines were finally subdued after their flight through the valleys from Mizpah.

I regularly arranged Sunday afternoon visits to Ain Karim, which were so popular that I invariably had to hire a special bus, which took the party to the village in the valley, and collected us later from the hilltop, which in summer was accessible for an Arab bus by means of a rough track. We would wander slowly between the cottages, exchanging greetings with the Arabs as they sat at their doors or at rickety tables outside a café, sipping coffee from tiny *finjans*; explore one or two churches, and watch the activity at the 'gracious spring' itself, where women would fill immense earthen water pots and balance them on their heads, whilst the children—girls, of course, not boys—would do the same with 2-gallon petrol tins. And we would finally mount the winding path through the Russian village on the western hillside and then toil upwards upon what seemed an interminable journey, resting occasionally to remove moisture from our brows and to admire the view, until we found the 'Shrine of Peace' on the very summit of the hill. Afterwards we would recline in deck chairs in the hostel garden and consume an immense tea. Grand and memorable days they were, days of exertion and of languid ease, of good companionship and of glorious views from a windy hilltop, views of misty hills with shadows between their folds, the Plain of Sharon dimly to the west and the spires of Jerusalem behind us.

The Shrine of Peace is a tapering sugarloaf of white stone which Miss Carey, a Guernsey woman and beloved Lady Bountiful of Ain Karim, has built on this eminence beside her hostel, which has been in recent years a holiday refuge for missionaries and others from Egypt, Palestine and beyond. One day, she hopes, it will be a convent for Anglo-Catholic Sisters of the Love of God. The men usually entered the little sanctuary when we arrived, and knelt on its blue woven rug to pray together for peace: peace in our hearts, peace in the Church, peace in the world. Crescents and stars of David are interwoven with crosses in its decorative symbolism, for it was designed as a place of prayer for Moslems and Jews as well as Christians. In one corner is a Greek cross with an oblique bar across it, representing the Penitent Thief who went up to heaven, and the other who went down to hell.

Since I have known Ain Karim I have understood better the choice of primitive peoples of a 'high place' for worship. It is easier to pray, somehow, on a hilltop. One feels nearer to God and more remote from the world. Religion began, I think, on high hills, where men could look down on the world about them and feel their kinship with the Divine. Jesus loved to go alone to a mountain-top to pray.

In the evening our bus would carry us on the winding track that goes along the top of the hilly range until it meets the Ain Karim road at the head of the valley, and we would go to church in Jerusalem that night browned of face from the sun and wind, weary and exhilarated.

The Byzantine and Crusader churches are now no more, for in that remote place they have known a more drastic fate even than that met by more famous churches in Jerusalem and Bethlehem; but beneath a modern one we were shown early mosaics, and beneath another, the Franciscan Church of the Visitation, a cave with Crusader crosses cut in the walls. A well is in this grotto, with pleasant cooling water from a spring said to have bubbled up at the moment that Mary greeted Elizabeth. The little church is modern and very pleasing, with graceful mural paintings of the legends associated with the birth of the Baptist. Perhaps for decorative reasons, Elizabeth is depicted as anything but 'well stricken in years'. On a hill slope above it we used to visit a church newly built on an ancient site guarding a rock chamber which was the reputed dwelling of Elizabeth, and with the modern interior decoration half-finished. Scaffolding still filled the nave and apse but under it we could see the intricate and in many ways beautiful Italian mosaic floor, and designs in coloured marble on the altar. Work had perforce ceased in wartime, but we could imagine the magnificence of the finished church, although it threatened to be, perhaps, a little too ornate. A queer-shaped rock was stored in a niche in the church below. In Latin a gilt inscription round it announced that here Elizabeth hid her child when Herod's soldiers slew the Innocents. . . .

But it was the Russian village that we loved best. As we descended the hill on the other side of the valley, we appreciated the view of its dark pencils of cypresses on the steep slope above the Arab village opposite us. We loved even more to roam its narrow, winding footpaths mounting in a labyrinth between tiny white-washed cottages hidden in a forest of cypress, olive, and fir trees, with here and there a burgeoning oleander or a fig tree with broad, dark leaves. There was an air of informality about the place, and of infinite calm. About 150 Russian nuns live in the compound, dwelling each in her own cottage and coming together for daily prayers in the tiny spotless church in the centre of the community. A cobbled yard with a lamp-post of Victorian design in its centre lies before the porch of the church, which from the outside looks more like a Methodist chapel than anything else. But once inside one steps into Russian Orthodoxy, for there are ikons everywhere: all round the walls and across the screen before the altar, countless crude and highly coloured ikons tied with ribbon and decked with wax fruit and flowers, ikons that are kissed a hundred times a day by pious, black-robed sisters bowing and crossing themselves repeatedly.

They are very sweet and simple folk, peasants for the most part, who pass their time in great devotion and extreme poverty. Seventy Palestine piastres a month (about 14s.) is each nun's allowance for food and clothing, even with the increased cost of living in wartime. Once a sister gave me tea in her garden, in the shade of a trembling pepper-tree. She spoke only Russian and a little Arabic, but Miss Carey, who had taken me there, acted as interpreter, for she had dwelt with the Russian nuns for twenty years. Sister Lisa was a voluble soul and a kindly one. She told me how they live only on milkless tea and sugar and a white bread made with sugar and milk which I voted excellent, and some home-made apricot jam. She told me something of their simple life in the compound, of their daily services and regular Eucharists and their celebrations on saints' days. It happened that the day of my visit was the Feast of St. John the Baptist, thirteen days later than the Western feast, as, of course, they follow the Orthodox calendar. They take no account of summer-time, either, following only 'God's time', as they call it. The sisters were all very sad that day, for Mary had left them. Elizabeth had gone with her as far as the fountain to say 'Good-bye', and they would not see Mary again until she came next year for her annual stay of three months. They were all disconsolate. And Sister Lisa wiped her eyes.

I was a little startled at all this. My thoughts went to the timeless story in the first chapter of Luke's Gospel, and I wondered whether Russian nuns took the parts of Mary and Elizabeth in a sacred drama, in the same way as the Orthodox bishops engage in feet-washing on Maundy Thursday. But I soon discovered that Sister Lisa was talking about ikons. Three days after the Feast of the Assumption a picture of Mary is carried in solemn procession every year from the Russian Cathedral in Jerusalem to Ain Karim, and is installed on a special stand next to an ikon of Elizabeth, where it remains for three months, to return to Jerusalem on the Feast of St. John the Forerunner. When it arrives it is carried with joyful circumstance into every room of every cottage in the Russian village. I had been in time to see the procession winding out of the village far below me as I descended the hillside from the hostel above, a little earlier that afternoon. The nuns, I learned, had all been weeping as Mary left them, and Elizabeth, who had met her at the 'Virgin's Fountain' on her arrival there, bade her farewell, the one ikon giving the other a loving kiss! I comforted Sister Lisa by telling her that Mary would soon be back again, although I secretly wondered why she should not be content with the picture of the Virgin that she possessed, or with the many others in her friends' cottages and the church.

The nuns are passionate royalists, and framed pictures of Tsar Nicholas hang in their cottages together with holy pictures and highly coloured views of Ain Karim and obscure villages in Russia from whence they have come and doubtless will never see again. Most of the sisters were in Palestine in 1917, at the time of the Revolution, although their numbers are now maintained by new-comers from Bulgaria and other Balkan countries, and they have a number of orphan girls, Orthodox Arabs, in their care, whom they hope will join their sisterhood.

The Georgians were the first of the Russian nations to have an interest in the Holy Land. They were known as Iberians in the Middle Ages and were popular with the Moslems for some reason. They had monasteries near Jerusalem in the sixth century and by the fourteenth century they were custodians of Calvary and possessed the keys of the Holy Sepulchre. Their influence thereafter declined, however, and they became victims of Franciscan intrigue. As the Iberians became poorer, they sold many of their rights to the Ortho-dox priests, and by the end of the seventeenth century they possessed only the Convent of the Cross, which in 1850 also passed into Ortho-dox hands. Credulous Russian pilgrims were for long the victims of the extortions of Greek priests until after the Crimean War, when Tsarist Russia demanded the erstwhile property of the Georgians. This startled the Greeks, who remembered that only a few centuries earlier the Iberians had been in charge of the Holy Sepulchre itself, and feared stronger Russian claims. They compromised, however, and in 1870 a Russian Mission was established in Palestine, and a certain Archimandrite Anthony, who appears to have been a great organizer, built many hospices for Russian pilgrims: churches, settlements, and later a cathedral in the Holy City outside the old walls. A hospice was built near the Holy Sepulchre, when excava-tions revealed remains of Byzantine Jerusalem. 1917 found many nuns and priests stranded in Palestine, with extensive property. £2,000,000 in the bank was claimed and appropriated by the Soviet Government. Rent from the land now maintains the Russians in the Holy Land, allowing a tiny grant for each of the 300 nuns, half of them dwelling in the Russian compound on the Mount of Olives and half of them at Ain Karim; and a grant for the priests, the bishop receiving, I believe, about 10s. a week. Two English women, Abbess Mary and Mother Martha, belong to the order, and have charge of a convent school at Bethany. The Wednesday Fellowship members went to tea there one Sunday afternoon, and the girls' choir sang songs for us in English, Russian, and Arabic.

It is a charming scene when evening falls on Ain Karim, and the nuns in their black peaked veils, each with a lantern, steal quietly along the footpaths for evening prayers in the church which is the centre of their communal life. They look like so many kindly gnomes in a fantastic forest with fairy-story cottages, white-washed walls and cobbled garden paths.

They told me about their services. At Epiphany they go down to the Jordan and dip themselves in the water. On the first day of their Lent, they confess their faults one to another, as we are exhorted to do in the Scriptures. Their priest first confesses to the congregation that he has made many grievous faults, and asks their forgiveness. The Abbess then does the same to him and to the other sisters; and then, commencing with the eldest, each nun admits her faults and begs forgiveness individually from those who have already done so, and collectively of the remaining congregation. The youngest, therefore, must speak personally to every other one, and I was told how delightful it was to see each sister raise the other up from her knees before her and embrace her as she asked pardon for her faults. I thought it was all very sweet, and realized that these humble nuns had the simplicity and sincerity of children.

Their liturgies were interesting to me. I discovered no less than three noticeable similarities to Presbyterian customs, of all strange affinities! The Presbyterians, those worthy Calvinistic Puritans without ikons or genuflections, in the following details resemble the Orthodox Church: The Bible is carried solemnly in at every service, giving honour to the Word; officiating presbyters sit behind the table at Holy Communion, presumably the earliest custom in the Eucharist (the fact that only the Pope to-day celebrates Mass whilst facing the people is a Roman Catholic reminder of this early practice); and it is customary to partake of the elements of Holy Communion only about four times a year. In the Orthodox Church the faithful are in the habit of attending Eucharist quite frequently, but they do not often partake. Both elements are taken at once, the bread being dipped in the wine. This was the custom in early times to prevent the holy wine being spilt in crowded churches. For the same reason, the Latins forbade the cup to the laity.

As I left the gracious hospitality of Sister Lisa, I saw a nun approach the door of the priest's cottage and mutter the *Kyrie Eleison*, the blessing, 'Lord have mercy upon us', before knocking at the door. This is always done at the house of the priest or the abbess. The sisters have an ikon in each room of their cottages, and bow and cross themselves before it whenever they leave or enter.

I was introduced to Sister Xania, a cultured woman who spoke perfect English, and who acted as physician for the community. She was returning from giving an injection to a sister suffering from heart trouble. One part of her little 'cell', as she called it, was crowded with bottles of medicine and the requisites for nursing the sick. The sisters contracted the usual maladies of old age, of course, as well as ailments due to an unbalanced diet—they never eat meat—and to unsuitable clothing. They were extremely conservative, and wore the voluminous garments they had worn in pre-war Russia, in spite of the heat of the Middle East. I imagine that six thick petticoats and a head-veil revealing only the face is not the healthiest of garb for the hot season in Palestine!

Sister Xania was an amazing woman. Upon her shelves were the *Dialogues* of Plato, Bunyan's *Pilgrim's Progress*, and a *Life* of St. Francis—none of them of interest to an Orthodox nun, one would think—and English, French, and Russian classics, medical textbooks and treatises on Byzantine and medieval art. She had some beautiful books full of reproductions of old masters, especially of famous Byzantine ikons, for she was an artist. Her cell was her studio, and on an easel was a half-finished painting of St. Helena, a queen who was of humble origin, I learned, and who had come seeking the holy places when she was over eighty. Round the walls were sketches and designs, and some completed ikons, painted on wood in the formal, decorative manner of the Byzantine period. She discussed with me the nineteenth-century tendency in England towards the richness of colour and detail that characterized the early days of Eastern art, but complained that it was so very English and insular. My thoughts flew to a discussion I once had in a St. John's Wood studio with a young artist of the 'modern' school, when he tersely and contemptuously condemned the Pre-Raphaelite Brotherhood. Here was criticism from the extreme opposite pole of the artistic sphere, yet how much more kindly and at the same time more penetrating it was.

Sister Xania was the young bride of a prosperous business man and engineer in Tsarist Russia, and fled with him to some property of theirs in Finland at the Revolution. They dwelt later in Geneva, and when her husband died she entered this order of nuns, choosing Palestine rather than a convent in Europe, and here she served the little community with her gifts and graces. She offered to paint me an ikon, so after much searching in her giant tomes I found a beautiful painting of the Feet-Washing and asked if she would copy it for me. It was of Jesus, girded with a towel, washing the feet of Peter, who was pointing to his head, with another disciple putting on his sandals, and the others in the background. She was delighted with my choice, and said she would take great pleasure in painting it. Her pleasure can be nothing to mine as I survey its glorious gold background ('gold for the beauty of the action', said Sister Xania) and its gorgeous hues of green and blue, of silver and purple.

Beside the porch of their beloved little church stands an irregular boulder of limestone which was brought from the bank of the Jordan. In a frame above it my party from Jerusalem and I had often read the translation in English of Russian words:

'On this stone St. John the Baptist said to the crowd his first sermon.'

This was an object of interest indeed. How the Russians knew that this was the Baptist's pulpit we thought it wiser not to inquire. I looked at it and wondered whether John was as nervous as I was when I 'said' my first sermon. Had his knees trembled as he stood on that somewhat precarious perch and gave out his text? I cannot believe that his voice had been as shaky as mine. I can imagine the boulder quaking with his thunderous 'Repent ye!'

'What was his first sermon about?' asked one of the men in my party. I pulled my Testament from my pocket and turned to the third chapter of Luke's Gospel.

'He called the people "snakes",' I replied, 'but in spite of that he seems to have been a very popular preacher. Perhaps preachers to-day would get a bigger following if they used stronger language. And this rock was apparently one of his illustrations, because he declared that God was able of these stones to raise up children unto Abraham. So he appears to have been opposed to the privilege of birth. In fact, he was a genuine social reformer, and preached about people's behaviour, and the redistribution of food and clothing.

'He gives soldiers some advice, too,' I added. 'He tells us to do violence to no man and to be content with our pay. His is ethical teaching of a very high order. He represents, I suppose, the best that man can do. Jesus said that he was the greatest of men. But he was inadequate. He had no good news; only good advice. Jesus was different. "The Kingdom of God," said Jesus, "is at hand. Repent ye, and believe the good news!" We cannot have social reformation without faith.

'People,' I added, 'always seem to want to know what to do. They asked, "What shall we do?" not only of John, but of Jesus and of Paul. It is significant that Jesus told the wealthy young M.P. to give away his wealth; not, I think, as a measure of social reform so much as the removal of an encumbrance, and to trust Him. That young man wanted to know what to do, and His answer was: "Follow Me." And when the jailor asked the same question of Paul the reply he received was a similar one: "Believe on the Lord Jesus Christ." '

It was a pity that we could never find the opportunity to walk for several miles round the hillsides beyond Ain Karim from Jerusalem to find the cave where tradition says John dwelt, not in an arid desert, but in a desolate place. But we found a tree hanging with locust beans, and bees buzzing amid the blossoms in the garden, collecting their wild honey.

CHAPTER XIV

GALILEE

... those holy fields
Over whose acres walked those blessed feet,
Which, fourteen hundred years ago, were nailed
For our advantage on the bitter cross.

SHAKESPEARE, *Henry IV.*

AFTER six months in Jerusalem, I was ready for a holiday, and when I was invited to attend a two-day Chaplains' Retreat on the Mount of Beatitudes by the Sea of Galilee, I took the opportunity to apply for a few days' leave, which was duly granted to me. So on a Thursday morning early in March I set off for Galilee by a round-about route, in order to visit a few friends—chaplains stationed at scattered points—and to see as much as possible of the Holy Land. The usual course taken by troops on leave in Jerusalem who wanted to see Galilee was to join a party of five or six, enough to fill a hired car, and in one day make a long tour northwards through Samaria and Nazareth to the lakeside and then to return by way of Haifa and Tel-Aviv. It made an exhausting journey to complete in one day, but it was usually entered upon with a good deal of enthusiasm. Later, notably on a certain memorable Whit-Monday, I acted as guide to some men making this long trip through Palestine; but on this occasion of my leave I was free for three or four days to wander as I pleased. I went therefore directly westwards from Jerusalem along the Jaffa Road to Tel-Aviv, the new Jewish city on the shore of the Mediterranean. The customary method of travel for casual passengers along the main thoroughfares of Palestine is to take a seat in a taxi, scores of which wait at certain garages and move away when they become full. They are usually modern, comfortable cars and one seldom must wait so long as half an hour before the car moves away. It was by this means that I travelled to Tel-Aviv in the company of a few troops on leave and a Jew and his wife who sat listening to our conversation.

The hour-and-a-half journey passed pleasantly enough. As a chaplain, I was imagined to be an authority on the events associated with places that we passed, and fortunately I was able to point out a few landmarks of interest, including Nebi Samwil, the Crusaders Montjoie I had climbed *en route* to Emmaus; the Pilgrims' Road winding off to the right along which the Roman Catholics make

pilgrimage on Easter Monday; Kolonia, where veteran Roman
soldiers once were settled, and where the ruins of their dwellings are
still to be seen; Abu Ghosh, the Kirjath-jearim of the Old Testament,
with its towering figure of 'Notre Dame Arche d'Alliance' above
the convent on the place where the Ark of the Covenant is thought
to have rested, and with its delightful Crusader church in the centre
of the village in the valley; the Trappist monastery nestling on a
hillside by Latrun; and Ramleh, believed as long ago as the days of
Eusebius to be Arimathaea, the home of the wealthy Joseph who
gave his tomb for the body of Jesus. We drove past the church
dedicated to him and his friend Nicodemus, on the site of one built
by Crusaders who found it a convenient stopping place for pilgrims
to Jerusalem. The Tower of the Forty Martyrs, or of the Forty
Companions of the Prophet, as the Moslems describe it, was of
interest to us, but we had perforce to move along the road as fast
as our impatient driver could take us. We were now in the Plain of
Sharon, fertile and green, with orange groves bright with fruit, and
wide fields of crops.

Before us were the minarets and domes of Jaffa, which is the
ancient seaport of Joppa, the dirty narrow streets of which gradually
gave way to the ultra-modern, jerry-built piles of flats and hotels
all huddled together which constitutes Tel-Aviv, the 'Hill of Spring'.
There is a great Jewish population here, the road traffic is thick, the
shops are busy, and advertisements in Hebrew characters are displayed everywhere. I stretched my cramped legs out of the taxi,
bade farewell to my companions, who were bound for a day of sea
breezes along the esplanade, and made my way to the Toc H hostel
to be the guest of the chaplain who acted as its warden. For a few
days I rested there, wandering about a little to see anything of
interest in the district.

I visited Jaffa, Joppa, the 'beautiful', as it was named in the dim
long ago. It stands on a promontory to the south of Tel-Aviv, and
when one evening I saw a crimson sunset behind its dark-towered
silhouette, with the placid sea beneath it for a mirror, I realized that
all the ravages of man and time could not rob it of a certain fantastic
Eastern beauty. But only from the distance and in the twilight does
it deserve its name. It was here that Perseus slew the monster and
rescued the fair Andromeda, chained to a rock by the shore. Josephus
declared that he saw the very chains in his day. It was a seaport in
Egyptian and Phoeni :ian times, mentioned often in the Old Testament, and the writer of the Book of Jonah says that the prophet set
sail from Joppa, when he ran away from God. Christians lived there
from Apostolic times, of course, for here Peter raised up Tabitha,

and here in the house of Simon the Tanner he had his dream about the unclean animals let down from heaven in a sheet. I explored some of the narrow streets and visited some missionaries I knew there, but did not tarry long in a town so unsavoury whilst I was on a leave that was all too short.

When I was ready to continue my journey, I found a seat in a taxi again, this time bound northwards past the ruins of Caesarea to Haifa, following the road parallel with the shore of the blue Mediterranean along what we used to call in college days the 'maritime plain'. Oranges and lemons shone in the sunshine amid dark green leaves, and fresh fields, emerald green, stretched away to the distant hills on my right. When I used to sit in the classroom studying the map of Palestine, I little dreamed that the time was not very far off when I would be following the route of the armies that marched to Megiddo in Bible days, and long after, up to the time of Napoleon and of Allenby, to clash with their enemies on the Plain of Armageddon. When afterwards I so often drew the easy outline of the eastern shore of the Mediterranean for the benefit of Sunday school teachers' training classes, and had been careful to zigzag it a little in the middle in the approved style, to represent the promontory where Carmel meets the sea, I did not imagine that soon I would be standing on its hilltop and marvelling at the loveliness of the view. It is indeed, from the Stella Maris Convent at close of day, one of the most memorable sights I have seen. The double, snow-tipped peak of Hermon rises in distant Syria, and Nazareth is on the hilltops to the east. Acre stands, battlemented as of old, along the curve of the bay, and below, like a toy harbour, lies the port of Haifa, with the Kishon, a river of winding silver through verdant meadows, below, and the sea under an evening sky still and lovely.

There is on this eminence a number of churches and monuments not only commemorating the victory of Elijah over the priests of Baal on the highest peak of the range, but in honour of Our Lady of Carmel, and in memory of Bonaparte's soldiers who died there. But I was intent upon continuing my journey to Galilee. So after a night at the German Hospice where dwelt a Methodist chaplain I knew and where I received kindly hospitality from the nuns, I inquired for means of transport across country to Tiberias, on the side of the Lake of Galilee. No taxis were available, but I was able to buy a ticket for the journey on a Jewish bus with the peculiar name of 'Egged'. I found this bus to be full, and had perforce to stand all the way clinging to a strap and jerked uncertainly about for two hours. The passengers were mostly Jews bound for Tiberias, which with varying periods of prosperity has been a centre of

THE Y.M.C.A., JERUSALEM.

[See page 218.

AIN KARIM

[Photo by C. J. Rawlings.

[See page 229

Jewish orthodoxy since a rabbinic school was founded there after the Jews were evicted from Jerusalem by Hadrian. Many of the men wore the long curls hanging in front of their ears that characterizes members of an orthodox mystical sect that originated in central Europe. They have confused the Mosaic injunction about leaving the fringe of the fields uncut so that the poor may gather a harvest of their own with rules about haircutting. Fur caps, incidentally, which have interested many troops in Jerusalem, are often worn by these Jews as a memento of the time during the Middle Ages when Jews in Poland were compelled to wear rabbit-skin on their heads.

I was too interested in the scenery to bother much about the discomforts of the journey. The road skirted the Plain of Esdraelon, scene of the Prophet's race against the rain after his triumph on Carmel, and fields of young green corn were spread out before us. The freshness of these plains was specially noticeable to me after the bare brown hills that surround Jerusalem, where peasants must scratch a precarious crop from patches of stony soil between great boulders of white rock. Until the Middle Ages, though, southern Palestine presented a far more fertile appearance than it does to-day, because trees covered the hills, and the country must have been rich with olives and figs in Bible days. Crusaders found trees covering even the heights of Nebi Samwil. But in the hundreds of years of Turkish rule the land was denuded of timber for fuel, and I am told that a tree tax was imposed at one time. Fortunately some valiant attempts are now being made at reafforestation.

Nazareth is about half-way across the old province of Galilee, between Haifa and the Lake, more than twenty miles by road from the coast and nearly twenty on to Tiberias. The bus started to climb the green Galilean hills as the road rose and dipped again and we approached the town which had been the home of Jesus. Bushes of yellow gorse were by the roadside, and spring flowers, daisies and buttercups and anemones, and something blue—was it speedwell or bird's-eye?—and the pale tint of bachelor's button, spangled the green grass with many colours. And so we came into Nazareth, truly the 'town of flowers', up a steep and winding road that gave us a fine view of the hills around.

I knew Nazareth well. I had been a patient in a hospital there for several weeks, and when I was recovering I had wandered about and climbed its hills. The sight of the scattered houses spread over the surrounding heights and hollows brought back happy memories of peaceful days and pleasant company, when I lay on my bed in the ward on hot afternoons, with the outline of the French Church of Jesus-Adolescent on the hilltop to be seen from the window, and I read the Gospels through again and listened to the bells of the Terra Santa Monastery sounding the Angelus at morning, noon, and evening. I called to my mind so much as the bus lumbered along the dusty main road of Nazareth: leisure hours in the District Commissioner's garden high on that hilltop; an evening Bible class with the good folk of the Edinburgh Medical Mission Hospital on the opposite slope; strange German sandwiches at the house of the Christian Jewish eye-doctor in a tiny back street (I suppose he was the only Jew in Nazareth); visits to the village carpenter, who had a shop beneath an old Turkish *khan*, hidden away where no tourist could find him, who showed me how he made simple ploughs, winnowing fans, yokes, and ox-goads, as he squatted on the ground and used tools as primitive as his craft; the cave I found just below the French church, where I loved to imagine Jesus playing as a child.

I felt myself very near to the youthful Jesus when I lived in Nazareth. I used to picture Him as He is shown in that lovely statue in the Church of Jesus-Adolescent: a lad of about sixteen, with sensitive features and the deep eyes of a poet, wandering about those very hilltops, with this carpet of colour beneath His feet and these glorious hills before His eyes, dreaming of the Kingdom of God. Did He imagine that rounded hill to the east would be called one day the 'Mount of Precipitation', and on the lesser slope dark cypresses would stand sadly around a chapel to mark the place where His mother stood weeping when the villagers hurried Him to the cliff edge to hurl Him over? Did He regard the dome of Tabor, scene of the victory of Deborah and Barak, and see it lighted with His own Transfiguration; or Little Hermon, with the village of Endor to the left and Shunem behind it where the prophet raised the dead, and know that He Himself would challenge the power of death one day at Nain, clearly to be seen on its slope? Hermon in Syria, with its snowy top, could be seen away to the north, Carmel to the west, and southwards Gilboa and Ebal and Gerizim. Only five miles to the north of Nazareth in the days of Jesus lay Sepphoris, or Zipporia, Herod's capital of Galilee until A.D. 18, where Jesus could have seen some of the life familiar to us from His sayings: a judge in a court, a prison, a market, soldiers, tax-collectors, a bank, even a king who made a marriage feast for his son. It is an ironic sidelight of history that, because this young Workman strode these hills, Sepphoris is now a tiny insignificant village, and Nazareth is the centre of the Galilee administration. We know that Jesus later preferred to climb the peak of Olivet or a mountain-place by the lakeside to be alone in prayer rather than be in the Temple or the synagogue. Is it not likely that He learned to find 'the calm of hills above' in His youth at Nazareth on these heights?

There are, of course, some 'holy sites' located in Nazareth, the most interesting of which was to me the village synagogue. A Greek Catholic church has stood over it since 1741, but the old stone floor is pointed out as the cover of the area of the early building. This is at the centre of what must have been the old village, not far from the only spring in the place, and it was a Jewish synagogue in A.D. 570, pointed out then as the place where Jesus learned the alphabet. It is reported, by the way, that the Jews in these Byzantine days were kindly folk, well disposed towards the Christians. There is no Jewish quarter in Nazareth to-day, and the town has a minority of Moslems. There are many churches: Roman Catholic, Greek, and Protestant, including the Anglican Christ Church with an Arab incumbent. The size of the synagogue is quite small, about half the size of the average Methodist chapel in an English village, and here it would be that Jesus went to school and worshipped on the Sabbath, and to which He returned to announce the fulfilment of the words, 'The Spirit of the Lord is upon Me'. Why did His neighbours not receive Him? We are told in Mark vi. He was a carpenter, with brothers and sisters like themselves, and therefore He was considered to be no authority upon the things of God. It was incredible to them that a young working-man so near to themselves could be a prophet, let alone anything greater.

Was He a carpenter? The Greek word is *tekton*, which means 'workman', and it is a very ancient tradition that He worked in wood. It is interesting to notice, however, that to-day the best stonemasons are to be found in Bethlehem, and they travel all over Palestine to do their work. The word *tekton* could mean mason or builder as much as it meant carpenter, and to-day the Arabs use a word which can mean either master woodworker or master stonemason. If this ancient craft flourished at Bethlehem as long ago as that, it is possible that Joseph was a worker in stone from Bethlehem and had found work in Nazareth. It is doubtful, in any case, whether there were specialists in joinery in those days, the probability being that a builder worked both in timber and in stone. Jesus never mentioned carpentry, but talked of a man building his house with a rock foundation, of the advisability of counting the cost before starting to build a tower, of the building of the Temple. One thing is sure, He worked by the sweat of His brow for most of His life, humble and obscure in a cottage home in Nazareth, and when He emerged to proclaim the acceptable year of the Lord He spoke with a Galilean accent and pleaded with men with hands marked by toil. He showed a special tenderness for widows. Was it because He had seen His own mother endure the hardships of a poor widow of those times? There were at least eight in His family, according to Mark. Was the reference Jesus made to 'the outer darkness, where there is weeping and gnashing of teeth' a memory of the crying of a naughty child, put outside the bright cottage living-room at night until he had learnt to behave himself in the fellowship of the home? So many thoughts and questions are in one's mind in Nazareth.

There is a series of caves under the Franciscan Monastery of the Holy Ground, in which some people believe the Holy Family to have lived. One has a church over it to mark the site of the Annunciation of Gabriel to Mary, and another is dedicated to Joseph; and others are pointed to as the kitchen, workshop, bedroom, and so on, of the domicile of Joseph and Mary. I was always very depressed when I visited these subterranean caverns, and I really cannot bring myself to believe that they are authentic. There is no reason whatever, beyond a doubtful tradition, to think that this was the home of Jesus. They were doubtless there in His day and He might have played in them as a child, but that is all one can say. Another holy place is the Virgin's Fountain, the only spring there, now built into a walled enclosure in the old town, and where no doubt Mary went for water, as the women do still, and it must have been familiar to Jesus. The effect is rather spoiled, however, by two ramshackle cinemas, one on either side of it.

I once found a tomb on a slope above Nazareth. It was a cave in a cliff-side in which had been buried the wife of a C.M.S. missionary some ninety years ago, and an inscription bore her name, including the Christian name 'Mary'. It had become neglected and remote, the entrance had been broken and, stooping down, I could see through the hole some scattered bones. A little Arab boy, to whom the place was familiar as a playground, came up and told me that it was 'Mary's Tomb'! I may say that when the Anglican clergyman in Nazareth was told of the tomb's condition he had the bones decently reinterred. But the incident brought vividly to my mind the memory of the Greek inscription of about A.D. 10 which was found recently at Nazareth and is mentioned in the *Palestine Exploration Fund Quarterly*. It reads:

'By order of the Emperor, I desire that all sepulchres and tombs which have been made out of respect of the dead, whether parents, children, or relations, shall remain undisturbed in perpetuity. . . . Anyone found interfering with the dead will be prosecuted. Great respect should be paid to the dead, and no one may lawfully disturb them.'

Perhaps it was in conformity with this order from the Emperor that Pilate ordered the watch and the seal over the tomb of Jesus.

The bus went between wide fields springing with corn which are known as the Fields of the Ears of Corn, the traditional place where the disciples plucked them on the Sabbath day. In the distance was a queer-shaped hill, the Horns of Hattin, where Saladin finally broke the power of the Crusaders. We went through the traditional Cana, with its well with sheep and goats flocked round it, its cactus hedges, its square white houses and various churches. The original Cana was probably some miles away to the north-west.

Finally, we saw the Sea of Galilee. It lay like a Scottish loch or piece of Lakeland shining below us, with hills all round. On this side the hills were green, but they looked wild and desolate beyond. The lake itself changed from an infinite variety of blues to green and indigo and silver almost whilst one looked at it, according to the changing cloudy sky above. It is a great moment when one first glimpses the Sea of Galilee from this hilltop. I was very surprised to see it so beautiful, so prepared was I to be disappointed. There it lay like a jewel, unspoiled by man. It is a coat of many colours spread in the valley. It is a mirror for Hermon's white head that is lifted to the north. Here, more than anywhere I know, can one see the background of the Gospel story and can understand better those—

> Sinless years which breathed
> Beneath the Syrian blue.

The road led steeply down past a sign marking the level of the Mediterranean, which is 680 feet above the lake, then, between waving palms, and white hotels with Hebrew names, to Tiberias by the edge of the water, and I was thankful to alight at the end of an uncomfortable journey. I had been invited to spend the day at the house of Dr. A. C. Harte, the venerable founder of the famous Y.M.C.A. in Jerusalem. I telephoned him to expect me and took a taxi to his house, a small building of black basalt about 2 kilometres to the north of Tiberias, by the edge of the water. As I passed the quay, I called to mind my previous visit to Tiberias at midnight on a bright moonlit night the year before, when with some friends I hired a fisherman's sailing boat and went out on to the lake to see an eclipse of the moon. It was all so unreal, I remembered, so ghostly, with the quiet water lap-lapping and the white sail above

my head and the fishermen calling softly to each other; and everything—the water, the boat, and our faces—drenched in the un-
natural light of the moon that waned and shone again and covered
us with a pale, frothy light. Then we had had a picnic near eucalyptus trees by the shore, and sang hymns under the moon. Now the
atmosphere was very different, bright with sunshine and loud with
men's voices as they worked. I passed the 'Galilee Lido'—sad
incongruity—and above the water a breeze-taut airsleeve for sea-
planes, and drove out on to the open road by a deserted shore to the
black, lonely house, though friendly enough as one approaches it,
that stands between the road and the sea.

I found Dr. Harte to be a wonderful old man of seventy-seven
years, retired now in that delightful retreat he had built, keeping
house for himself (in spite of severe arthritis) with the aid of a black
servant. He had travelled in many lands, and was full of stories of
his life in India, Burma, and Ceylon, where for many years he was
in charge of the Y.M.C.A. work, and of Germany and Russia
during the First Great War, when he had the care of the Y.M.C.A.
welfare work among prisoners of war. In that period he made
fifty-two sea voyages either across the North Sea or the Atlantic.
As a minister of the Methodist Episcopal Church in the U.S.A., he
was a chaplain to troops in the Spanish-American War of 1898. It
was when he paid a visit to Jerusalem between 1914 and 1918, and
sat on the Mount of Olives with his New Testament, that he
dreamed of creating a worthy centre of young men's Christian
activity in the Holy City. His declining days were being spent in
good works in this lonely spot, giving rest and refreshment to troops
on leave, and taking an interest in the needs of the poor round about
him.

He led me through his garden, containing, I should think, every
sort of spring flower that grows in Galilee, and at that time of the
year it was simply riotous with colour, and the air was heavy with
fragrance. He pointed out a semicircle discernible in the rock cliff
on the other side of the road. It was the remains of a tomb with a
rolling stone inside it—a most unusual thing. The garden lay on a
steep slope down to the water and was terraced and planted with
trees and informal patches of fruit and vegetables. The little lagoon
he had made into a swimming pool was the most charming corner of
all and by its side bubbled up a hot spring, always at a temperature
of 70° F., in which myriads of fish moved about in the clear water.
He had concrete steps going down to it, and two dressing-rooms,
and anybody who pleased could have the key from him and enjoy
a bathe. He told me about the fish, many tons of which are caught

in the season along this little piece of shore, and which spawn under these sheltering cliffs. The Arab fishermen are forbidden to gather in the young ones, but they were constantly breaking the law. I saw a police motor-boat cruising along on the look-out for lawbreakers.

Because of the warm springs that bubble up into the lake at this point, there are always more fish here than elsewhere in Galilee. Very likely the disciples came here to fish, and afterwards to bathe in the pleasantly tepid water. From the steep bank it is possible to see the fish in crowded shoals in the water when they are invisible to men in a boat. Many times Dr. Harte has stood in his garden and called to fishermen below to cast their nets on the other side of the boat. . . .

'There are two main kinds of fish in this lake,' he said. 'A little chap two inches long that the natives call *sardin*, and a larger fellow called *musht*, which is Arabic for "comb", on account of the shape of its fin. The small ones are not sardines, for our word probably derives from Sardinia, but they are the sort of fish easy to put within a roll for a sandwich, two of which the lad might have had, with five rolls, when Jesus fed the five thousand by these shores. The people still fry them in olive oil, and eat them cold. The *musht* is known as "Peter's perch", because it might have been in one of them that Peter found the coin.'

He went on to explain that the male fish has a little sac under his mouth. They are often attracted by a bright object, like a ring which has slipped off a finger into the water. It was not impossible, therefore, for a *stater* to find its way into a fish's mouth.

He pointed across the far side of the lake.

'Draw a line,' he said, 'from Gergesa there to this house, and north of it took place all the events of Jesus' Galilean ministry. There the swine went over the cliff; here was probably Dalmanutha.' And he pointed out the sites located by George Adam Smith and by Gustaf Dalman, the British and the German authorities on Biblical geography. Bethsaida was undoubtedly on the far side of the lake, Capernaum possibly where a clump of trees stood at the northern end where are the ruins of a synagogue, Chorazin farther away on the hills behind, and Magdala between here and Capernaum. Magdala was important politically, but there is no record of Jesus having visited it or Tiberias. The calling of the disciples and the Resurrection breakfast might have been at Tabgha, but the Sermon on the Mount would scarcely be where the Italian Hospice now stands on the low mound called the Mount of Beatitudes. If it was a connected discourse on a hilltop, then it was probably in a more remote place, to the north. It is a significant thing that there is not a vestige of remains of the two cities whose woe Jesus foretold: Chorazin and Bethsaida.

There was a fairly large population round these shores in the days of Jesus, perhaps 140,000, so it presents now a much more peaceful aspect than it did in His day. The fish-curing factory of Tarichae was along the coast to the north here somewhere, and not to the south as was formerly believed, for Vespasian in his northward march captured it after he had taken Tiberias. Josephus said that Tarichae had a fleet of 330 fishing boats, a fish market and place for salting fish, as well as a hippodrome. Galilee fish were known all over the Roman Empire, and there was a large export business from this centre. Perhaps Peter sold his miraculous draught of fishes there, and they went to some noble patrician's table in far-off Rome!

The old gentleman led me into his house and gave me lunch— fried chicken in the approved American style—and told me many stories of famous people he had met in the course of his travels: of Gandhi in India, of Sarah Bernhardt (who told him 'I have no ideals; only an ideal'), of Hindenburg and Lenin and Rasputin, of German and Russian royalty, including Princess Louise of Baden, the Kaiser's aunt, who, like many another prominent figure in public life, loved to talk with this modest little American welfare organizer about personal religion. She said, he told me, that when she was a child she said her prayers, when she was older she prayed, 'and now', she said, holding her wrist, 'every pulse-beat is a prayer'. He talked on quietly and unassumingly, of the past and of the present, and of the joy he had in these latter days in dwelling on the peaceful shores of Galilee, where Jesus called His disciples.

'When the wind echoes round the house,' he said, 'I fancy I can hear it echoing His words. The sound it makes is exactly like "Follow Me!"'

After lunch he showed me some of his treasures. He had a little black ball found in the sea, made from the local rock and intended for a missile from sling or catapult when Titus put out a fleet on to the lake and attacked the Jews here in A.D. 64. He showed me a stone with a hole through it which was used for weighting fishing nets, possibly in Jewish days. He opened a silver pen-container on a writing box and displayed the sort of sharpened reed with which Aramaic characters once were written. And strange old scissors, lamps, pictures, antiques of all kinds, objects of art and interest, were everywhere. There was a Burmese planter's chair in the library and a low, circular copper table no more than 9 inches above the carpet under a seventeenth-century Damascus ceiling, and walls of wood painted to resemble rich brocade.

He made me lie full-length at the table, my left arm upon a pillow, and my body continuing its radius. It was, he said, the sort of table used at the Last Supper, and it was easy to understand how thirteen people could recline round it in comfort, how John could lean back his head upon Jesus' bosom and how Jesus could speak to one and not be heard by the others. Elsie Anna Wood, the artist of the famous picture 'Hilltops in Galilee', who visited this house, had drawn a picture of the scene in the Upper Room, making, however, the mistake of depicting Jesus holding high the chalice in the European manner of proposing a toast. He would 'take the cup' in a very different way, touching it upon the table.

While Dr. Harte rested in the hot afternoon, I swam in his pool, lying in the warm spring with 'Peter's perch' tickling my legs, or striking out into the colder water of the lake. The setting was perfect. I felt I could pass all my days in this heavenly place. A eucalyptus tree cast its shade over the old Roman wall that once enclosed the pool, two kingfishers sped by with a flash of blue and gold, a cormorant stretched its long black neck as it stood on a distant rock, great dogfish rose to the surface at times, and I saw herons and gulls by the shore. Round a tiny promontory I discerned a party of blue-frocked little girls paddling in the lake in the care of a nun. The smooth water, sometimes ruffled by a breeze, sometimes still, had a dream quality, misty and silver, on this hot afternoon as, years before, I had sometimes seen Lake Maggiore from Stresa. What tranquil, gracious days this fine old gentleman was spending! After a life full of years and hopes fulfilled, he was still listening to the Voice of his Master coming to him over the lake: 'Follow Me!'

The Chaplains' Retreat was to be held on the Mount of Beatitudes, and it began that evening. The place had been a Catholic hospice for pilgrims and lay some five miles to the north of Dr. Harte's house. I was able to reach it comfortably, as I had previously warned a chaplain who would be passing that way in his car to be ready to give me a lift, which he obligingly did. As I came out under Dr. Harte's bougainvillea, which hung in a rich purple mass at the door, the many-toned camel-bell hanging aloft was shaken by a wayward breeze and tinkled out a farewell from the house of rough black stone amid its profusion of colour. The journey then was past green meadows and occasional clumps of trees by the water's edge which may mark the site of some of the ten cities. This is the Plain of Genesareth, and beyond a further rise of land lies the delightful little inlet known as Tabgha. The so-called Mount of Beatitudes is a green hill beside Tabgha, and I settled myself in its hospice, in a room overlooking the spreading Galilean hills, for the next two days.

It is no part of this record to tell of the Retreat, save to say that it was a source of inspiration to all of us, chaplains of various Churches, and was led by an Anglo-Catholic monk from Mirfield who had become an Army chaplain. He followed an abbreviated course of the devotional exercises of St. Ignatius, and although I found it difficult to concentrate my mind on his somewhat discursive addresses, I was deeply impressed by the atmosphere of the chapel where we gathered, with an altar before an open window through which we could gaze at the blue lake and circling hills, with the altar cross silhouetted against the scene. Never have I sung a hymn so apposite as I sang Whittier's

> O Sabbath rest by Galilee!
> O calm of hills above,
> Where Jesus knelt to share with Thee
> The silence of eternity,
> Interpreted by love!

Under the window a late orange tree was in flower, and its heavy, sickly fragrance rose to us in the still air like incense.

There were opportunities to explore the neighbourhood, which I did in company with a good friend of mine, a young High Church chaplain with whom I shared a room. We walked down the hillside to Tabgha to see the famous mosaics and the Mensa Christi. There are seven springs in this little valley, bubbling and rushing in eccentric courses amongst the rocks and by the lush grass. Many trees, cattle, sheep, and goats were about as we came down, with a few fishermen's houses by the beach and a tiny black stone church perched on a rocky ledge. Boats were pulled up the mouth of the stream, and fishing nets were spread out to dry, while out in the shallow water a man was wading, and casting in a net with a skilful, circling movement. This is how Simon and Andrew must have been working when Jesus called them, for they could hardly have been out in a boat. They were obviously by the shore, and were able straightway to leave their nets and follow Him. Indeed, there are not many places along the lakeside where it would be possible to fish in that fashion, especially near to Capernaum, so it is overwhelmingly likely that the tradition is true that it was at this very place that the words were spoken: 'Come ye after Me, and I will make you to become fishers of men.' It is very likely that Capernaum fishermen mostly gained their living at this convenient anchorage, and the whole scene that lay before us, with the rushing streams and the hills beyond, must have been very familiar to Jesus.

It seemed to me not unlikely also that it would be at this place, so familiar to them earlier, where the Risen Christ awaited the disciples who went back to their fishing after the Crucifixion, and where He prepared their breakfast. Peter doubtless went back to his work at the old place, and thus it would be where he was first called that he saw again the Resurrected Jesus, and heard the divine Voice: 'Feed My lambs.' There is a piece of rock believed by the Franciscans to be the Table of the Lord, and over its rugged whiteness, so long exposed to wind and rain and sun, they have recently built a little chapel of black basalt. My companion remarked that he believed the Franciscans, if they could, would drain dry the whole lake, build a church over it, and say, 'This is where the Sea of Galilee used to be.' We found some Arab boys and asked for the key, for nobody seemed to be in charge and the door was locked. Fortunately, I remembered the Arabic for 'key' and other appropriate phrases, and from a nearby house they produced it, and we entered the little sanctuary. The floor was almost wholly virgin rock, rising at the east end in the form of an altar, with a cruciform window in the wall above it. There was not much to see, and soon we went out again to the sunshine.

The name Tabgha is a corruption of Heptapegon, the Seven Fountains, and is mentioned several times in the accounts of the visits of early pilgrims. One, and only one, of the springs is a hot one, and possesses medicinal qualities. I remembered a story that a friend of mine in Jerusalem told me of a visit he paid here once. He is a fluent Arabic scholar, and was able to converse with an old Arab he met by the seven fountains. He asked the Arab why one of them had healing properties, and the reply was that the prophet Job, whom the Moslems respect, was sitting here, sad with his troubles, especially after the sermon his wife had given him (to be found, incidentally, in the Septuagint, but not in our Old Testament), when a fair damsel arrived and offered to be his wife. This offer Job accepted, but when she began to attend to his wants she found that there was no bread, so she went into a nearby village for it, leaving him sitting there disconsolate, aching with his sores and his poverty. When she returned with three loaves she found a handsome young man seated by a stream, and inquired of him for Job. He replied that he was Job, and that in her absence an angel had appeared to him and told him to dig into the sand, and water would come up in which he should bathe himself. He did so, and behold, his boils and sores disappeared, and he was completely renewed. He found also a new suit of clothes which he donned. On his part, however, he demanded to know what had become of her two long plaits of hair. She explained that the sheikh of the village had refused her bread, but she besought him to give it her, so he demanded her two plaits in exchange for loaves, and thus she had lost them. This annoyed Job very much, and he insisted that she should return to the village for her hair; she did, and he was able to restore it to her head, for everything is possible to Allah. The spring has retained its healing powers unto this day.

I was very keen to see the famous Tabgha mosaics, which were discovered in 1932, and we found the place several hundred yards in from the shore. A low corrugated iron roof covered the site, which did not make it appear very attractive, and our entrance was impeded by a mob of very dirty Arab children who clamoured for *baksheesh* amid a cloud of flies. Inside the concrete building, however, we were rewarded by the sight of the most beautiful old mosaics I had ever seen. They date from the fourth century, and covered the floor of the Byzantine church that was built on this site to commemorate the Feeding of the Five Thousand, which it was believed took place in this little valley. Perhaps there was a confusion with the feeding of the disciples here by the Risen Lord, or the fact that there is 'much grass in the place' misled them, but certainly it was not here, a busy fishing centre and adjacent to many villages, where the hungry multitude was fed, but somewhere beyond Jordan, on the deserted east coast of the lake where grass grows in the valleys, in the spring at any rate.

The church that stood here, therefore, was the Church of the Multiplying of the Loaves and Fishes, and A. M. Schneider, the excavator of the site, quotes, translating from the Latin, a description of Tabgha which is believed to have come originally from the lost *Peregrinatio* of Aetheria, who came here in A.D. 386 from Spain:

'There is a fertile field near the Lake of Galilee with plenty of pasture and many palm trees, and nearby seven springs, from each of which gush copious streams of water, and in this field the Master fed the people with five loaves and two fishes. Indeed the stone on which the Master placed the bread has been made into an altar, and from this stone visitors chip off pieces for their healing, and all benefit thereby. Near the wells of this church passes the public road where the Apostle Matthew took toll, while close to the church rises the hill where the Saviour, having ascended to an eminence thereon, preached the Beatitudes.'

The church was ruined by the Persians in A.D. 614, or possibly by the Jews of Tiberias, who were known to aid the Persians in destroying Christian churches. The artist who made the mosaic pictures has been called the 'Tabgha Master', and certainly every picture, across the wide nave and the apse, is a masterpiece. The gay colours of the birds and beasts and flowers of Galilee are woven into a carpet of intricate design, and we marvelled at the skill and artistry that could create, like a tapestry, so much beauty with the medium of a myriad little pieces of coloured stone. The artist had shown a flock of birds searching the leaves of plants for food, preening their feathers, ruffling their plumes, fighting with snakes, or contentedly rocking themselves on giant leaves. Perched impudently on a flower bell was a little bird with sharp eyes, and two ducks appeared to be chatting amicably together like old housewives; one big bird stretched itself, flapping its wings, a peacock proudly displayed its long tail, and geese curiously investigated the contents of a basin. Two partridges held in their beaks the either end of what appeared to be a snake. The whole effect was one of individuality and charm. The artist had caught the characteristic pose of a duck's neck or a flower's graceful curve. He was obviously a careful student of animal life, and a lover of Nature. He was, as Schneider says, 'a sensitive man endowed with the full knowledge of the aesthetic charm and the stirring beauty of the things of this world'.

I was particularly interested in the picture of a badger cowering before a pugnacious bird approaching him, and raising his right paw, possibly in self-defence. Round his neck was a ribbon or collar of some kind, so it can scarcely have been meant to be a wild creature. Was it a pet of the artist, who had seen it in this very attitude, and set the scene in stone for posterity to see and marvel at?

Little houses were shown in the mosaics with conical roofs on triple columns, but no human figures. Did this man possess, we wondered, a survival of local Semitic prejudice against making 'graven images' of human beings? It was interesting to appreciate the cheerfulness of those early Christians who chose to decorate their church, not with the solemn symbols of religion, but with representations of the world around them, of the profusion of Nature and the beauty of earthly things. Near the altar, though, stood two fishes on their tails on either side of a basket containing five loaves, as though, when he reached the altar the artist, who had been enjoying himself with putting gaily coloured pictures of creatures of the fields all over the floor, recollected the purpose of the building he was decorating, and paid this tribute to the miracle the church commemorated.

We went for a row on the lake in the afternoon, in a boat we hired from a bearded fisherman who was the very picture of St. Peter. His two boys, like the sons of Zebedee, were fishers too, and took the oars for us while we undressed and bathed and half-heartedly

fished in the lazy heat and watched the ploughman pushing a
lonely furrow in a field by the water's side. After a couple of hours'
pleasant dalliance on the lake surveying the peace all around us,
and the water glittering and sparkling in the sunlight spread out
before our eyes away to the enveloping hills, we picked up from the
shore the boys' father, 'Peter'. He sat on the bows as we returned
to Tabgha, smiling and talking to us the while in Arabic. My friend
propounded the theory that the climate tends to produce similar
human types, and that these fishermen were very like the men who
toiled in boats here in the days of Jesus. It was easy to believe it as
I watched him sitting there with his hardy, open face, curling
beard and cheerful mien.

Next day we went to Capernaum, or rather to Tel Hum, which
tradition and Professor Dalman say is Capernaum, but which was
not accepted as such by Adam Smith, who believed it to be farther
west. The place is in a clump of trees on the northern shore, about
a mile from our hospice in the opposite direction from Tabgha.
We walked over fields thick with spring flowers: anemones and
daisies and ranunculas, tangled vetch of blue and chrome, and the
pale wind-blown cyclamen—a living mosaic of colour in a green
matrix. When we paused to rest on a rock and watch a herd of
cattle go by, I picked a specimen each of twenty different kinds of
flowers within about a square yard of ground and pressed them in
my Testament to send home from Galilee in spring-time. The lilies
of the field of which Jesus talked may have referred to daffodils, or
anemones, or to almost any flower there, perhaps to the fine gladiolus
which grows wild near Tiberias and wears the purple of a king. The
white Easter lily is foreign to Palestine. When I visited these fields
some months later, in the heat of summer, they were bare of grass
and flowers, and were graced only by twisted gorse bushes and the
slender, tapering asphodel.

Tel Hum to-day consists of a modern house for Franciscan monks
by a little stone quay, and some well-kept ruins behind the trees. A
Christian Arab youth explained everything to us in French: the
famous columns standing facing the sea and the surrounding flagged
courtyard and broken masonry lying about. He was sure it was the
synagogue that Jesus knew in Capernaum, and said that its Roman
architecture was due to the fact that it had been built for the Jews by
the centurion whose servant Jesus healed, a reference, or course, to
Luke vii. 5. Several flagstones outside the actual area of the synagogue were marked in a fashion very similar to Pilate's Judgement
Hall pavement in the Ecce Homo Convent at Jerusalem, for there
were squares and circles presumably intended for games of some

kind. Another area of flagged courtyard our guide declared had
been *pour les enfants*, presumably the 'Sabbath School' of Capernaum. I was particularly interested in two inscriptions which were
discernible on recumbent broken columns. One in Greek read:

> 'Herod [son] of Monimos and Joustos . . . with their children,
> erected this column.'

And the other, in Hebrew:

> 'Alpheus the son of Zebidah, the son of John, made this column.
> May it be to him a blessing.'

Both inscriptions bore names familiar to the reader of the New
Testament, the Hebrew one particularly recording Alpheus,
Zebedee, and John, all Galilean names mentioned in the Gospels.

As I have said, George Adam Smith did not believe that this is
the original Capernaum at all, and Gustaf Dalman, who thinks it is,
declares that these ruins are of second-century date, possibly a
reconstruction of the synagogue that Jesus knew. Certainly a large
town was here once, with a main road down to the sea and a Jewish
place of worship facing Jerusalem. The Star of David, the Ark of
the Covenant, and the seven-branched Candlestick were plainly to be
seen among the decorative work carved in the stone. If it was here
that Jesus taught, and healed the lunatic and the man with the
withered hand, then it was near here that Peter's wife's mother was
cured and the palsied man lowered through a roof and the maiden
arose at the word of Jesus: *'talitha cumi'*. Where this quay lies, was
there a custom house where Levi sat to take toll? Is 'Tel Hum' a
corruption of *telonion*, a custom house? Or can the name Capernaum be from Caphar Tanhum, the Tomb of Tanhum, Tel Hum?
Certainly Capernaum was located here in Byzantine times. We
inspected an octagonal enclosure with a few mosaics within it
which our guide told us marked the site of Peter's house. Possibly
it was the remains of a fourth-century church built there by the
famous Count Joseph of Tiberias.

In the monk's house were diagrams to show the appearance of the
synagogue when it was new: walls enclosing interior columns, and
a low double-sloping roof with exterior stairs above a gallery for
women worshippers. In some such building, maybe not so imposing
as this later prosperous one, Jesus joined in the ancient prayers of His
people, and taught them as one having authority.

We walked silently back across the fields of Galilee in the heavy
heat of that afternoon and contemplated the sparkling sea with
circling hazy hills, a few white sails in the distance, and the slow

cattle knee deep in lush grass of the meadows by the water's rim. The green was spangled with red and gold, and the sky above us was blue and enormous. Before we found the welcome shade of silver birches on the hilltop, we tried the acoustics of that natural amphitheatre. My friend stood by the shore and spoke in a normal voice. High on the slope I could hear him perfectly. Was it here that Jesus taught the multitude by the lakeside?

When the Chaplains' Retreat was over next day, a car carried me swiftly back to work. I passed the southern point of the lake where the Jordan resumes its interrupted course to the Dead Sea; the fertile plain of Jezreel, with Gideon's spring at the foot of Gilboa; and then the mound called Dothan, where the young man's eyes were opened and he saw horses and chariots of fire round about Elishah. It is still true, I thought. 'More there are with us than them'.

We sped rapidly through the amazing country of Samaria, up great winding roads which dipped suddenly down again, passing Sebastieh, the ancient city of Samaria itself, high on a hilltop to our left. This fortress of Omri has been excavated in recent years, and relics of Ahab's 'ivory palace' have been revealed. We could see from that distance the exposed gateway of the city, the very gates before which the chariot of Ahab arrived, and the dogs licked the blood from its wheels. It is an interesting commentary on the Hebrew historian's sense of values to reflect that because Omri had the reputation for 'doing that which was evil in the sight of the Lord', his reign is dismissed in a verse or two in 1 Kings xvi. But such an influential ruler was he that Israel was known to surrounding nations as 'the land of Omri', and the Israelites were called 'Omrians'. Our route then lay along the valley between the mighty Ebal and Gerizim, through populous Nablus with its many minarets, and past Jacob's Well by the roadside. Then it was a straight road back through the picturesque Robbers' Valley and over a switchback of hilltops to the Holy City.

[Photo by Lee M. Terrill.

THE SEA OF GALILEE.

Dr. Harte's house is by the lakeside.

EMMAUS.

The present name of this village is Abu Ghosh.

CHAPTER XV

EMMAUS

We, every day and every hour,
Would walk with Thee Emmaus-ward
To hear Thy voice of love and power.

J. A. NOBLE, 1844–96.

TWO of us decided to walk to Emmaus. My Church of England colleague and I had long planned to take a day's holiday, and one Friday morning a little while before Easter we found ourselves free to journey along that memorable route together. Later, perhaps at Easter, when the members of the Fellowship could ask for a day free from duty, I would take a party of men there, all the better for having seen it first myself.

In spite of the fact that the whole atmosphere of the story suggests a lonely walk of two dejected men who were glad of the company of another traveller, they might have been walking on a main highway, for the busy thoroughfares we know to-day are the products of modern traffic. The Emmaus walk could very well have been along the principal road which ran from Jerusalem to the coast, and there is good reason to believe that it was. However, we did not intend to walk along the present main road, noisy with cars and buses moving swiftly between Jaffa and Jerusalem. We decided that an old track winding over the hills a little to the north of the modern highway would be the Emmaus road for us. Perhaps it was not the exact route the two disciples took, but the main road in their day must have looked very much like it. Only thus could we recapture something of the spirit of that Resurrection morning.

There are four places which different people at different times have believed to be the village to which those two were travelling when the Stranger walked with them. It is not surprising that a small group of dwellings in the Judean hills, distinguished for nothing save this lovely story, should lose its identity in the changes and chances of the turbulent generations in Palestine. The only clue in the New Testament to its whereabouts is its distance from Jerusalem, which Luke tells us was sixty *stadia*, or furlongs, about seven and a half miles. There are not many roads out of the city, and the choice of direction is further limited by the fact that the land is desolate eastwards of Jerusalem almost unto Jericho. Southwards on the Hebron road through Bethlehem there is no village at a distance from Jerusalem which at all corresponds with Luke's story, and the same is true of the directly northern road. Westwards, however, the land has hamlets and villages in greater number, and it probably was so in the days of Jesus, since similar geographical considerations applied then. Furthermore, the main road to Jaffa runs westwards, with a number of footpaths and bridle tracks winding over the hills to the villages in that direction.

Emmaus is probably the village of Abu Ghosh. It is about seven and a half miles from Jerusalem along the Jaffa Road. Josephus refers to several places named Emmaus, a word which possibly meant a 'bath', and one of them he describes (on p. 458 of Everyman's Edition of the *Wars of the Jews*) as being sixty *stadia* from Jerusalem. He says that a settlement for retired Roman legionaries was established there. At Abu Ghosh there are Roman remains, and relics of the Tenth Legion, so this was probably the place he meant, and Luke's Emmaus is most likely the one mentioned by Josephus. It is very doubtful if there can have been two places of that name at the same distance from Jerusalem. The macadamed road of to-day follows an ancient route, for a milestone of the seventh century has been found on it, and a piece of the old road over a hilltop can still be seen to the left just outside the city. Every one of the hundreds who travel daily along the Jaffa Road, driving at speed and looking usually with callous eyes at their surroundings, are passing over the ground which those holy feet trod on the first Easter Day.

The Crusaders believed that Abu Ghosh was Emmaus. It is mentioned as such on their official lists of holy places, and they built a beautiful church there. But pilgrims in the thirteenth century were only permitted to enter the Holy Land by restricted routes, and the main road was forbidden to them. They were compelled to journey to Jerusalem by a road that went farther to the north, and in time they located Emmaus on that road at a village named El Kubebieh, which means the 'domed tomb', and is sixty furlongs from Jerusalem. A Crusader village was there, with a local church. To-day the Franciscans point to it as the site of Emmaus. They have built a new church on the place where the old one stood, and Easter pilgrimages are made to it along the 'disciples' road', a track which partly follows the Jaffa Road and is probably the route that pilgrims were allowed to take in the Middle Ages.

This is principally a Franciscan tradition, however, dating from the time when they became the Custodians of the Holy Land. The Benedictines, who have the care of the church at Abu Ghosh, do not accept the Franciscan claims. A Dominican father has suggested that Kolonia, an old Roman colony a little nearer to the Holy City on the main road, is the Emmaus of Josephus and St. Luke, but all the evidence seems to point to Abu Ghosh. The Byzantines apparently thought that the town of Emwas, called in their day Nicopolis, was the Emmaus of the Gospels. There are Roman baths there, and the remains of a Byzantine church. Both Jerome and Eusebius, who lived in Palestine in the fourth century, decided that this was the place. But it is too far away. It is out on the plain, about twenty miles west of Jerusalem.

Emwas was a city, not a village, as Luke plainly describes Emmaus. Some encouragement for the theory that this is the place is found in the version of this Resurrection story in the Codex Sinaiticus, the fourth-century Bible that was bought a few years ago from the Soviet Government and is now in the British Museum. There we read in Luke xxiv that Emmaus was 160 *stadia* from Jerusalem, instead of the usual sixty *stadia* shown in other manuscripts. But even Tischendorff, who found and loved the Codex Sinaiticus, did not accept this reading as authentic. Probably some early pilgrim's knowledge of a place named Emwas in the Holy Land caused him to insert a note in the margin of his manuscript Gospel about its distance from Jerusalem, which was copied by a later scribe into the text. One cannot imagine how those disciples, having travelled twenty miles until it was 'towards evening', and having partaken of supper, could have been able to retrace their steps over that same distance and arrive in Jerusalem in time to find the city gates still open and the disciples and women still up and about and, possibly, with broiled fish on the table for supper. It is uphill all the way back to Jerusalem, and we are told that they were walking.

My friend and I decided to walk to Abu Ghosh by way of El Kubebieh along a lonely winding track over the hills. Only in that way could we recapture something of the spirit of the Gospel story, and walk the way the Master went. For us, that track was the Road to Emmaus.

With packs on our backs and stout Army boots on our feet, we made our way through some straggling suburbs on to a rough track that descended a valley, and in a surprisingly short while we were completely remote from the sight of any habitation. It was a delightful day, with the sun bright in a cloudless blue sky, and on either side of us the hillsides sloped up, scattered with stones and white rocky patches in the brown soil. A dry watercourse lay in the bottom of the valley, and the grassy verge was stained crimson with anemones. Afar on a hillside a flock of sheep and their lambs searched between the stones for blades of grass, and a shepherd in a brown *galabieh* and a flowing white *kafiyeh* over head and shoulders leant on a staff and called in a high-pitched note to some wandering sheep. We went downhill and then up a long incline past a few cavernous holes in the cliff, and glimpsed in the distance to our left a few square white houses leaning against a hillside. Everything was at peace. Nothing here was changed from time immemorial. The quiet air held the stillness of memory. The voice of the Risen Jesus was in the far cry of the shepherd and the low momentary murmur of the wind. Cleopas and his friend had trod a track like this, weary with hope spent and hearts heavy with dismay, to find as we could surely do in these modern days of warfare and turmoil that Christ is risen indeed. It was difficult to remember, surrounded by all that peace and beauty, that the world was at war; and we ourselves, men called of God for the pursuit of peace, were clad in khaki, to be at one with our fellows.

On a hilltop we paused to look back. The road, light brown in the darker brown of the hill, wound down and up again to the horizon, and far off on the way we had taken two Arabs were driving several heavily laden donkeys, and a camel paced solemnly along behind them. There was a gentle wind on this hilltop, and we seated ourselves by a disused well-head among the grass-grown ruins of some ancient village. The rolling countryside stretched before us, and ahead stood the minaret on the height of Nebi Samwil, by which our way would lead us. The scene was glorious. Never had I realized the unutterable loveliness of the Holy Land until I sat on that eminence and saw the view. Few students of the Bible realize, I think, that those mighty dramas were enacted before a gorgeous backcloth of beauty. What a scene for a Resurrection story was this winding track uphill and downhill, with all this glory round about it! It was so ordinary and yet so unearthly, somehow. It seemed to me that its solitude and unnamable peace and beauty combined the things of earth with the things of heaven. I could well believe the Risen Jesus had walked here, not a ghost at dead of night, but a living personality in the full light of day.

We talked of many things as we strode onward. Who was Cleopas, the only one of the two whose name is given? Obviously he was one of 'the rest' mentioned in Luke xxiv. 9, disciples of Jesus in addition to the original twelve. The physical appearance of Jesus was familiar to them, for 'their eyes were holden that they should not know Him' during their journey, and later the familiar act of Jesus in breaking bread enabled them to understand who He was. It is possible that they recognized a characteristic gesture or, more likely, they saw the marks of the nails in His hands. They had the messianic expectation that Jesus should be the redeemer of Israel, and maybe that reveals a misunderstanding of the nature of His mission prevalent among even His closest followers, and which Jesus then corrected as He interpreted to them the Scriptures. We know nothing else of Cleopas, though tradition has it that he was the father of St. Simeon, the second Bishop of Jerusalem. It has been suggested that his companion might have been a woman, since the name is not given and the sex is not indicated, and that it was to a man and his wife that Jesus appeared. There is no evidence whatever for this suggestion, which is completely opposed to every tradition. They were certainly walking, for that word occurs in both Mark's and Luke's accounts of the story, so presumably they were too poor to afford the customary donkey. It is, of course, not completely impossible that they were the Cleopas and Mary, kinsfolk of Jesus, mentioned in John xix. 25.

We could but make idle guesses at the reason for their journey. They might have lived at Emmaus, and were returning home, their adventure in following Jesus as the Messiah being, as they thought, over. Perhaps they had business in Emmaus. Perhaps, since they were afoot, they had decided after this shattering of all their hopes to go for a long walk, as Mark puts it, 'into the country', to leave Jerusalem for a while in order to get over the reaction after the tension of the previous few days. It is possible that this suggestion was an unjustifiable use of our imagination, for we had no reason to think that the modern love of a long hike into the country for the pleasure of it, such as we were enjoying, had a part in the lives of those of ancient times.

We wondered whether Jesus had walked beside any other travellers that day, and talked with them to make their hearts burn, and yet they, and history, knew it not because the travellers did not ask Him in. He is still walking the dusty roads of human life as a Stranger, waiting to be invited in. Men's hearts glow sometimes as they get a glimpse of Him, yet we do not realize the glorious truth of His presence and His power. We turn aside to rest when evening comes, still intent upon our worries, and Jesus is forgotten.

When we reached the top of Nebi Samwil we paused to look at a great cistern, possibly of Roman origin, by the roadside. Two lads with donkeys passed us. We hailed them: 'Do you speak English?'

One shrugged his shoulders, but the other, an Arab youth with a lean brown face and keen eyes, walked over to us.

'Yes, very well,' he said truthfully. We asked him the way to Emmaus, but he had never heard of it, so we mentioned El Kubebieh. He knew that all right, it was just over the hill; and he offered to lead us there. We declined with thanks, for we preferred to tramp on alone.

'Where did you learn English?' I said.

'In the American University School in Beirut. My home is in Beit Anan. I asked my father to send me to school in Syria, and he did so.'

'How old are you?'

'I am fifteen,' he replied.

We asked him his name.

'Farik,' he said. 'I am not able to get a job.'

'What sort of job to do you want?'

'Anything. I am taking my donkeys back from Jerusalem. I take them there every day with milk which I sell to some Jews. But I want a job.'

We inquired where Beit Anan was. He said it was five kilos beyond Kubebieh. So this Moslem lad, to all appearances just an Arab donkey driver, but with an excellent knowledge of English and of good education, walked every day along this road, ignorant, of course, of the significance it had for us that day; and, like many another in the world, wondering how he could find employment.

He gladly accepted a piastre, politely shook hands, and departed after his donkeys, who had continued on their familiar path.

We explored a grove of fig trees by a stream back from the road, and then sat in the shelter of a cliff and ate our lunch. The water issued from a fissure in the rock and watered a tiny mossy *wadi*, and disappeared away to our left. Several rock-cut tombs were there, making a honeycomb in the cliff-face, and a ruined peasant's hut was half hidden in the trees. Bees droned about us and lizards ran in and out of the holes in the rock.

It was a peaceful scene that we surveyed. The whole country lay about us like a giant relief-map. In the distance we could see the towers of Jerusalem, which had been hidden from us hitherto. It was from this very height that Crusaders, journeying from the coast, had caught their first sight of the Holy City, and had named the hill Mons Gaudii: the Mount of Joy. Somewhere near where we were sitting Richard Cœur-de-Leon had come, and refused to look upon Jerusalem, for he knew that he might never enter it. Eusebius and Jerome declared that this hill corresponds to the Mizpah in Benjamin where Samuel judged the people, but they were wrong. Mizpah has been located farther to the north of Jerusalem, at the recent excavations at Tel en Nasbeh. The association of this height with Samuel led both Jews and Christians in later times to believe that his tomb was here, and the Moslems accordingly venerate it as

such to-day and have given it its present name, for *nebi* is Arabic for
'prophet'. The mosque is built on the site of a Crusader church,
which was ordered to be built by Baldwin II in 1131, and was
dedicated to 'St. Samuel of the Mount of Joy'. Only the old transept
remains. The mosque was shelled by the Turkish guns on November 30th, 1917, when British troops held the hill, but the minaret
was soon rebuilt.

When we had rested and eaten, we climbed the steep, filthy
streets of the Moslem village surrounding the mosque, and a woman
admitted us into its coolness, out of the haze of dust and flies and
stench. We saw through a grille in the thick Crusader wall a green-
draped cenotaph covering the reputed tomb of Samuel, and then we
mounted the narrow winding stairway of the minaret to stand at
last on its tiny balcony, with the most glorious view imaginable
around us. This Nebi Samwil minaret is one of the best-known
landmarks in Palestine and it commands a better panorama perhaps
than any building in the land.

Away to the north were the peaks of Gerizim and Carmel, and
to the west the great plain towards the sea; eastwards lay Jerusalem
and the hills of Transjordan; and as we looked southwards we saw
the beautiful village of Ain Karim, 'Gracious Spring', as it is called
by the Arabs, nestling among the hills with the rounded shrine of
peace above it. We could see the Franciscans' road to Emmaus
winding up towards us, and on the far horizon the flat-topped
Frank Mountain so clearly seen on the Bethlehem road. We could
even see the heights of Hebron from where we were.

We continued our journey westwards and presently came to the
village of Biddou, a group of poor Arab cottages at the junction of
the mountain path. Men were at work in the fields with the same
style of lowly plough we read of in the Bible. Children were playing
by the roadside, and as we watched them a file of women with great
earthen waterpots balanced on their heads padded past us with bare
feet, and busied themselves about the well, chattering shrilly to each
other. We went on our way, and it was not long before we came
to the brow overlooking El Kubebieh. It lay within a sweeping
valley, and the now-empty German Hospice stood among trees
on the opposite hill. The tower of a church rose above surrounding
roof-tops, and we heard an echo of the English countryside as the
sound of its bells came up to us.

We sat on a rock on the hilltop. It was a sleeping village like this,
cradled in the hills, dropping slowly with a quiet beauty, that had
confronted the heavy-hearted disciples as they drew near to it with
their Companion when it was towards evening. I drew my Testa-

ment from my pocket. It had been my companion for seventeen years. Little did I think when I first held this book in my hands that one day I should turn its pages as I sat on a rocky ledge near Emmaus, and read that matchless story at the place where those things had come to pass. There were more memories now to make that slight volume precious to me. I read the story aloud as my companion sat staring at the village below. . . .

At the bottom of the path we tugged at the bell-pull of a door in an old wall, but only its rusty noise came back to us. We learned later that in normal days that hospice was busy with pilgrims; but in this remote spot in time of war it was standing desolate. A little way beyond it we found the Franciscan Church of St. Cleophas, and monks in brown habits were passing slowly in to their devotions. We entered also, and when we had prayed and looked about us at the high ceiling and far-off altar we tiptoed across to that lovely painting by Martinetti which shows the two travellers recognizing Christ as they sat at table with Him. On their faces was the light of morning as the knowledge of Him dawned upon them. Through an open portico were portayed the very hills that are round about Emmaus. The church is a conventional Italian one, and was built in 1901. In a triptych over the central altar we saw a sculpture representing the breaking of the bread.

Outside the church we explored some excavations the monks were making of the site of the Crusader village around the church, tracing the old walls and unearthing a wine-press of stone hidden by the soil and overgrown with grass. The bones of an early pilgrim, jumbled all together in a trench, were pointed out to us, and I wondered if he had been an Englishman like ourselves, one who had dreamed of home on that same hilltop, and had been too deeply moved for speech as he trod the holy way from Jerusalem to what he believed was Emmaus. A proud horseman no doubt, and a man of courage and piety in his day, but now only a dusty heap, stirred for a moment by the accident of an excavator's spade. He laid himself down for his last rest after a weary journey to a country not his own; and yet it was no alien land, but, for him, another holy home, the land his Saviour knew.

Before leaving the village we explored the deserted grounds of the German Hospice, and found in a desolate spot in the shade of some fir trees a pathetic little pile of rusty tin hats and broken shell cases, with a cross of wood bearing a date in 1917. What a find to make in 1942, when the whole dreadful story was being told again! Death was all around us. We had seen the tomb of a prophet, the bones of a pilgrim, a memorial to Turks and Englishmen, and never

absent from our minds was the knowledge of the clash of armies in
the wider world. It all conspired to throw into stronger relief the
Gospel story. In the midst of death we were in life. The sun was
bright over our heads and the birds were singing, the Holy Land
lay around us with its timeless serenity.

We climbed up out of the valley and turned south-west for a long
hard tramp across the hills to Abu Ghosh. The path was hardly
discernible at times among the rocks and patchy soil. Little blue
flowers winked up at us, and anemones and a few dog-violets grew
at our feet. Very soon we came to a better road beside a sloping
field dotted with sheep, many of them clustering around the sheep-
fold: a horseshoe of banked earth with its aperture forming 'the door
of the sheep'. A shepherd boy played a weird and haunting tune on
his reed pipe. The Old Testament was alive before our eyes and ears.

We walked some miles before we rounded a hillside by an ugly
Jewish settlement and saw our destination far ahead. Jewish boys
and girls in shorts toiled with rake and mattock in the fields, and
their crude modern huts stood upon the skyline to our right. We
walked straight from the Bible into modern days, for we had not
gone far before we passed a young lady carrying a music case and
clad in high-heeled shoes and the latest thing in millinery. She had
evidently stepped from a bus on the main Jaffa Road below us and
was returning to the settlement from Tel-Aviv.

We neared the village of Abu Ghosh, lying in the crook of the
busy highway. Above us to our right stood the great figure of the
Virgin above the Franciscan Convent of Our Lady, and to the left,
square among the houses of that large village, the beautifully-
preserved Crusader church which is cared for by French Benedictines.

Abu Ghosh was the name of a famous brigand of the early part oı
the last century who had his headquarters here, and the place is
named after him. Bishop Gobat, the second Anglican Bishop in
Jerusalem, came to Palestine as a young man in order to learn
Amharic from Abyssinians in Jerusalem before going to Ethiopia as
a missionary, and while he was travelling he encountered the
notorious robber. He did what perhaps nobody else had ever done.
To the surprise of Abu Ghosh, he exhorted him to leave his life of
crime and brigandage and become an honest man. His plea was not
successful. The robber heard him courteously, but declined to
follow his advice, though he assured him of his goodwill towards
the young priest. Years afterwards, when Gobat became Bishop in
Jerusalem, Abu Ghosh presented him with a slender silver vase as an
expression of that goodwill. I have held it in my hands, a finely

wrought and delicate piece of craftsmanship, probably part of the robber's booty. Many respectable citizens of that district, descendants of the brigand, bear the name of Abu Ghosh. There are no less than three of them in the Palestine Police Force.

This village, also called Kiryat el Enab, is Kirjath-jearim of the Old Testament. It marked the border of Benjamin's tribe, according to Joshua xviii. 14, at 'the goings out thereof'. So this road was a highway even in those far-off days. It was known not only as the 'City of the Forest', but as Kirjath-baal, the 'City of Baal'. It was the men of Kirjath-jearim, of course, who brought the Ark of the Lord from Beth-shemesh to their own city and kept it there for twenty years. The story of its surrender by the Philistines in I Samuel vi is a graphic one. It describes how the Ark was drawn in a new cart by two milch cows who 'went along the highway, lowing as they went, and turned not aside to the right hand or to the left'. The golden tumours and golden mice they sent with it prove that the Philistines perceived that their plague was connected somehow with the presence of mice. It is a source of astonishment to me that this was never realized all through the Middle Ages. Apparently it did not occur to our fathers, in spite of this clue, that rats and mice carried the plague, and it was left for scientists of modern days to rediscover the truth. What a great difference it would have meant to history if those who battled against disease through the centuries had learned the significance of those golden mice in the Bible story!

It is very likely that the Franciscan convent high on the eminence north of the village stands on the site of the 'house of Abinadab on the hill', where the Ark was left with Eleazar for safe custody. The tremendous figure, a well-known landmark, is of Notre Dame Arche d'Alliance. She is represented as standing upon the Ark of the Covenant, which rests upon a gigantic and none-too-pleasing framework of concrete.

We went through the narrow lane that leads to the Benedictines' church, and pulled the bell at the gateway. A solitary black-robed father with a grey beard welcomed us in. He spoke excellent English, so there was no need for our halting French. He was kindness itself, and when he heard that we had walked over the hills for fourteen miles he bade us rest ourselves in his guest-room, and poured out for us his home-made wine. We were eased by the grateful comfort of the cushions of an immense settee, and as we rested he chatted to us. He had dwelt as a lad at Buckfast Abbey in Devon, familiar to us both, and after a few years in the United States he came to Abu Ghosh some eighteen years previously. Only he and another father and brother lived there, and as the Superior was away for a few days he was in charge. Sometimes he had no visitors for days on end, and he was always delighted to see people. He plied us with more refreshment, and bade us inscribe our names in the visitors' book. Then he showed us his church.

It was a delightful place, so unexpectedly perfect. We passed through a crypt whose low arches remained as they were when the light from those gothic windows in the thick walls had fallen upon pilgrims of the twelfth century as they clustered about the well in its centre. The monk turned on an electric bulb for us to see its transparent depths, and when we craved a drink from its coolness, he lowered a bucket and poured out a clear flow that was ambrosia to our thirsty tongues. This spring, he told us, had fed not only the Roman colony that once was here, but the Crusaders on their way from the coast, and a multitude of pilgrims before and after them.

Upstairs we stood in the bareness and the gloom of that wondrous place. The pillars towered above us in columns of loveliness, and the silence of the shrine was awesome. So it had stood through generations—one of the finest Crusader churches in Palestine, possibly the best of its kind in the world. Quietly the three of us knelt before the altar, and prayed where knights and ragged pilgrims had prayed in days long past. We should have loved to remain there for a while, to explore the precincts of the church and the old tombs round about it, still sealed by rolling stones as the tomb of Jesus was. But the day was drawing to its close and we had to return to Jerusalem.

The priest led us to see an inscription of the apparently ubiquitous Tenth Roman Legion. The Crusader masons had found the plaque and built it into the wall of their church. Beneath, by the outside of the church wall, lay the tomb of an early abbot under a semi-arch which was recently built over it to protect the old stonework. Only a few years ago, comparatively, had this great church been restored to its former beauty. We saw some photographs of the church as it was last century when rubble filled the crypt and to half the height of the nave. The whole place had been neglected, left desolate except for occasional use as stables, for some hundreds of years. But it had not been destroyed, and the valiant monks had cleansed it and restored it not only as a worthy monument of days gone by, but as a sanctuary where to-day it was easy to worship and find peace.

In the days of Knights Hospitaller this shrine was an object of pilgrimage, but now tradition guides the pilgrims' feet elsewhere. Few people realize that this quiet byway from the busy thoroughfare is where Jesus revealed Himself to the faint-hearted disciples in the breaking of bread. The Kirjath-jearim of the Old Testament is the

Emmaus of the New. That is a parable. Where rested the Ark which for them of old was the Presence of the Lord, there came One who makes known to men, even to weary travellers, the eternal living Presence on every road, in every village, at every table, for those with eyes to see and hearts to love.

We left that old church with kindly memories, and accepted our host's pressing invitation to visit him another day. When I did so, a few weeks later, I beheld the side of the church covered with sarsaparilla flowers, hanging like a rich tapestry of blue; and below, in a flower-pot, a solitary yellow Sussex primrose, lading that alien air with its delicate perfume. Some monk who loved Sussex as I do had brought it to the Holy Land. I had seldom been so homesick as I was when I held up that flower-pot and breathed its sweetness.

Father Raphael insisted upon accompanying us so far as the main road, and he walked between us, pulling the cowl of his black habit over his head and making a strange, medieval figure, grey-bearded as he was, beside our rough battledress.

We intended to wait for one of the rickety buses that ply to Jerusalem along this road, and prepared to take our stand beside the heedless traffic until one arrived. But Father Raphael would have none of that. Directly he saw a fast car approaching, he stood out from the roadside and signalled it to stop. To our astonishment, it did so. Drivers of military cars usually flash past with a fine scorn of hitch-hikers. But the sight of this bearded monk clad in the garb of the Middle Ages and busily waving to him caused the driver to apply his brake. With the boldness of one who could wear such garments in a modern world, our friend inquired if we could have a lift to Jerusalem.

'Certainly', was the dazed answer. So we promptly entered and settled ourselves, with our thanks to the monk for the hospitality we had enjoyed. We shall not quickly forget his spontaneous smile and his twinkling eyes. We looked back and saw that dark, rather forlorn figure waving to us as we passed rapidly out of his sight, to go through Kolonia and up the curling highway to brave the intricacies of the corners known as the Seven Sisters, and so into the Holy City.

O Lord Jesus Christ, Thyself the Beginning, the Way, and the End; grant to us who have trodden in Thy earthly footsteps that we may not err from the Way of Holiness, but that, faring forth in Thy Blessed Company, we may feel our hearts burn within us, and know Thee face to face at the day's end. *Amen.*

BIBLIOGRAPHY

ALBRIGHT, W. F. *Archaeology of Palestine and of the Bible.* (Revell, N.Y.)

ASHBEE, C. R. *Palestine Notebook.* (Heinemann, 1923.)

BADÈ, W. F. *Manual of Excavation in the Near East.* (University of California Press, 1924.)

BENTWICH, N. DE M. *Palestine.* (Benn, 1934.)

BESANT and PALMER. *Jerusalem.* (Scribners, 1890.)

BLYTH, E. *When We Lived in Jerusalem.* (John Murray, 1930.)

BOULTON, W. H. *Palestine.* (Sampson Low, London.)

BRIDGEMAN, C. T. *Jerusalem at Worship.* (Jerusalem, 1932.)

Bulletin of the American School of Oriental Research, Jerusalem.

CAIGER, S. L. *Archaeology and the New Testament.* (Cassell, London, 1939.) *Bible and Spade.* (Oxford University Press, 1936.)

CONDER, C. R. *City of Jerusalem.* (John Murray, 1909.)

CRAWLEY-BOVEY, A. M. *Garden Tomb of Golgotha.* (Covenant Publishing Co., Ltd.)

CUST, L. H. *Jerusalem, a Historical Sketch.* (Macmillan, N.Y., 1924.)

DALMAN, G. *Sacred Sites and Ways.* (S.P.C.K., 1935.)

Department of Antiquities Quarterly. (Government of Palestine.)

DOWLING, T. E. *Orthodox Greek Patriarchate of Jerusalem.* (S.P.C.K., 1913.)

DUCKWORTH, H. T. F. *Church of the Holy Sepulchre.* (Hodder and Stoughton, 1922.)

DUNCAN, J. GARROW. *Digging Up Biblical History.* (Macmillan, 1931.)

FINN, J. *Stirring Times.* (Kegan Paul, 1878.)

GARSTANG, J. & J. B. E. *Story of Jericho.* (Hodder and Stoughton, 1940.)

GASTER, M. *Samaritans.* (Oxford University Press, 1925.)

GILBERT, V. *Romance of the Last Crusade.* (Appleton, N.Y., 1931.)

HAMILTON, R. W. *Guide to Bethlehem.* (Department of Antiquities, Jerusalem, 1939.)

HANAUER, J. E. *Walks in and Around Jerusalem.* (C.M.J., 1926.)

HOLLIS, F. J. *Archaeology of Herod's Temple.* (Dent, 1934.)

JEFFERY, G. *Holy Sepulchre.* (Cambridge University Press, 1919.)

JOHNS, C. N. *Excavations at the Citadel, Jerusalem.* (Department of Antiquities, Jerusalem, 1940.)

JONES, A. H. M. *Herods of Judaea.* (Oxford University Press, 1938.)

JOSEPHUS, FLAVIUS. *Antiquities.* (Dent, Everyman's Library.) *Wars of the Jews.* (Dent, Everyman's Library.)

KENYON, SIR F. G. *Bible and Archaeology.* (Harper, N.Y., 1940.)

LAGRANGE, M-J. *St. Étienne et son Sanctuaire à Jerusalem.* (A. Pickard et Fils, Paris, 1894.)

LUKE, H. C. *Prophets, Priests and Patriarchs.* (Faith Press, London.)

MACALISTER, R. A. S. *Century of Excavation in Palestine.* (R.T.S., 1925.) *History of Civilization in Palestine.* (Cambridge University Press, 1921.)

MATSON, G. O. *Jerusalem and Environs*. (Matson, Jerusalem, 1942.)

MEISTERMANN, B. *Guide to the Holy Land*. (Burns, Oates and Washbourne, 1923.) *Palestine Pilgrims' Texts.*

PETRIE, HILDA. *Side Notes on the Bible*. (Search Publishing Co., 1933.)

PETRIE, SIR F. *Palestine and Israel*. (S.P.C.K., 1934.)

PIEROTTI, E. *Jerusalem Explored*. (Bell, London, 1864.)

Quarterly Statement of the Palestine Exploration Fund, Jerusalem.

RICHMOND, E. T. *Sites of the Crucifixion and Resurrection*. (Jerusalem, 1934.)

SAYCE, A. H. *Fresh Light from the Ancient Monuments*. (Revell, N.Y., 1895.)

SCHNEIDER, A. M. *Church of the Multiplying of the Loaves and Fishes at Tabgha.* (Ouseley, London, 1937.)

SCHOFIELD, J. M. *Historical Background of the Bible*. (Nelson, 1938.)

SMITH, SIR G. A. *Atlas of the Historical Geography of the Holy Land*. (Hodder and Stoughton, 1936.) *Historical Geography of the Holy Land*. (Hodder and Stoughton, 1931.) *Jerusalem*. Vols. I and II. (Hodder and Stoughton, 1908.)

SUKENIK, E. *Third Wall of Jerusalem*. (Hebrew University Press, Jerusalem, 1930.)

THOMSON, J. E. H. *Samaritans*. (Oliver and Boyd, 1919.)

VINCENT, L-H. *Garden Tomb* (in French). (V. Lecoffre, Paris.) *Jerusalem Nouvelle*. (Paris, 1926.)

WALKER, J. B. *Jerusalem and Bethlehem*. (Nile Mission Press, Jerusalem, 1934.)

WALLACE, E. S. *Jerusalem the Holy*. (Revell, N.Y., 1898.)

WATSON, C. M. *Golgotha and the Holy Sepulchre*. (Palestine Exploration Fund, Jerusalem.) *Story of Jerusalem*. (Dent, 1918.)

WILLIAMS, G. *Holy City*. (Parker, London, 1845.)

WILSON, C. W. *Recovery of Jerusalem*. (Appleton, N.Y.)

Young Men's Christian Association, Jerusalem. (Jerusalem Y.M.C.A.)

INDEX OF PLACES

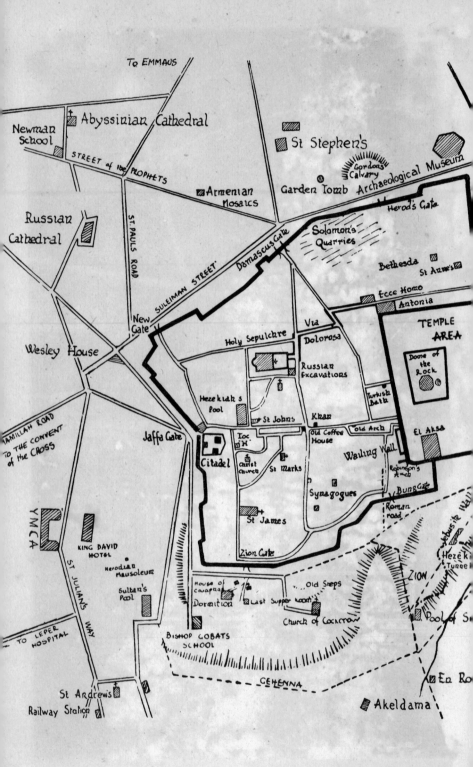

To EMMAUS

Newman School

Abyssinian Cathedral

St Stephen's

Gordon's Calvary

Garden Tomb Archaeological Museum

STREET of the PROPHETS

Herod's Gate

Armenian Mosaics

Russian Cathedral

ST PAULS ROAD

Damascus Gate

Solomon's Quarries

Bethesda
St Anne's

SULEIMAN STREET

Ecce Homo

Antonia

New Gate

Via

TEMPLE AREA

Wesley House

Holy Sepulchre

Dolorosa

Russian Excavations

Dome of the Rock

Turkish Bath

Hezekiah's Pool

St Johns

Khan

Old Arch

El Aksa

MAMILLAH ROAD
TO THE CONVENT of the CROSS

Jaffa Gate

Toc H

Old Coffee House

Wailing Wall

Citadel

Christ Church

St Marks

Robinson's Arch

Synagogues

Dung Gate

YMCA

Roman road

King David Hotel

St James

ST JULIAN'S WAY

Herodian Mausoleum

Zion Gate

Hezek
Tunnel

Sultan's Pool

House of Caiaphas

Old Steps

ZION

Dormition

Last Supper Room

Pool of S

TO LEPER HOSPITAL

BISHOP GOBATS SCHOOL

Church of Cockcrow

GEHENNA

En Ro

St Andrew's
Railway Station

Akeldama